Prawns
in the game

Best Wishes

For Dad

PRAWNS in the game

•◆ Paul French

dewi lewis media ltd

PRAWNS IN THE GAME
by Paul French

This edition first published in the UK in 2006 by
Dewi Lewis Media Ltd
8, Broomfield Road
Heaton Moor
Stockport SK4 4ND
www.dewilewismedia.com

> Front Cover Design
Peter Rogers

> Design and Artwork Production
Dewi Lewis Media Ltd, based on an original design concept
by Arco da Velha – Design e Ilustração, Lda, Portugal

> Print and Binding
Biddles Ltd, Kings Lynn

ISBN 10: 0-9546843-8-9
ISBN 13: 9780954684389

12   11   10   9   8   7   6   5   4   3   2   1

>> CONTENTS

"Sometimes you wonder,
do they understand the game of football?
We're 1-0 up, then there are one or two stray passes and
they're getting on players' backs. It's just not on. At the end of
the day they need to get behind the team. Away from home
our fans are fantastic, I'd call them the hardcore fans. But at
home they have a few drinks and probably the prawn
sandwiches, and they don't realise what's going on out on the
pitch. I don't think some of the people who come to Old
Trafford can spell 'football', never mind understand it."

Roy Keane
Manchester, 2000

FOREWORD

It all kicked off on a cold, wet afternoon in Grimsby. The date was Saturday November 29th 1986 and the occasion was my first football match: Grimsby Town vs Birmingham City in the Today Football League Division Two. Back then, Division Two was the second division of English football not the fourth and Today was a newspaper as well as a description of the here and now. The programme cost 50 pence, was wafer thin and rather bizarrely featured people of various ages wafting Grimsby Town scarves in the air under the words – 'the family club'. Remembering that this was a time when football was more about fighting than fussing my friends, I think this must have been an attempt by the club to try and get you to see it their way rather than representing any kind of reality.

Good honest names like David Felgate and Brian Rice dominated the team sheet and, thanks to a handwritten score I handily inked in next to the team names in the centre pages, I can inform you that Birmingham ran out 1-0 winners. Whether it was deserved or not, I don't know. The only thing I can remember about the match is the boats tripping past in the fog, disappearing and reappearing like ghosts behind the main stand. And the cold. The bitter, icy cold you only seemed to get in the 1980s. In Grimsby.

But something must have happened. Whether it was a scandalous refereeing decision or a sumptuous goal or the carnival-like atmosphere on the terraces, I don't know. But something got inside of me that day; an addictive, irresistible drug that I've been doing every weekend since: football.

The Mariners didn't have quite the same effect. Although I did go and see them again [not for another two years, mind] they never became my team. Whatever. The crucial thing is that they introduced me to Planet Football.

I've watched hundreds if not thousands of games since, at various levels in different places around the world. Like all football fans, I've stood in the freezing snow, the baking sun and the drizzling rain. I've travelled thousands of miles, spent thousands of pounds, suffered countless disappointments and letdowns, yet still I come back for more. Why? Because I love the game of football. I've never worked in it, I haven't played it to any great standard, but I love it. I really, really love it.

And that's why I get angry when I see the state of the game today:

arrogant, millionaire footballers arguing over whether it's a king's ransom or a Quinton Fortune in their pay packets; clubs whoring themselves to the corporations with the deepest pockets and fans watching meekly from beautifully crafted seats whilst munching blithely on a prawn sandwich. Yes sir: Planet Football is a very different place now to the one I walked into on November 29th 1986.

Roy Keane was the first in a long line of people to inspire me to write this book. When, in 2000, he talked about the prawn sandwich brigade at Manchester it set me thinking about how massively the game had changed in the last 20 years. As time wore on, more things began to boil my blood – G14, Rio & Ashley, The Emirates stadium. To me it seemed as though everyone was taking a slice of the football pie: the players, the clubs and big business were all doing very nicely thanks out of the beautiful game, whilst the fans were left footing the bill.

I don't begrudge anyone making a living out of football, but I'm not so keen on people making a killing out of it. And, having chatted to fans of clubs all over the country, I found that many people felt the same. What was missing was an understanding of how we've ended up here. Most fans wrongly lash out at The Premiership and at Sky, not realising that they are just cogs in a wheel that has been turning for nearly 150 years.

So I set out to uncover the truth: to find out what, in the name of John Barnes' rap, has happened to the game of football? How has it gone from being a load of blokes kicking a bag of wind around to a multi-million pound industry? And how did the prawn sandwich join the chicken and balti pie as the half-time snack of choice?

There are a couple of books which have examined the idea of commercialisation, most notably David Conn's excellent *The Football Business*. I wanted to take the idea and put it into context – to examine the history of commercial activity to see if it would throw up any clues as to how football got where it is today. And if, buried in there, there were any hints as to how it might get out again.

Before we kick off, we need to establish one thing: I'm not saying that the commercialisation of football is evil *per se*. It's not. As you will see, it can have a positive influence on football.

The biggest single threat posed to the future of our game is greed. Money used to be distributed around the game, now it's hoarded by the magnates at the top of the sport. But, if the Fat Cats keep milking their cash cows to the extent they are now, the only thing that's going to be left to flog in a few years' time will be a dead horse.

This book does not contain all the answers to the game's ills, but it may help you understand how it got so sick. And, with a bit of luck, it might make you want to kiss it better.

Paul French

PRAWNS IN THE GAME

> CHAPTER I
A DANGEROUS GAME

1   A DANGEROUS GAME

Tightropes: who'd walk 'em? Wobble your girth too far to one side, you lose your balance and end up dead on the floor. Make it to the other side and you get a luke warm round of applause and the chance to live another day. Not exactly a win-win situation, but such is life for the 92 Football League clubs and scores of their non-league chums who, on a daily basis, have to try and keep their balance on football's high wire. Business or pleasure? Team manager or bank manager? Fans or customers? Football clubs are playing a dangerous game.

It hasn't always been this way. There was no such thing as a football club until May 1857, when solicitor Nathaniel Creswick and his wine merchant friend William Prest, both keen cricketers, stumbled upon the idea, while out on a country walk. They'd been racking their brains to think of a way to keep fit during the winter months so they'd be in peak physical condition when the cricket season started. Eventually they settled on the game they'd discovered at college and they agreed to start what would go on to become the most beguiling, glorious, hateful, untrustworthy, ludicrous concoction known to man: the football club.

Football had been played in various guises for centuries all over the world, but no one had ever set up a club independent of a university or college specifically to play the game. In fact, no one could even agree how to play it. Each college and university played by its own set of rules, so the chances of the game becoming popular with the masses looked slim. How could people from different places play each other if there was no common set of rules?

With this in mind, Creswick and Prest wrote to as many public schools and universities as they could, asking for copies of their rules. They took what they deemed to be the best bits from each and produced the Sheffield Laws.

Viewed now, the laws, [re-printed in full at the end of this chapter], make about as much sense as a Paul Gascoigne team talk. Catching and punching the ball was allowed, pushing with the hands was allowed but hacking wasn't. And each player had to provide himself with a red and dark blue flannel cap, to allow differentiation between the sides. Not for our nineteenth Century cousins, the indignity of having to 'play in skins'.

With some playing rules established, Creswick and Prest turned their attentions to putting into practice the idea they'd come up with on their walk. On 24th October 1857 they called a meeting at the greenhouse and potting shed of former master cutler Thomas Asline Ward, and the world's first football club was born.

That club was Sheffield Football Club and, although its principle role was to give its cricket-loving perpetrators a way of keeping fit during winter, the business of setting up the club was taken seriously, with each member required to pay an annual sub-scription of 'no more than 2s 6d.' Officers were elected, with Creswick installed as honorary secretary and treasurer. Prest joined the committee and other prominent Sheffield folk took the rest of the positions. The incumbents then set about establish-ing a set of rules for the club. These included a note that the season 'shall commence on the first day in November and end on Easter Eve in each year,' and that 'the play day of the club be Saturday from two o'clock until dark.'

24th October 1857... the world's first football club was born

Being pioneers of football was all well and good but it did throw up a rather practical problem. As the world's first club, who on earth do you play? For three years the members of Sheffield FC played amongst themselves, dividing up the players any way they could think of – married men against unmarried men, professionals against unskilled labourers, the first half of the alphabet against the last. Then, finally, in 1860 they were presented with some real opposition by the formation of Hallam and Stumperlowe [now just Hallam] by fellow Sheffielders.

Suddenly the purpose of the football club was not so fluffy. The element of competition meant that, rather than just being a means of keeping fit, the players of Sheffield FC and Hallam wanted to win. Badly. After one of the world's first ever derby matches on December 29th 1862 at Bramall Lane, the following report appeared in the *Sheffield Independent* newspaper:

"Hallam played with great determination. They appeared to have many partisans present, and when they succeeded in 'downing' a man their ardent friends were more noisily jubilant. At one time it appeared the match would be turned into a general fight. Major Creswick had got the ball away and was struggling against great odds – [against] Mr Shaw and Mr Waterfall [playing for Hallam]. Major Creswick was held by Waterfall and in the struggle Waterfall was accidentally hit by the Major. All parties agreed that the hit was accidental. Waterfall, however, ran at the Major in the most irritable manner and struck him several times. He also 'threw off his waistcoat' and began to 'show fight' in earnest.'

By this time lots of people had taken Creswick and Prest's idea and founded football clubs of their own. In 1862 there were 14 clubs in and around Sheffield, with a similar number springing up in London. However, in the capital, they took things a step further.

On October 26th 1863, members from Barnes, the War Office Club, Crusaders, Forest of Leytonstone, No Names Club, Crystal Palace, Blackheath FC, Kensington School, Percival House [Blackheath], Surbiton and Blackheath Proprietary School and Charterhouse gathered at the Freemason's Tavern on Great Queen Street. Although Mr B.F. Hartshorne, the captain of Charterhouse, refused to join, the remaining ten clubs banded together to form the Football Association.

It appeared the match would be turned into a general fight

By joining together rather than trying to exist in isolation, the clubs in the south were able to take the game forward. One of the first tasks of the newly-formed FA was to try to establish a commonly-accepted set of rules but, like patting your head and rubbing your tummy at the same time, it was to prove more difficult than it first appeared. At one meeting, the representative of the Blackheath club stormed out because the rules allowing running with the ball in the hand and 'hacking' an opponent had been removed.

The two superpowers of football, London and Sheffield, collided on March 3rd 1866 at Battersea Park, London, in the first ever inter-city match. After some common ground had been found on the rules front, the game took place in a downpour, with London running out eventual winners by the bizarre margin of two goals and four touches down. This worrying dalliance with the world of rugby was finally ended in 1871 when Richmond, who in 1863 had played in the first football match using FA rules, left the kicking game behind and set up the Rugby Football Union.

Since the birth of Sheffield FC in 1857, football had been a gentleman's game, played mainly by public school and university graduates and undergraduates. In the early 1870s a new player burst onto the scene: the working class man. As football fever gripped the nation, it wasn't unheard of for people to take days off work from the factory to watch or play football. In Sheffield, as in other parts of the country, people made use of Saint Monday – a Victorian sickie pulled by factory workers to allow them to enjoy recreational activities. This led to an increase in the skill levels of footballers and an increase in the general interest of the game. It also led to one of the fiercest battles the football world has ever known.

THE GREAT WAR

It wasn't long before the masses began to take hold of the game. Everton and QPR were born out of church movements and many clubs were formed by groups of workers. Arsenal began life as Dial Square – a works team from the munitions factory at Woolwich, West Ham was formed by workers at Thames Ironworks and Manchester United by railwaymen from Newton Heath. The purpose of these clubs was to give the men something to do. They were a means of keeping fit and provided some light relief from the harshness of factory life. But it wasn't long before this began to change.

In 1867 twelve Sheffield clubs took part in the world's first organised football tournament. The Youdan Cup, named after a local theatre owner who provided the trophy, saw Hallam beat Norfolk in the final at Bramall Lane. The cup was never contested again, although it provided a blueprint for competition that was swiftly picked up by the FA.

For the 1871/72 season the FA introduced its own tournament. Being a challenge cup and the brainchild of the FA, the wheezes in the corridors of power wasted little brain power when settling on a name: the FA Challenge Cup. The fifteen entrants of the inaugural FA Cup almost reads like a who's who of pub quiz teams: Barnes, Civil Service, Clapham Rovers, Crystal Palace, Donnington School, Hampstead Heathens, Harrow Chequers, Hitchin, Maidenhead, Marlow, Reigate Priory, Royal Engineers, Upton Park, Wanderers and Queen's Park [yes, the Scottish one – as no such tournament existed north of the border, these jocular jocks scaled Hadrians Wall for a crack at taking the silverware off the Sassenachs. They failed].

In 1872 Kennington Oval played host to the first-ever FA Cup final and, in front of a crowd of 2,000, Wanderers beat Royal Engineers 1-0. The victorious team bagged the trophy, a bye into the following season's final [where they beat Oxford University 2-0] and the chance to nominate where that final should be played [they chose Lillie Bridge, because it was the nearest stadium to the Thames, where the then-popular Varsity boat race was taking place].

The FA Cup was hugely instrumental in the development of English football. The fact that 2,000 people turned up for the final cemented the idea that there was a section of society which was happy just to watch the game, rather than play it, confirming the birth of a new phenomenon: the football fan. These fans would play a crucial role in the commercialisation of the game in the not-too-distant future.

Just as significantly, the FA Cup gave the world its first glimpse of competitive football. It was a way of giving all games the intensity of the Sheffield FC-Hallam derby. It was also an encouragement for teams to become better than others. If they wanted to do well, they'd have to have the best players. And if they wanted to be sure of securing the services of the best payers, they'd have to get their purses out.

The FA Cup quickly changed some clubs from being places where people could turn up and play football, to places where good players could turn up and play football to help the club win matches. By the mid 1870s, clubs had started to pay players in order to make sure they got the best men on their team. Technically it was illegal, but clubs found ways around the law, such as accidentally leaving money in players' boots at the end of a game. Professionalism was the game's worst-kept secret and it sparked one of the greatest wars the game has ever seen. It pitted north against south, upper class against working class, pride against prejudice. It was also the first great victory in the march towards the commercialisation of football.

The supporters of professionalism were mainly northern and midlands-based and almost exclusively working class. Their argument was that, as interest in football grew, more spectators turned up to watch and the pressure to win increased. Players began taking more time off work to hone their skills, and should therefore be entitled to some form of compensation for loss of earnings.

This caused much nervous twitching and parping amongst the southern and upper class football men. They argued that being paid to play was against the spirit of the sport, which ought to be played for its own sake. It was an easy argument for them to make, seeing as none of them had to earn their living in a mine or factory. But the toffs did have a point. They warned that paying players would mean that player's livelihoods depended on matches and that this could lead to cheating, and that the involvement of football crowds could lead to the abuse of players and officials. Their crystal ball-like vision even extended to future England teams, with their warnings that the new professional game could lead to opportunities for drinking and gambling.

The 'to be or not to be' debate first came up officially at an FA meeting on June 24th 1884. The representative for Blackburn suggested that if compensation for players for loss of earnings was not introduced, the game would die out in Lancashire. A spokesman for Sheffield, who vigorously opposed the 'growing evil' in the game, stood up and argued against this. Eventually the idea of compensation was put to the vote. The proposal was voted out.

Fearing the uprising in the north, the southern-based, public school-founded FA decided to try and smash the idea of professionalism once and for all. They concluded that the problem lay with players coming from out of town to play for clubs, as they were often paid inducements to travel and play. So the FA asked members for written clarification of the personal details of all 'imported' players, hoping to weed out those that 'weren't from round 'ere' and thus put an end to the professional menace.

The move caused outrage in factory-dominated Lancashire, a working-class football hotbed where professionalism was seen as necessary for the future of the game. They not only refused to cooperate with the FA, but even set up an organisation of their own, the British National Football Association, through which they hoped to wrest power away from the rich public school boys of the south.

Matters came to a head on January 19th 1885, when over 221 clubs and associations were represented at a passion-filled meeting in London. Both sides trotted out their by now familiar arguments and again the matter was put to the vote. This time the pro-professional lobby won 113 to 108, but not by the two thirds majority needed to effect change. When the motion was again defeated in a vote in March, it looked as if the toffs had won. Yet, just four months later, professionalism was legalised in English football.

"Whilst deploring the new practice of professionalism, FA secretary Charles Alcock felt it preferable to control and contain it rather than allow a split to develop in the English game," says football historian Dr Graham Curry. "Generally speaking the southern amateurs, led by Alcock, as well as maintaining their grip on the administration and law-making arms of the FA, felt secure enough in their status to accept professionalism. Relying on compromise and negotiation the cooler heads of the FA had probably saved the game from self-destructing."

With victory in the bag, the northern monkeys disbanded the British National Football Association. It was pointless. The game had now gone professional and the first big barrier to the commercialisation of football had been smashed from its hinges.

TAKING CARE OF BUSINESS

Like Elvis, football clubs had been taking care of business long before Spurs floated on the stock exchange and Man U got a mega store. In 1888 Small Heath – AKA Birmingham City – became the first football club in the world to become a limited company. Following the advent of professionalism, football clubs suddenly had a dual role. They were still important members of their communities, providing a club for local people to play for and support. But now they had to make money too. They had to become more business-like if they didn't want to die on their arse. Like Elvis.

In those days the only income a club had was gate money. This was often haphazard as some teams didn't attract many fans and sometimes games were scrapped at the drop of a hat to accommodate cup matches. To solve this problem Aston Villa Chairman William McGregor wrote to a number of other big clubs proposing the formation of a league comprising ten to twelve of the 'most prominent clubs in England'. The idea was that with a regular supply of big games, the clubs would all be assured good crowds, and could therefore afford to pay the best players top money.

Although some were scared off because they thought the FA wouldn't be happy, McGregor managed to get the support of 11 other clubs and in April 1888 the Football League was formed in Manchester. The 12 founder members, all from the pro-professional north and midlands, were: Aston Villa, Everton, West Bromwich Albion, Bolton Wanderers, Blackburn Rovers, Derby

County, Wolverhampton Wanderers, Burnley, Stoke City, Preston North End, Notts County and Accrington [as-in 'Stanley? Who are they?!'].

The role of the football club had changed beyond recognition. Now they were employers, with wage bills and a responsibility to bring their grounds up to scratch for the growing number of people who wanted to come and watch them play. That was the inspiration for Birmingham City to become a limited company. And knowing a blueprint when they saw one, all the top clubs followed suit, although not without some opposition.

"People howled," sniped Chairman McGregor, talking about when he first suggested that Villa become a limited company. "But then people will howl at anything if its novel."

Smelling a rat bigger than Roland, the FA moved with a level of cunning that seemed to elude them when the Premiership was formed nearly 100 years later. In 1896, sensing that football clubs might become oil wells to be mined by the wannabe rich and infamous, they introduced Rule 34, which put a cap of 5% on the maximum dividend that could be paid out to shareholders. They also prevented directors from being paid.

People will howl at anything if its novel

However, then as now, those of a certain persuasion will find their way around any law, and so it was with Rule 34. Although unable to draw wages from their clubs, enterprising directors ensured there were some financial benefits to their positions. The Sir Norman Chester Centre For Football Research notes that 'directors in the building trade could expect to win the business to build the stands, those in hosiery provided the playing kit and director/bakers sold the club pies for home games.' It was hardly a passport to that desirable second home in Bognor, but it was better than a kick in the bowler hat.

Safe in the knowledge that the cash they made would stay with them, thanks to the protection of Rule 34, clubs set about the task of making themselves financially viable. Aston Villa became the first club to introduce turnstiles in 1892, part of a nationwide race to build grounds suitable to house spectators, who through their admission money paid the wages of the players on the pitch. It was a simple equation for clubs in those days, when ideas of merchandising and other such deals would probably have been enough to have got you hung up in a bottle and shot at. Money came in from the gate, went out to the players, and what was left was used to run the club.

There's no doubt that early Football League chairmen would have welcomed some of the extra revenue streams open to today's incumbents. Suddenly they had to have at least 25 players on the payroll, as failure to produce a team would lead to a fine. And the very nature of competition meant that they wanted to win, and to do that they needed the best players.

By 1900 Wolves were paying some of their top players £7 a week, whilst Villa were paying £6-10s. When you consider that in 1901 the average working wage was 14 shillings and 11 pence [around 75p], it shows that top footballers then were not far removed from the Rio Ferdinands and Ashley Coles of today.

Because they had more money, the top clubs were able to stay well ahead of their poorer rivals and the players were quids in. As a competition, the Football League was becoming stale with moneybags Villa and Sunderland winning the title eight times out of nine between 1892 and 1900. Something clearly needed to be done if the competition wasn't to be devalued and, in 1901, it was.

The FA, which was traditionally an amateur organization that disliked the new commercialisation running through football, was disgusted at the amount of money changing hands to secure the services of the top players. Like mums and dads who come home early to find their kids having a party, they decided to put a stop to the fun then and there. Instead of pulling the plug on the hi-fi and ordering everyone out the house, the FA introduced a maximum wage. Clubs could, they ruled, no longer pay their players more than four pounds a week.

Although clubs were now businesses, the normal rules of business did not apply. Successful companies did not force weak ones out of the market. In fact, the maximum wage, in tandem with the prohibitive retain-and-transfer system which chained players to their clubs for as long as their clubs wanted them, ushered in a golden age for football clubs. With wages limited and transfers drastically reduced, it was easy for clubs to make money and, because of the maximum wage, there was no way for clubs to out-do each other, so the gap between the haves and the have-nots was minimal.

Another crucial factor was that when the Football League was formed the clubs agreed to share the gate money, so that away teams were guaranteed a percentage of the match revenue. This, it was felt, would stop clubs with big attendances from yomping away with the title every year: if the big clubs were allowed to pocket all the cash they made off the gate, they'd be able to afford all the best players and the league would become unequal.

By 1924, when the Football League had grown to 88 clubs, the number of supporters [and thus the amount of money] was spread much more evenly between the clubs than it is today. In 1947 basement division Notts County broke the English transfer record when they signed England striker Tommy Lawton from Chelsea for £20,000. Barring the arrival at Spotland of a billionaire Cossack benefactor, it's hard to imagine Rochdale slapping £35m on the counter at the Man U mega store and declaring that Wayne Rooney shall be theirs.

This remarkable parity [well, as close to parity as you can get in a league that numbered 92 clubs by 1950] lasted until the start of the 1960s, when Jimmy Hill won his battle against the FA and the maximum wage, swiftly followed by the retain-and transfer system, was abolished.

BIG GUNS BLAZING

Suddenly clubs were free to pay players what they liked and players, no longer bound by archaic contracts, were free to move around and look for the best deals. This new freedom suited the big clubs best. The more supporters they could get in their ground, the more money they could make and the more they could afford to pay their players. There were exceptions of course – brilliant managers [Brian Clough at Derby and Forest] or clubs with rich benefactors suddenly snaffling up the best players [Sir Jack Walker's Blackburn in 1994] – but since the maximum wage and retain-and-transfer bit the dust the league has been dominated by clubs with big attendances – Manchester United, Liverpool and Arsenal.

As the 60s rumbled on, a new phenomenon entered the game: television. Increased media exposure turned Manchester United and Liverpool into superclubs. Through their success on the field, Man U and Liverpool were able to seduce a whole new set of fans sat in armchairs across the country and, later, the world.

"The modern day football 'brands' are all products of the post TV age," says Dr Rogan Taylor, Head of Liverpool University's Football Research Unit. "It's hard to say just why some are chosen and others not. I think a lot depends on a combination of disaster and success, plus remarkably durable fan bases. The current 'brands' were all established by the end of the 1970s, and no new 'brands' have emerged in the last 25 years. It's probably all about 'love' in the end and, as John Lennon said, money can't buy it."

It's no surprise, then, that these two clubs were instrumental in gradually shifting the balance within football clubs towards a more business-like approach. By being the first to explore ways of making money outside the traditional bums-on-seats model, Man U and Liverpool blazed a commercial trail.

In 1966 Man Utd became the first club in England to incorporate executive boxes – a means of charging blokes in suits loads of money – into their ground. At first the boxes went for between 250-300 quid for the season but by 2006 their value had shot up to an eye-popping £44,215 per box. Not a bad little earner, even if it was, at least partly, accidental.

As John Lennon said, money can't buy it

"The architects wanted to install some private boxes as they had done something similar at a race track and thought it would work for football," says Ken Ramsden, the assistant secretary who has been working at Man U since 1960. "The directors took some persuading and to this end, the architects put some kitchen chairs on the back seating deck where the boxes were to be situated. On seeing this, the directors instructed the architects to proceed with a small number to 'test the water'. I think that by the time the stand was complete, we had built and sold boxes from goal line to goal line."

The following decade, Liverpool became the first league club to have their shirts sponsored, when Hitachi paid the club to allow them to splash their name across the famous red jersey.

"We were very proud to be sponsored by Hitachi," says England's most decorated footballer Phil Neal. "But we weren't allowed to wear named shirts when playing in Europe. I can't tell you how much the contract with Hitachi was worth, but it saved us going to the wholesaler in the high street when we wanted to purchase anything."

In the 80s, as Thatcher's Children came of age and yuppies barked orders into over-sized mobile phones on the streets of London, football caught the entrepreneurial bug. Spurs became the first club to float on the stock exchange in 1983, cementing themselves a special slot in the commercialisation of football hall of fame. Not so much because they were brazenly going after pots of cash, more for the fact that they were about to tear up the rule book and open the doors for football clubs to be used as businesses.

Way back in 1896 the FA had introduced Rule 34, which placed a 5% limit on the amount of share capital that could be divided up amongst a club's shareholders. The aim of this was to stop greedy directors getting fat off the land of their clubs. Although this was raised to 7.5% in 1920, 10% in 1974 and 15% in 1981, the principle still held firm. Or at least, it did until Tottenham stuck their snouts in the trough.

The FA's rules prohibited Tottenham from distributing the club's profits to shareholders without limit. However, there wasn't a darn thing the FA could do when Spurs set up a holding company which was outside the jurisdiction of FA rules. The crafty cockerels were then able to siphon off as much cash as they wanted to the shareholders, making it a more attractive proposition for investors.

Or at least that was the theory. After an initial surge of interest in football clubs (Man U, Millwall and a host of others followed hot on their heels), the city lost interest and share prices tumbled. Spurs carried on largely as they had before, reasonably wealthy and susceptible to winning the odd cup, and investors returned to wiring cash to the nearest pharmaceutical company.

The big difference was the abandonment of Rule 34. With several clubs following Spurs down the holding company/stock market flotation route, the honourable law was abandoned. It meant that football clubs could be run just like any other business. There was nothing to keep the balance, nothing to push clubs back towards their more noble, community-based edge.

"The FA didn't do anything because they didn't think about it," says David Conn, football journalist and author of *The Football Business*. "Spurs' lawyers discovered it. The rule was introduced in the late nineteenth century because the FA wanted clubs to be different. The FA used to do a job that needs doing even more now than it did then. I only found out about it because I had a lawyer bragging to me about how they'd got around it. The FA just didn't think about it."

Clubs were now potential cash cows and directors at the top clubs immediately reached for the marigolds and started to milk the udders. 'Tat', which had previously been the preserve of local 'entrepreneurs', was suddenly deemed to be part of the club 'brand', and brought under the jurisdiction of the club.

"Football merchandise was a cottage industry all through the 50s, 60s and 70s with more memorabilia being sold outside the grounds than in," says The National Football Museum's Mark Bushell. "Clubs took hold of things in the mid 80s when Manchester United and Spurs developed mega stores."

As with all powerful businesses, top football clubs began sucking too hard on the greedy balloon. Not content with match day revenue and new found merchandise opportunities, the big boys wanted a bigger cut of the money in the football pot. In 1983, after shining a bright torch in the eyes of the Football League, gate sharing was abolished, meaning the clubs with the biggest attendances pocketed even more money. Two years later, the thumbscrews were put on again, this time over the issue of TV and sponsorship money. In 1965 when The League did a deal with the BBC to show highlights of games on *Match of the Day*, the £5,000 prize was shared equally amongst all 92 league clubs. Twenty years on, the big clubs threatened to breakaway unless the money was distributed more 'fairly'. In the end, the 'Heathrow Agreement' prevented them from stomping off, by giving top division clubs 50% of all TV and sponsorship deals, with 25% to the second division and the remaining 25% split between the third and fourth division. It was an important event in the movement of power from a collective of clubs towards the top end of the game. But it was nothing compared to what happened in July 1991.

TIPPING THE BALANCE

It's late afternoon, July 17th 1991. There are 22 suits packed into a meeting room at the Royal Lancaster Hotel in London. It's been a long day tinged with argument, but no one is checking their watch or yawning. This is important. It's one of the first meetings of the new Premier League chairmen since they broke away from the Football League and the very fabric of the bright new dawn is being argued over by the biggest names in English football. Sky TV has agreed to pay £305m for the rights to show the new league's games and how to distribute the whopping windfall is proving tricky. Eventually, many hours after entering the Royal Lancaster, the chairmen emerge blinking into the early evening air, having shaken hands on the Founder Members Agreement.

"We all agreed to stick to the principle, and we said it was cast in stone, about how the money was going to be distributed," says Premier League Chairman Dave Richards. "We spent a lot of time arguing the principle of how the money was going to be distributed, because there were the big clubs, the medium clubs and the small clubs. It was supposed to be a league of equality. So we spent a lot of time arguing the philosophy. We eventually finished up where we'd got 50% of domestic TV money equally spread among the 22 clubs, 25% on the ladder payment [money is awarded according to where teams finish in the league] and 25% on TV appearances. That was the Founder Members Agreement. We said 'that is cast in stone' and we all vowed that we would never break that. People have tried to break it but it's stood ever since. That was a little bit visionary. Whether it's right today or not, because the money has gone from there [gestures down] to there [gestures up] is questionable, but the principle is right. There were lots of arguments over it. I can remember Batesy, Martin Edwards, Sir Philip Carter, Irving [Scholar], Old Sam [Hamman], yeah, lots of arguments. Everybody was vociferous because these guys were young, entrepreneurial guys. We're talking about 15 years ago. It was done by continual argument and trying to get consensus. We got consensus and then we had a constitution on how we could vote."

The Premiership opened up a commercial goldmine. The deal they negotiated with Sky TV meant that the £305m the TV company agreed to pay would be split solely between the new Premier League clubs, with more money going to those who appeared more often [Man U, Arsenal, Liverpool]. Redistribution, that had done so much to maintain some kind of parity between clubs over the years, was dead. And the enormous coverage on Sky TV helped turn mere football clubs into household brands. Increased exposure of the product meant clubs could now shift more merchandise to an even wider audience.

"The Premiership had a far-reaching effect across football," says Mark

Bushell, of the National Football Museum. "Clubs needed to grow revenue to pay the bigger salaries being demanded by players. Since the Premiership came in, clubs have been run more like businesses, looking to make money in any way, shape or form. Suddenly clubs were saying 'let's get into Asia', and looking to sell merchandise to people in different countries who'd never even seen them play."

Players used the creation of The Premiership to set themselves up for life. They began putting pressure on their clubs, demanding ludicrous deals that the clubs, now flushed with TV cash, were happy to sign off.

"When the Sky money came in, wages went up and when the second Sky deal hit in '96 they went crazy," says Andy Hosie, former commercial director at Everton. "Suddenly clubs had an extra £25m they'd never had before. That money went straight into salaries, but the wise clubs also invested it in bringing in commercial people. Commercial positions within football clubs had traditionally been filled by football men who'd worked their way up. Suddenly people starting coming in from television and big business."

Even with the big clubs upping the commercial ante, the main sources of revenue for those at the top are TV money, European cash and the old constant, bums-on-seats. The latter is the reason Man U keep extending the capacity at Old Trafford and it's why Arsenal swapped the beautiful, art deco Highbury Library for the Corporate-oriented Emirates Stadium.

"Sky is the biggest revenue generator for most clubs, then matchday sales," says Andy Hosie. "Everton made £60m in the financial year ending May 2005. Of that, £49m came from Sky and ticket sales, with £11m from commercial activity. I don't know what it's like for the very top clubs, but for a mid-tier Premiership club, that's reality."

The glitz and glamour of The Premiership has also introduced another revenue stream for clubs, or rather, afforded certain clubs the luxury of operating without the need to make money by conventional means at all. Tapping their arms furiously and preparing to mainline freshly-cut power into their veins, certain club chairmen have pumped their own personal fortunes into their clubs in an attempt to manufacture success. The deep pockets of Sir Jack Hayward, Sir Jack Walker and Dave Whelan have ensured that Wolves, Blackburn and Wigan respectively have all basked in The Premiership sun.

But the prominence of off-field individuals hasn't led all clubs into the Garden of Eden. The work of men like Peter Ridsdale, who took to his task as

Leeds Chairman like a kid in a toy shop, has produced the phenomenon of Icarus Clubs, those that, in the pursuit of greatness, fly too close to the sun and end up going down in a ball of flame. Fans at Sheffield Wednesday, Barnsley, Bradford and Nottingham Forest have all seen Premiership dreams turn into third division nightmares, whilst Leeds chucked so much cash at trying to become the Big Dogs of England, they ended up having to sell the goldfish out of the boardroom.

And now there's Chelsea. The Blues of SW6 have a chairman so rich, they don't have to bother with commercialisation at all if they don't want to. They could play to empty stands week in, week out and still Roman's Roubles wouldn't run out. They can field almost two teams of players who would walk into most

They ended up having to sell the goldfish

other Premiership sides, which is why since José Mourinho added his considerable management skill to the Cossack's cash, they've steamrollered their way to two league titles out of two and made The Premiership about as exciting as a re-run of *Last of the Summer Wine*.

The gulf between English football clubs is now bigger than it has been at any time in history. With each passing year that the top clubs have access to huge vats of TV and European cash, whilst their Football League counterparts get practically nothing, the gap widens. Throw in extra gate money and merchandise sales for the big boys and you can see why, according to Deloitte and Touche, in 2003/4 Premiership clubs made a profit of £151m whilst their Football League chums made pre-tax losses of £68m.

One thing that all clubs have in common, Chelsea, the rest of The Premiership, the Football League boys and the Icarus clubs, is that they all share the same purpose as the 12 clubs who set up the Football League in 1888. They all have a community responsibility and a need to make money. The only thing that's changed in the last 150 years is the balance.

Ironically, as football clubs become more business-oriented, the onus on them to maintain more of a balance grows. Corporate governance encompasses the system of laws, codes and regulations that control the way corporate organisations are run. Good corporate governance for football clubs means clubs looking after the interests of their supporters and being more transparent in their monetary dealings.

"It's a big thing you have to look at," says Andy Hosie. "Man United had to do it when they were a public limited company. There's a big gap between what they do and what a private company has to do. The Premier League has laid down guidelines about customers and accountancy standards."

It's not just clubs coming under a harsher spotlight. Premier League Chairman Dave Richards says his life is run by corporate governance now.

"I am regulated to the hilt – government, Inland Revenue, VAT man, FA, UEFA and FIFA – all with different rules, all with corporate governance," he says. "If you look at the Premier League over 14 years you can see how it's changed. It used to be run by chairmen, it's now run by boards, directors, chairmen, commercial directors and financial directors. All of that has come out of corporate governance and proper governance of a business. It's a standard of how the business should be regulated."

And therein lies the problem, according to Dr Adam Brown, senior research fellow at Manchester Institute for Popular Culture and former member of the government's Football Task Force. Football shouldn't even be attempting to keep its clubs in check using corporate governance.

"Football clubs are not corporations, they're not traditional businesses," he says. "Therefore there should be no corporate governance. But if clubs are going to be PLCs, they need to act like it and follow the correct corporate governance procedures. If you follow this to its natural conclusion, Chelsea has most money = win league. It's the end of the game."

Whether clubs are right or wrong to follow corporate governance, the fact remains that if that's what they're doing, it's not working. The community aspect of football clubs at the top level has been neutered. Sure, all top clubs pay lip service to the idea of being a 'community club', but how many of the players actually do the community service they are meant to enter into each week? And how many people from the communities of Premiership clubs can actually afford to go and watch their local team? When the Premiership started in 1992, you could get into Chelsea for a tenner. Thirteen years on, the cheapest ticket at The Bridge is £48. Worse still, recent press reports suggest that some clubs are now charging their young fans for being matchday mascots. Not very community spirited is it?

It's not just the financial restrictions that are killing the football club. It's the attitude. Many are operating as pure businesses who look at their fans as pound signs. Chelsea chief executive Peter Kenyon calls Chelsea fans customers. Crowing about a deal he'd just struck with Samsung in 2005, he said: "Samsung has a key part to play in the future global development of Chelsea and we believe we can play a similar role for them in their strategic aims. There is a great synergy between the two brands in terms of recent dramatic growth and success, levels of performance and market targets."

The bad news is, it's not going to get better. In fact, according to Andy Hosie, it's going to get worse.

"It'll become more business-like," he says. "Top clubs are major brands now. The major opportunity for them is affinity products. It's about using the club brand to sell commodity products – savings accounts, credit cards, telecoms products. If you put clubs' names on them, fans will sign up. If a direct mail comes through from MBNA, people will throw it in the bin. But if it comes through from their club, people will buy it. Tesco have led the way with this – you can buy anything from them. But top football clubs are the most trusted brands in their fans' lives. They should be able to do it better than Tesco. Arsenal is currently endorsing a property development in Spain. It's already one of the biggest-selling developments in the country."

And don't be fooled into thinking it's just Chelsea or Arsenal or even just teams in The Premiership. When basement division Boston United re-launched their website in 2005, they did so with a checkout on the home page and awarded fan points to customers who'd bought things from them. The implication being the more you buy, the better fan you are. It's as if football and business are one and the same.

"Football isn't any different," says Premier League chairman Dave Richards. "It's pure perception. There's no difference between Marks and Spencer PLC and Manchester United, Arsenal, Newcastle and Liverpool. There's absolutely no difference, except with the one or two clubs that are owned by wealthy entrepreneurs. When you've got millions of pounds and it's your money, you can decide what to do with it. When you're a PLC, you are governed by the rules of the board and corporate governance. Fans? That's a terminology isn't it? What's the difference between a fan and a customer? You stick with your club through thick and thin. Isn't that part of our heritage? Isn't that part of our breeding? Through thick and thin. We talk about customer service in football now. We don't talk about fan service. We talk about customer service. We talk about how we can deliver better things for the customer. We call them fans but there is an element that says some of these people are customers, because they come into our shops and they buy our brands. We're much more switched on to fans and customers. We have customer relations in clubs now. Like Marks and Spencer."

This is the attitude that is killing the game. Football supporters are not customers, they are fans. How many customers would rally around and save a local business that was about to go bust? How many customers remain loyal to businesses that operate so badly on a regular basis? And how many businesses have customers that turn up every other week to cheer and sing and actively partipate in raising the business's performance?

"It's not right," says Alan Bloore, deputy chairman of the Football Supporters Federation. "I can't understand it. Customers are people who flip from place to place. If they don't like what's on offer at Sainsburys, they go to Tesco. Supporters don't do that. They support one club and stick with them through thick and thin. That's because football clubs are more than just businesses. Our view is that football clubs are going to drive people away from the game if they continue to push for market forces and push the prices up."

The Football Supporters' Federation is not alone. Football fans from Southampton to Northampton via Newcastle and Tynecastle are sick of being sold to.

"As fans in the 1970s and 80s, we would have been glad to be treated as 'customers' if it meant we didn't have to stand in two inches of piss and pay for the privilege," says Dr Rogan Taylor, Head of Liverpool University's Football Research Unit. "But Clubs have to be careful how far they take this. No one is spreading the ashes of their dead granddad down the aisles of Tescos. There's a limit to how far clubs can commercialise the relationship they have with supporters. Those who go too far will pay the price."

Football clubs, you have been warned. From Sheffield to SW6, it's been an incredible journey. Football clubs have enchanted, bewitched, delighted and exacerbated us on a weekly basis for the best part of 150 years. But, until clubs realise they need to be a bit more Creswick and a bit less Kenyon, the edge of the tightrope draws ever closer. Business or pleasure? Fans or customers? The future of the humble football club is hanging in the balance.

ORIGINAL FOOTY RULES EXPLAINED

These are the rules of football, as set down by the world's first football club Sheffield FC.

1. **THE KICK OFF FROM THE MIDDLE MUST BE A PLACE KICK**

   Author's note: What they mean is, place the ball on the centre circle and hoof it out of touch, muttering "ave it!" under your breath.

2. **KICK OUT MUST NOT BE FROM MORE THAN 25 YARDS OUT OF GOAL**

3. **FAIR CATCH IS A CATCH FROM ANY PLAYER PROVIDED THE BALL HAS NOT YET TOUCHED THE GROUND OR HAS NOT BEEN THROWN FROM TOUCH AND IS ENTITLED TO A FREE KICK**

   Author's note: I thought these were football rules?

4. **CHARGING IS FAIR IN CASE OF A PLACE KICK [WITH THE EXCEPTION OF A KICK OFF AS SOON AS THE PLAYER OFFERS TO KICK] BUT HE MAY ALWAYS DRAW BACK UNLESS HE HAS ACTUALLY TOUCHED THE BALL WITH HIS FOOT**

   Author's note: Commonly known as cabbaging. Frowned upon these days, especially from the penalty spot. John Aldridge, beware.

5. **PUSHING WITH THE HANDS IS ALLOWED BUT NO HACKING OR TRIPPING UP IS FAIR UNDER ANY CIRCUMSTANCES WHATEVER**

6. **NO PLAYER MAY BE HELD OR PULLED OVER**

7. **IT IS NOT LAWFUL TO TAKE THE BALL OFF THE GROUND [EXCEPT IN TOUCH] FOR ANY PURPOSE WHATEVER**

8. **THE BALL MAY BE PUSHED ON OR HIT WITH THE HAND, BUT HOLDING THE BALL EXCEPT IN THE CASE OF A FAIR KICK IS ALTOGETHER DISALLOWED**

9. **A GOAL MUST BE KICKED BUT NOT FROM TOUCH NOR BY A FREE KICK FROM A CATCH**

10. **A BALL IN TOUCH IS DEAD, CONSEQUENTLY THE SIDE THAT TOUCHES IT DOWN MUST BRING IT TO THE EDGE OF THE TOUCH AND THROW IT STRAIGHT OUT AT LEAST SIX YARDS FROM TOUCH**

11. **EACH PLAYER MUST PROVIDE HIMSELF WITH A RED AND DARK BLUE FLANNEL CAP, ONE COLOUR TO BE WORN BY EACH SIDE**

    Author's note: Now we're talking. What about goggles?

> CHAPTER 2
TOO BIG FOR THEIR BOOTS

2:   TOO BIG FOR THEIR BOOTS

Something grotesque is going on in the beautiful game. Footballers used to be heroes, men who'd run through brick walls for their supporters and play their hearts out because they loved the game. Now you can't turn on the TV without seeing an overpaid Premiership star scowling and telling the ref to f*** off and you can't open the paper without reading about a player's latest sex scandal or exorbitant wage demands. Footballers, it seems, have become too big for their boots.

The work of men like Jimmy Hill and George Eastham, who did so much to release footballers from the contractual bondage that condemned legendary players such as Wilf Mannion to die in poverty, has been abused. Since Jean-Marc Bosman won his test case at the European Court of Justice, player power has become so great that footballers seem to believe they can do and say as they please. Commercialisation is not in itself necessarily a bad thing, but greed is, and it's ruining this great game of ours. Nowhere is this trait more evident than with today's top footballers.

In 2005 Rio Ferdinand was roundly booed by Man United fans after he stalled over signing a new £100k-a-week contract because he wanted an extra £20,000 a week. Around the same time, Ashley Cole met illegally with Chelsea, saying he was unhappy with the £50,000+ deal Arsenal had offered him. He later said that the club he claimed to support, Arsenal, had 'hung him out to dry' and 'fed him to the sharks'. Really? Would that be the same Arsenal that had invested in Cole since he was a boy and turned him into one of the best left backs in the world?

It's no wonder footballers are arrogant. Many top players earn more in a single week than the average man-on-the street does in a year. How can this be? Some of the answers lie in the law courts, where footballers over the years have fought battles as important as any they have had on the pitch. Another reason clubs can pay such ridiculous wages is the sheer amount of money in the game since the Premiership clambered into bed with satellite TV. And one, often over-looked aspect of footballers' salaries is force of habit: footballers have always earned more than the common man.

When the newly-formed Football Association created the FA Cup in 1871, they inadvertently ushered in the age of professional football. Desperate to steal a march over their rivals, clubs began giving sneaky payments under the noses of the FA so they could attract the best payers and advance in the competition. When Boston United employed this tactic to get into the Football League in 2002, they were hit with a massive fine and a four point deduction. But in the late 19th Century, the FA weren't so sharp.

Clubs would leave money, usually half a crown, in a player's boot

Clubs would simply leave money, usually half a crown [around 12p], in a player's boot at the end of the game, safe in the knowledge that they'd be able to afford it because people were paying to come through the gates. By the mid 1880s so many clubs were paying 'boot money', that the FA could no longer bury its head in the sand and professionalism was legalised.

In 1888 the Football League was founded and competition between clubs began to really hot up. Grounds were developed and clubs began paying higher wages to make sure they got the best players. This caused outrage in the press, a good 125 years before the likes of Rio Ferdinand and Ashley Cole, with one hack huffing: 'This is truly the golden harvest for football professionals. When a second-rate forward receives a genuine offer of £4/10s a week and others even more, we may well ask what we are coming to?'

The wages explosion began to drain clubs of their finances and in 1893 they came up with a solution: the maximum wage.

This proposal was actually defeated at the league's AGM in 1893 but as two clubs' domination of the league continued [sound familiar?], the campaign for the maximum wage gathered momentum. Sick of seeing the names Aston Villa and Sunderland at the top of the league table [sound familiar? Thought not], other clubs rallied around and in 1901 when the idea of a maximum wage was put to the vote, it coasted in. The figure was set at four pounds a week, which wasn't to be sniffed at considering that for working your fingers to the bone on a farm you could be expected to pull in 14 shillings and 11 pence [about 75p] a week. Having said that, men such as Billy Beats and Tom Baddelly [they don't make names like that anymore] could feel aggrieved, as they'd been on seven pounds a week each at Wolves.

In 1909, a good 90 years before David Beckham started demanding image rights, top footballers successfully argued that they should be paid more than the make-weights in their team, as they were the ones the crowd was coming to see. They were paid an extra payment – 'talent money' – to supplement their basic wage. By 1920 'talent money' amounted to two pounds for a win and a pound for a draw in league and cup games.

It wasn't long though before massive unemployment caused attendances to drop and clubs again looked to cut costs. Again they decided to put the squeeze on the players and the maximum wage, which had been bumped up to nine pounds a week, was cut back to eight in 1922. The players, who'd threatened to go on strike, soon shut up when they realised they could spend 50 hours a week toiling the land and still only pull in one pound and eight shillings.

Legendary footballers retired with little to show for their efforts

By 1946 the average weekly footballer's wage had risen to 12 pounds, double the average of a manual labourer, and by 1961 it had risen to 20 pounds a week, a fiver more than a manual labourer and the same as a non-manual labourer. But men such as Johnny Haynes, who captained England and entertained thousands of fans every week, no doubt ought to have expected to be earning a lot more than a non-manual labourer. Legendary footballers like Tom Finney, Stan Mortenson and Nat Lofthouse had carved out illustrious careers on the pitch yet retired with little to show financially for their efforts.

If the latest crop of superstars was to fare any better, they were going to need a champion, someone to stand up to the clubs and take on the system on their behalf. And, in April 1957, they found him.

A WEAPON OF MAXIMUM DESTRUCTION

The Players Union AGM of 1957 was a tense affair. Over 100 footballers from around the country converged on the Great Northern Hotel in Manchester. It didn't take long to realise the mood was black, as they took it in turns to take pot shots at Chairman Jimmy Guthrie. Some objected to the fact that he was paid, others didn't like his methods but everyone seemed united behind the idea that Guthrie was a crap Players' Union Chairman. They'd wanted him out at the previous AGM, an outcome which had seemed certain until the new delegate from Fulham had stood up and defended the Chairman; pointing out that his lack of popularity with Football League bigwigs meant he must be doing something right for the players. But after another year of Guthrie the players could take no more and when it came time to re-elect, not a single hand was raised in favour.

At the next meeting of the Committee of Management, which ran the Union, it was decided that the very pup who'd spoken up in support of Guthrie in 1956 was the man who should lead the Union forward. And so on February 11th 1957 Jimmy Hill became chairman of the Players' Union. Although he didn't know it at the time, it was the beginning of a chain of events that would set players on the road to untold riches, fame and power.

"I had no idea at that time what an enormous difference it would make to my life," says Jimmy. "Or to the lives of professional footballers. Or that it would eventually lead to the vast sums of money now paid to today's superstar players."

At the time when Jimmy took over as chairman of the Players' Union, there were two ways footballers could earn extra money. The legitimate way was to advertise a product. Denis Compton bagged a nine year contract with Brylcreme worth £1000 a year in the 1950s, but for those who didn't want to be involved in adverts which said things like *'when up for the cup…make smartness your goal. Brylcreme your hair'*, there was another, less cheesy way: clubs simply passed money to the players 'off the record'.

One of Jimmy's first acts as chairman was to defend a group of Sunderland players who'd been accused of receiving improper payments. It was this perceived injustice that kick-started the war against the maximum wage.

The feeling was that footballers shouldn't have to go sneaking around to earn the cash they felt was rightfully theirs. The star players believed that, since they attracted the fans through the gate, they should be entitled to see more of the profits. The maximum wage had been in place for nearly 60 years and footballers had had enough.

Before he could contemplate taking on the established football order, Jimmy Hill recognised the need to modernise the Union, so he convinced the Committee of Management to ditch the name Players Union and go for the more professional-sounding Professional Footballer's Association [PFA].

The first meeting between the PFA and Football League, on December 7th 1959, was a disaster. Not only did League Big Knobs sit stony-faced throughout whilst the PFA outlined their vision of a better future, they followed it up with a letter guffawing at their ideas and insisting that they never appear on the agenda in future.

At the AGM in 1960 outraged footballers, perhaps thinking they'd suddenly been imbued with Mafia-like qualities, instructed the PFA to take 'any steps necessary' to bring an end to what they saw as Football League tyranny.

No one ended up sleeping with the fishes, but there were some ugly stand-offs and lots of table-thumping meetings. Essentially the Football League wasn't prepared to concede anything to the players which would significantly weaken its own position. The players cried that they only wanted a fair crack of the whip.

Showing a Churchillian grasp of propaganda, the players took to the airwaves. Bobby Robson, Jimmy Greaves, Bobby Charlton, Tommy Docherty and Johnny Haynes were amongst the avalanche of footballers that appeared on radio and TV, stating the case of the players in order to win public support.

The ploy worked and, with public opinion swinging against them, the Football League buckled and offered to raise the maximum wage to 30 pounds a week. By now it had become a matter of principle for the players and, instead of accepting the improved terms, they voted at a meeting in London on December 13th to go on strike. They wanted the right to earn as much as a club was willing to pay them. Similar meetings were held in Birmingham and Manchester and by the end of the week the strike vote was won by a majority of 694 to 18.

The threat of strike action split the football world down the middle, with clubs planning to carry on playing using amateur players and players threatening to adapt club names and carry on themselves.

In the end it didn't come to that. After much to-ing and fro-ing, a meeting was convened on Wednesday 18th January 1961. Within four hours the maximum wage, the scourge of footballers for the best part of 60 years, the legislation that had prevented the likes of Dean, Matthews, Mortensen and Finney from earning enough from the game to be able to retire without the need to find another job, had been abolished. But, if the players stood back and watched the floodgates wrenched open, waiting for a wave of new money to flood into their coffers, they'd have been dismayed.

"It didn't go crackers," says Jimmy Hill. "It crept up steadily. Income wasn't sufficient to support massive increases, so clubs paid what they thought was a businesslike amount. In those days directors were extremely well looked after. We used to turn up to play matches and they'd have luxurious lunches and all the wine they could drink. It was like a holiday from business for them. When we got rid of the maximum wage we turned things in another direction."

FIGHTING THE POWER

Jimmy Hill was the icing on the cake, but the road to player power had actually begun being paved at the tail end of the 19th Century. From the start of the 1893/94 season, the Football League introduced a new system which meant a player had to be registered with the club he intended playing for and, once registered, he couldn't play for anyone else. This 'retain and transfer' system was brought in to stop big clubs scooping up all the best players and was designed to keep some kind of parity in the league. It was great news for the clubs but less good for the players, who suddenly found that if they wanted to move clubs at the end of a season, they'd have to get the permission of their current club, even if they had no intention of playing him in the new season. In principle, a club could refuse to release a player's registration, preventing him playing football again.

The first rumblings of player power appeared in 1897, when the Scottish League banned its members from taking English players, slamming the door shut on many an English journeyman's escape route. An attempt was made at forming some kind of union, but with membership never rising above 50% of players, the idea was ditched amidst a whirlpool of apathy. It was in this climate that the maximum wage was pushed through in 1901.

Six years later though, the players' ire was stoked to such high levels that it could be held back no more. The straw that broke the camel's back was Welsh wizard and all round rogue Billy Meredith, who was banned for 18 months in 1905 for attempting to bribe opponents into throwing matches. His club Manchester City, who had fully supported Meredith, got cold feet and pretended to know nothing about it. In a rage, Meredith became the first player to squeal like a pig about the corruption in the game. He detailed City's illegal signing-on payments to new players, the club officials' role in bribing opponents and their persistent violations of the rules on the maximum wage and player bonuses. As a result of Meredith's blabbing, every single member of City's FA Cup winning team was suspended from the game and banned from playing for the club ever again. As soon as his ban was up the cantankerous Meredith gave City the biggest two fingered salute possible by joining hated neighbours Manchester United. Other footballers, perceiving Meredith to have been stitched up by City to some extent, realised that Zebras are right: you really are safer in numbers. And so, in 1907 in Manchester, the first Player's Union was formed.

The Union's first attempt at getting a slice of power pie revolved around the mysterious case of Herbert Kingaby. Kingaby was chuntering along in the Southern league with Clapton Orient when Aston Villa, one of the most powerful sides in the land, paid £300 for his services. Two months later, the Villans realised they'd dropped a rickett of Bosko Balaban-sized proportions and offered Kingaby back to Orient for £150. Clapton couldn't afford that kind of money and things started to turn nasty. Even though they had no intention of offering him a new contract, the law stated that Villa could keep hold of Kingaby's registration, so they did. This meant he wasn't getting a penny from Villa and couldn't play for anyone else. The cunning Kingaby then got a gig with Fulham, a Southern League side, and therefore not bound by the League's retain-and-transfer handcuffs.

Things were going swimmingly until Kingaby joined second division Leyton Orient in 1910. Just after he moved, the Southern League and Football League did a deal over the issue of retain-and-transfer, which prevented League players dropping down into the Southern League to escape the draconian system. The deal saw Kingaby's registration winging its way back into the hands of Aston Villa, meaning he couldn't play for anyone unless Villa agreed to transfer him. Villa did agree to transfer him to Leyton Orient, but not until Orient agreed to stump up £350. That kind of cash was way out of the Londoners' reach and an impasse erupted that was as impregnable as if Gandalf himself had thumped two sticks on the floor and said "they shall not pass".

Making the reasonable observation that Villa were unlawfully restricting his ability to trade, Kingaby decided to take the matter to the law courts. The newly-formed Players' Union, sensing an opportunity to make their mark, agreed to help out with the financial cost of the case. Legal Eagles told the Union they had a strong case and it was with great confidence that the Union approached the Kingaby v Aston Villa Football Club case.

What they didn't legislate for was an error of judgement of Eric Djemba-Djemba-sized proportions. Inexplicably, the player's counsel attacked Villa's malicious use of the retain-and-transfer system, rather than challenging its legality. The case proceeded on the presumption that the system was legal and, as such, it didn't matter if Villa had acted out of malice or not, as that alone couldn't render a lawful act unlawful. The case was slung out and the future of the Players' Union looked bleak. They were forced to pay costs and made to look like imbeciles in the press.

However, the Union's next foray into the legal arena was more successful. After the end of the First World War there was mass unemployment and football attendances dropped. The Football League decided to cut the maximum wage back from £9 to £8 a week and force players who weren't on the maximum to be paid less, reasoning that, if the money had to come from somewhere, it might as well come from the players. Players were legally entitled to be paid what they'd been contracted to play for, but after the Kingaby case, the League thought they could do as they please.

What they hadn't bargained for was a Superman-esque appearance from the Players Union, gallantly appearing out of nowhere to guide the innocent victims to safety. In May 1923 Chesterfield's Henry Leddy, assisted by the Union, won a case against the League which established the player's right to earn what they'd been contracted to earn. It was a minor victory, both the maximum wage and retain-and-transfer were still in place, but it was the first battle won by the Union in a war against the League – a war which would run for the next half century.

They were made to look like imbeciles in the press

The Union trudged on, helping players out where possible, but not really making much of an impact until Jimmy Hill appeared and fought, like a man possessed, against the prohibitive maximum wage and the retain-and-transfer system. The wars raged simultaneously for a number of years. All the meetings, the press coverage and the threats of strike action mentioned earlier revolved around both these points, and the issues didn't get separated until Wednesday 18th January 1961, when Jimmy Hill emerged from a meeting at the Ministry of Labour believing he'd secured the end of both the maximum wage and the retain-and-transfer system. It turned out he was only half right.

The maximum wage was gone but on April 14th League clubs met and refused to accept the end of the retain-and-transfer system, as had been agreed at the Ministry of Labour meeting.

'The Football League, born 1888, died of shame at high noon yesterday,' screamed one paper, reflecting the public opinion that was now firmly weighted behind the footballers.

If a miracle was required it appeared in the form of Newcastle player George Eastham. The Blackpool-born forward had made several unsuccessful attempts to get away from the Toon Army before eventually throwing his hands in the air and storming off in a huff. He took on a job outside football but, starting to smell an idea, the PFA approached him about using his experience as a test case.

He agreed and, in the summer of 1963, the case of Eastham v Newcastle United was heard in the Chancery Division. Newcastle had already relented at this point and Eastham was knocking in the goals for Arsenal, but it was now the principle the PFA were fighting for and it was one that would change football forever.

When Judge Wilberforce found in favour of Eastham, citing the fact that the retain-and-transfer system was an unreasonable restraint of trade, it was a small step for men but a huge leap for footballers.

"I'd had to resign as Chairman of the PFA by the time the result came through, because I'd had to stop playing," recalls Jimmy Hill. "I was manager at Coventry when the verdict came through, but that didn't stop me celebrating. Cliff Lloyd and I had taken the decision to take the authorities to court because they'd cheated. They'd given their word and gone back on it. We knew we were right and the court's decision showed that. It was justice."

In 1963 a new transfer system was put in place which meant every player's contract was a matter of free negotiation between him and the club [without, of course, the restriction of the maximum wage]. At the end of a player's contract the club could only renew if the terms were as good as the old ones or better, for at least the same amount of time, otherwise a free transfer could be granted. Also, if there was a dispute between player and club, it could be referred to an independent transfer tribunal. The days of players being imprisoned by their clubs were well and truly over. Herbert Kingaby and George Eastham were princes in the battle for player power but it wasn't until a year after the new transfer system was put in place that the king was born, in the unlikeliest of kingdoms: Belgium.

ACCESSION TO THE THRONE

As soon as the maximum wage and the retain-and-transfer system were abolished, life began to look a whole lot rosier for footballers. Fulham chairman Tommy Trinder had boasted, from behind the safety of a maximum wage system, that he would pay star player Johnny Haynes £100 a week if he could. As soon as the footballer's Berlin Wall came down, he was as good as his word, making Haynes the first £100-a-week footballer.

"It didn't change my life all that much," Haynes told the FA's website a year before he died in 2005. "I put a few pounds in the bank. Having said that, I think I got a car soon afterwards! It was an S-type Jaguar and I think I paid £3,000 for a brand new one. Apart from that, I didn't go throwing my money round."

The floodgates may have opened but salary rises only trickled through at first. But, as the years went by, footballers' wages went up and up, breaking new barriers.

"The question of the first £1,000 a week player is difficult," says PFA Historian John Harding. "Once the maximum wage was abolished, there was no clarity about who got what and a lot of concealment. Kevin Keegan was on about £2,000 a week in the 1970s while in the 1980s John Barnes was said to be the best paid player in Britain on £500,000 a year and when Paul Gascoigne went to Lazio he was on around £1.3m a year."

However, it wasn't until a previously unheard of footballer from Belgium hit the headlines that wages started to go insane. Until Jean-Marc Bosman pitched up, the most famous person to come out of Belgium was Hercule Poirot. And he wasn't even real. Bosman's 1996 European Court of Justice win not only elevated the Low Country briefly out of its well of mediocrity, it also turned the man himself into the unlikely figurehead for player power and secured him a spot in the dictionary alongside other modern luminaries, Tong and Dyson.

The Bosman case came about because Jean-Marc Bosman's contract with

RFC Liege had run out and he wanted to sample the spirit of Dunkerque. Liege wouldn't let him move without money changing hands and Dunkerque were unwilling to pay a fee. Bosman argued that as a European citizen he had the right to freedom of movement within the European Union if he wished to find work. The European Court of Justice agreed, finding that transfer fees for out of contract players were illegal if a player was moving between one EU Nation and another and so were quota systems [where leagues restricted the number of foreign players in their leagues].

Football's top brass and the European Union have been fighting like Capulets and Montagues ever since. The European Union wants to homogenise football practice so it is in line with the rest of European employment law, whilst football's big squeezes stick their tongues out and say 'ya boo sucks, leave our game alone'. Always with a keen eye for danger,

Jean-Marc Bosman ...the most famous person to come out of Belgium

FIFA tried to head off trouble at the pass by bringing in new transfer regulations in 2001, which included compensation if a club nicks a player under 23, a transfer window system and the creation of an independent disciplinary and arbitration system to deal with contractual disputes.

The practical fall-out from the case was an increase in power for players. Clubs started offering higher wages and longer contracts to keep players happy to avoid the nightmare scenario of someone 'doing a Sol'. In the summer of 2001 the then Tottenham captain Campbell ran down his contract and simply walked across the Sven Sisters Road and into the all-too-welcoming arms of deadly rivals Arsenal. Sol got a fat signing on fee, Arsenal got a top class central defender for less than they would have had to pay out in transfer money and Spurs got a bad case of the yips.

But what does the man himself make of it all? Not content with the fame and the power he's given his fellow professionals, it seems that Monsieur Le Bosman wanted the part of the holy trinity he didn't get his hands on: dirty cash.

"I look at all these big stars earning a fortune today and they are all able to negotiate contracts thanks to me," Bosman told *UEFA.com* in 2005. "I personally never thought about earning a lot of money, I was only trying to earn a living but the fact remains that without the Bosman ruling, Real Madrid wouldn't be the club they are now. Nor would Chelsea. If I'd done the same thing in America, I'd be a multi-millionaire by now as a reward for giving everyone their freedom. But we don't think like that in Europe."

However, the Bosman case did open the cashgates for footballers to live like kings. Prior to the 1966 World Cup, England's Geoff Hurst earned £45 a week at West Ham and would have netted an extra 300 quid for winning the tournament. Forty years later, England's John Terry earned around £100,000 a week and would have pulled in an extra £300,000 if England could have emulated the '66 side, rather than crashing out on penalties. Again. How come the drastic, disproportionate up-turn?

"Clearly the advent of Sky put millions into the top clubs' coffers," says PFA Historian John Harding. "That combined almost simultaneously with the extra freedom players at the top now have after Bosman. Together these factors have contributed to the dramatic surge in top players' weekly wages."

WHEN WILL I, WILL I BE FAMOUS?

A mix of personal crusade and legal expertise have combined to put players in a position of previously unassailable power. This in turn has allowed players to achieve wealth beyond most rock stars' dreams. And, as surely as Palmer always comes after Emerson and Lake, fame comes hot on the heels of money and power.

It's not a new thing. Even in the days of grainy black n' white footage, long before 24 hour coverage on Sky TV and T'internet, George Best had to employ three secretaries to sift through the 10,000 fan letters he got each week. These days the likes of Beckham, Rooney and Lampard can't go anywhere without a minder.

Fame can work two ways. David Beckham has harnessed his spectacularly, negotiating a deal for his own image rights whilst at Man Utd that reportedly added another £20,000 onto his salary. Since then, he's developed himself into a brand, complete with his own clothing range, football academy and a slew of endorsements that have seen him use his fame to sell Adidas football boots, Pepsi, Police sunglasses, second hand Japanese cars, Japanese chocolate, the Tokyo Beauty Centre, mobile phones, Castrol lubricant, Jaffa

Cakes, trading cards, hair products, KLM airlines and Gilette razors. Not to mention his own ill-feted DB7 range for Marks and Spencer [er, can we make that DB23?].

"I get many offers for commercial associations, but I only ever consider the ones that I feel are right," gushed Beckham following the announcement of his Gilette deal. "I have always tried to associate myself with the best brands, as my existing relationships with Adidas and Pepsi show. This new Gillette deal is exactly that – they are the best at what they do and I'm proud to be a part of it."

Beckham's fame has turned him into a commercial phenomenon. In 2005 the accounts of Footwork Productions, the company set up by Beckham to 'provide the services of David Beckham', revealed an influx of £17.4m into the Beckham coffers for the year. Taking into account the £4.4m salary at Real Madrid and the odd bit of cash for appearances, that means about £12.5m of Beckham's cash comes from advertising. Footballers, it seems, have come a long way since Denis Compton's £1,000-a-year Brylcreme deal.

However, fame can also work against footballers. As any hairy, fairground-dwelling coconut will tell you, the problem about living life on a pedestal is: you're there to be shot at. Footballers may not have to have their bellies slashed in order to provide the world with vile-tasting milk, but life in the sports lane can bring its own tortures.

The heady cocktail of fame, money and power makes footballers targets for people who realise that, unlike on *Bullseye*, there's everything in this game for two in a bed. Kiss-and-tell stories have been appearing in the papers since George Best started playing the field off the field. If a girl felt hurt by a night she'd had with a footballer or just simply needed to make a few quid, she could pose for the camera in her bra, dish out a few secrets and make herself some cash. No one really got hurt [unless, of course, the player was married], it just provided a bit of entertainment for readers and some pocket money for the girl. Then, in 2003, things started to get heavy.

In most walks of life, roasting means nothing more sinister than basting a chook in hot oil and cooking it in the oven. Not on Planet Football. For footballers a weekend roast seems to involve getting together with at least one other footballer and gang banging a girl. Carlton Cole and Titus Bramble were amongst four footballers famously accused of roasting a 17-year-old girl at the Grosvenor House hotel against her will in 2004. The Crown

Prosecution service dropped the case because there was insufficient evidence.

The last few years have seen an explosion of incidents in which footballers have been accused of sexual assaults. The 'Leicester City six' – including Paul Dickov, Frank Sinclair and Keith Gillespie – were accused of raping three German tourists in a hotel in La Manga. After a torrid time in a Spanish jail, and subsequent release on bail, all charges were dropped. Arsenal striker Robin Van Persie was held for two weeks in Holland after being accused of raping a beauty queen, whilst Man Yoo winger Christiano Ronaldo was arrested after a woman claimed he'd raped her at a central London hotel. In both cases the charges were dropped.

What goes on? Are all these footballers victims of their own fame, set upon by girls hungry for a quick buck? Or are they arrogant young millionaires who think they can do whatever they want without fear of retribution? A straw poll of men-on-the-street would point to a belief that rich, young footballers think they can, and do, take whatever they like from whoever they like. However, Dr Rogan Taylor, Director of Liverpool University's Football Industry Group, sees it another way.

"It's hard for ordinary people to imagine what it's like to be a young, successful football player," he says. "For a start, you've probably lived inside a special bubble since your talent was first identified in your early teens. By the time you're 18, someone is giving you £10,000 a week pocket money. How many of us would survive that? The world says it loves you but it is also a malevolent place. Every time you leave the 'bubble' and head into the ordinary world, it is full of dangers. There's a pack of wolves waiting at every turn: smart suits, old hacks, pretty girls. They all have one thing in common: they are intent on using you for their own advantage. You are a target. We shouldn't be surprised that some young players fall prey. The surprise is rather that they don't more often! But even if you don't go upstairs with the pretty girl, you may well find her claiming that you did [in a national newspaper] and even if you did go to bed with her, the next thing you hear about it is that you 'raped' her. That's what life is like for these young guys."

WHAT NEXT?

The power struggle between footballers and their clubs has been long and traumatic. No one can be in any doubt that for 60 years footballers had a raw deal. Unable to leave their clubs when they wanted to and unable to earn above an amount set by the Football League, many players likened their position to serfdom. Then along came Jimmy Hill and later Jean-Marc Bosman, The Premiership and Sky TV, and now there's a feeling that things have gone way, way too far the other way.

Footballers are now so arrogant it beggars belief. Who else could perform so miserably in public then expect people to fork out to read about the failure, as England's footballers did post-World Cup 2006? The slew of books that emerged from England's failed campaign was nothing short of an insult to the English public. Still, the players will shrug, who are the real idiots here – the losers who didn't turn in a single performance of note in Germany or those that are buying their books?

The trouble with the high wages of the Premiership is that for every Thierry Henry, there's a Lee Bowyer. In short, some players accept their outrageous wages with good grace, whilst others seem from the outside to be rather nasty, arrogant pieces of work who let it go to their heads.

And there are other problems too. With such high wages, the Premiership is a very uneven battleground these days. Since Roman Abramovich's private jetski landed at Chelsea, they have simply been able to buy whoever they want whenever they want, for however much they want. Genuine fears are surfacing that a one horse race does not a title race make. And no one wants to turn up and watch a foregone conclusion every week. So what's the answer? Going full circle, according to Wigan Athletic Chairman Dave Whelan, who would like to see a salary cap re-introduced.

"Fifa will have to look at limiting salaries to about £20-25m," he told the BBC in September 2005. "Chelsea is paying £100m a year in wages and have virtually three teams of players that would get into any other team in the Premiership. It's not going to be good for the game. The competition will become devalued and attendances will go down, so clubs will lose more money."

Whelan is qualified to speak because as owner of the once all-conquering Wigan rugby league club, he's been on the receiving end of salary capping.

Wigan were pretty much untouchable until the league introduced a £1.8m salary cap.

"It has taken about six years to get the transparency needed and I think every club now abides by it, with the rules strict," Whelan said. "It works in rugby league and I'm sure it would work in football throughout Europe."

However sensible a salary cap might seem, the chances of getting the pampered stars of today to accept such a ruling are virtually nil.

"Some figures in the game have recently suggested there should be a wage cap for today's footballers," George Best noted in his book *Hard Tackles and Dirty Baths*. "I doubt you would ever persuade players to accept a situation that previous generations fought so hard to end. But I do wonder if the Football League would have capitulated, had it been able to foresee not just the astronomical sums now paid out to players but also the power this gave individual players."

And what of the man who gave them that power? Does he ever survey the wreckage of The Premiership and think 'I wish we'd never got rid of the maximum wage'?

"No," says Jimmy Hill. "Even as a chairman, when I was working hard to keep Fulham alive, before Al Fayed came on the scene, I thought the same. Players should be entitled to earn a fair percentage of what they earn for their club. I don't mind how much a club pays their players as long as they can afford to do it without going into the red. The trouble comes when clubs pay too big a percentage of their income. When I was chairman of Coventry I made a rule that we wouldn't pay more than 50% of our income out as wages. At one point, Wimbledon were paying 165% of their income on wages. That's as clear an example as you can get. Why do clubs do it? The pressure comes from supporters. They don't care, they just want to see their team win on a Saturday afternoon and if they don't, they don't turn up. That's the silly thing about the game, 90% of players are overpaid in the sense that clubs are paying them more than they can afford, because of the pressure from supporters to win things."

Wimbledon were paying 165% of their income on wages

One beacon of hope comes from Italy, where Roma legend Damiano Tomassi became the world's first footballer to demand a pay cut. After suffering a bad knee injury in 2004, it was touch-and-go whether he'd play again. But he battled back and, when Roma offered him an extension to his contract, he said he'd only accept if they agreed to pay him 1,500 Euros a month, the minimum wage in Italy.

"I did it because I love the Rome Club and football," he said. "Kids see us as idols and we have to give a good example. I do a job that I love and I get a lot of money for doing it. This is a joy but also a big responsibility."

If more players had captured the spirit of football the way Tomassi has, perhaps the game would be in better shape. As it is, the likes of Rio Ferdinand and Ashley Cole have such power that they can demand more money in their weekly pay packet than the average Joe earns in a year. And the frightening thing is: it could be about to get a whole lot worse.

"Things may get even better for players," says PFA Historian John Harding. "At the moment things are held together by a thread – the transfer system is illegal under EU legislation and only a 'gentleman's agreement' between the Premiership and the European Commission allows clubs to ask for transfer fees before a player's contract expires. If players obtain the freedom to simply talk to whoever they wish whenever they wish about moves and salaries then the Sky's the limit. It's all in flux, and continues to develop, but top players will continue to reap the financial benefits until the game fades in popularity."

THE TOP 5 ADVERTS INVOLVING FOOTBALLERS

1. PAT JENNINGS / UNIPART

Surely the most bizarre advert of all time, this 70s oddity featured Pat Jennings flinging himself around a muddy goalmouth whilst the crowd chanted *"Unipart! Unipart!"* To try and make some sense of the madness, the voiceover informed us that "a goalkeeper is like an oil filter." Maybe at Unipart FC, mate, but on Planet Earth goalkeepers are more like…men with gloves and, when it's cold, long-legged pantaloons.

2. IAN RUSH / MILK

Although he never actually appeared, the very mention of Ian Rush was enough to coerce two young scouse scamps into drinking more milk. Why?
"Ian Rush says if I don't drink lots of milk, I'll only be good enough to play for Accrington Stanley."
"Accrington Stanley! Who are they?"
"Exactly!"

3. DIXIE DEAN / CARRERAS CLUB CIGARETTES

Brylcreme came out with some cheesy ads in their time but for sheer brazenness of pun, Carreras Club gets the vote for their Dixie Dean campaign. *"Carreras Club – the cigarette with the kick in them."* Ugh!

4. KEVIN KEEGAN / BRUT

You could see where Brut were coming from when they hired Henry Cooper [a bit of a brute] to advertise their aftershave but things got a bit confused when they threw Kevin Keegan into the mix, then made them frolic together semi-naked in a shower room. Still, at least he got to act alongside a real person. When he came back into advertising 20 years later, KK had to put up with enormous yellow fool The Honey Monster pretending to score goals for Newcastle. Yeah right: like anyone scores goals for Newcastle.

5. GARETH SOUTHGATE / PIZZA HUT

When Gareth Southgate, Stuart Pearce and Chris Waddle profited from their penalty shoot-out buffoonery by appearing in adverts promoting pizza, it left a sour taste in the mouth. Profiting from the nation's doom just seemed... wrong. At least dear old Gareth was made to work hard for his cash: it reportedly took him 27 takes to film his scene.

> CHAPTER 3
DANCING IN THE STREETS OF
TOTAL NETWORK SOLUTIONS

3: DANCING IN THE STREETS OF TOTAL NETWORK SOLUTIONS

It's a typical English Saturday afternoon during the football season. Those that can't get to a game are slumped in their armchairs, transfixed by the multitude of scores flashing across their TV screens. To keep things interesting the presenter has a head full of stats to put things in context or, if you're really lucky, he'll unleash one of his catchphrases.

As the clock ticks around to 4.47pm a familiar scoreline trickles through from the Welsh Premier League. Fans of *Gillette Soccer Saturday* brace themselves for a golden catchphrase moment. Jeff Stelling grins impishly as he delivers the line for the umpteenth time this season: "they'll be dancing in the streets of Total Network Solutions tonight."

The studio panel of ex-footballers falls about laughing, a scene replicated in living rooms around the country. But scratch under the surface of the Raith quip – Kenneth Wolstenholme once famously said "they'll be dancing in the streets of Raith tonight," after a victory by Raith Rovers, even though they played in Kirkcaldy – and you'll find a much darker layer of meaning. Football: for sale!

The journey to Total Network Solutions began in 1885, when professionalism was legalised and football clubs suddenly found themselves with the dual responsibility of being community clubs and businesses. The need to make money was largely sated by gate receipts but, by the late 1970s, with falling attendances and players freed from the maximum wage wanting more cash, clubs were forced to seek funds elsewhere. As luck would have it big business, a dull sphere of life with pots of cash and the charisma of a Doberman, was looking for a way to make itself more sexy. The solution was obvious.

The unholy matrimony has existed ever since – with football shirts, stands and grounds sold off to the highest bidder. Although fans don't particularly like it, most realise it's an evil worth tolerating. For the sake of having a firm's name splashed on the front of your teams' shirt, you might be able to afford that journeyman left-back who would be the missing piece in your trophy-hunting jigsaw.

Like Jeff Stelling, erstwhile WWF wrestler, Million Dollar Man, used to have a catchphrase. As he bounced flabbily into the ring, his voice could be heard growling over the tannoy: "everybody has their price."

And do you know what? He was right. In the 1970s Led Zeppeliln supposedly sold their soul to the devil in exchange for the track *Stairway to Heaven*. In the 1980s TV show *The Legend of Tim Tyler*, a teenage boy sold his laugh to a mysterious businessman known only as The Baron. And in the 1990s Llansantffraid FC sold their name to the firm of local businessman Mike Harris.

"It was 1997," says Mike. "Llansantffraid had just qualified for the UEFA Cup, after winning the Welsh Cup. They asked me if I wanted to get involved in sponsoring their shirts, so I said OK. At the time we had trouble attracting staff. We were working out of a back street shed. No one had heard of us, even in our home town, so we did the shirt sponsorship. The shirt sponsorship helped raise the profile of the business a bit, but there were no great changes. When they asked if I wanted to sponsor the shirts the following season, I said, 'sorry not this year.' I said 'if you'll change the name of the team to the name of our company we'll do it.' I thought nothing more about it but 24 hours later they rang back and said 'what can you offer us?'"

Change the name of the team to the name of our company... we'll do it

What Mike Harris offered them was a quarter of a million pounds spread over five years in return for Llansantffraid taking on the name of his technology company. The club accepted and Total Network Solutions was born.

The new club didn't get off to the best of starts. They couldn't buy a win on the pitch and some fans, upset at suddenly having to shout "come on you Total Network Solutions!" sought refuge elsewhere.

"Llansantffraid was seen as the local football side with local players," says TNS fan Angharad Jones. "But many fans who used to support the old team have now changed teams for other local sides following the takeover."

After a disastrous start to the 1997/98 campaign, which saw seven straight draws followed by a 10-0 thrashing, the club phoned Mike and asked him to get more involved in the running of the club. He took up the post of managing director and the club hasn't looked back.

"Initially there had been a strong feeling amongst supporters of 'why change the name?'" he says. "But they needed the cash. They faced the choice of either staying in the top league or slipping back into oblivion. They chose to stay in the top league and we've taken them onto a new level. I think it helped that we didn't mess with the structure – they've got the same chairman now they had before we came in. Now we're the best-run club in Wales. Wrexham, Cardiff and Swansea have all had financial problems over the last five years but we've got a clean balance sheet, we've gone full-time and we're in Europe every season."

"Now we're the best-run club in Wales"

Indeed, since Llansantffraid sold its name, its fortunes have transformed on the pitch. The one-time Welsh Premier League also-rans have picked up three league titles, three runner-up medals, a plum Champions League game against the reigning European champions and a celebrity fan who's fast on his way to becoming to the new millennium what Des Lynam was to the old.

"I can't remember exactly when I started saying it, but it was around the 2002/03 season," says Jeff Stelling, referring to his dancing in the streets quip. "Nobody had ever given the Welsh football results before. Sky were encouraged to do so, as they gave the Scottish results. I was looking through the list at all the unpronounceable names and TNS stood out. I tried to think of something witty to say and used the Raith thing as inspiration. Now 90% of the time, if TNS win, I say it. It's really appreciated by the club. They've invited me to a couple of European games and send me a bottle of something nice at Christmas. They've become my Welsh team."

Llansantffraid might not have been the first club to flog off their name – Mike Harris points to the example of Inter Cable Tel in their league and clubs like PSV in Holland who did it first – but, partly thanks to Jeff Stelling, they're the most successful example in Britain of a sponsor-named team.

"My business has grown year-on-year," says Mike Harris. "When we first changed the name no one in our own town knew who we were. Now you could call up anyone in the Welsh phone book and they'd have heard of us. This deal has been very good for me, the business and the football club. Both parties have got what they wanted out of it. We've got the name recognition and the club has had success."

Total Network Solutions has set a precedent and, Mike Harries believes, it won't be long before clubs in the English league start to follow it.

"It's inevitable," he says. "Outside of the top two or three clubs, exposure from shirt sponsorship disappears. Can you tell me who was on Villa's shirt last year? Or Bolton's? How are these clubs going to generate the money to compete with a club like Manchester United? If they're getting £1m a year for shirt sponsorship, they could get £35-40m for selling off their name. It won't matter – people will still know Bolton is Bolton but they'll be able to compete. With TV money being reined back and wages still spiralling, it's one of the ways football will go. It's been a great way for us as both sides have got what they wanted out of it."

In 2005 Total Network Solutions were taken over by British Telecom, bringing an end to one of football's most celebrated sponsorship deals. Keeping the acronym TNS, the club changed its name to The New Saints, but they'll be dancing in the streets of Total Network Solutions no more.

A MASTER STROKE

The World Cup is still the Greatest Show on Earth ™, but these days the action off the pitch is just as high tempo as anything you'll see on it. The biggest businesses in the world spent tens of millions of pounds for the right to attach their names to the 2006 World Cup. It wasn't just for the exposure, although the expected global audience of 40 million was better than a kick in the face, but for the favours sponsorship could bring. Official sponsors Adidas supplied the clothing and the footballs, whilst co-sponsors Coca Cola enjoyed the luxury of their drinks being the only fizzy pop allowed to be sold in the stadiums. And all sponsors will have felt the sweet impact of tickets caressing their palms, whilst tickets sold directly to fans for the greatest celebration of football since Japan and Korea 2002 accounted for only 8% of the total.

The run-up to Germany 2006 saw one of the fiercest off-field battles in the history of the game, as Mastercard and Visa fought like siblings vying for mummy's attention. Both are jockeying for the slot of Credit Card Champion of the World and both see official partnership with the World Cup as key to achieving that success. That's why Mastercard felt like cocks of the school when they bagged the deal for the 2006 World Cup and the same again without the 'of the school' bit when it was announced that Visa would be the official partners of the 2010 and 2014 World Cups.

"This action by FIFA is a blatant and deceitful violation of our right of first refusal," spat Noah Hanft, general counsel of MasterCard International, on hearing of FIFA's deal with Visa. "Particularly as we had already signed and accepted FIFA's offer."

Mastercard filed a suit in a New York Court in April 2006 to try and prevent FIFA's deal, reported to be worth between £80m and £110m, going ahead. It's not hard to work out why. As part of their 2006 deal, Mastercard had the global army of football fans sewn up. If you wanted to buy a ticket using a credit card or use a credit card in a World Cup venue, the only one that would be accepted was Mastercard. Add to that the brand association with the Greatest Show on Earth™ and you're talking money. Loads of money.

"For a company like Mastercard the World Cup ticks a lot of boxes," says Phil Carling, head of worldwide football for marketing company Octagon. "The cumulative audience for the 2006 World Cup was forecast to be between 30 and 40 billion worldwide. Mastercard's involvement guaranteed them presence within the TV picture with boards up at the grounds. In terms of raising awareness and building authenticity as a football brand, it represented tremendous value for Mastercard. The World Cup also allows Mastercard to drive other business criteria. They will have 11-14 key global accounts like HSBC. The collateral from FIFA, like tickets for games, is something Mastercard can give to the banks to use for customer promotions. This is massively important for a company like Mastercard. There are also 3 to 4,000 merchants who accept credit cards who don't care whether it's a Mastercard or an Amex they take. Mastercard's involvement with the World Cup allowed them to offer what they call priceless engagements, things like tickets and guided tours of the stadiums, which is important for driving business. I've seen the figures for the 2002 World Cup and, rest assured, they were very impressive figures in terms of business creation and generating dollars."

Whilst the ferocity of companies clamouring for involvement might be a new thing, the attachment of their brands to the World Cup is not. Coca Cola has had boards up at grounds during World Cup games since 1950, although formal association didn't come until 1974 and official sponsorship didn't flower until Argentina in 1978.

The 70s was a key time for competition sponsorship. In England, with crowds on the dip and players freed from the shackles of the maximum wage demanding more money, football needed to find extra funds from somewhere, so it batted its eyelids in the direction of big business and sponsorship was born.

Before the start of the 1970/71 season a new competition was launched. It pitted the two highest scoring teams from each division against each other in a straight knockout and, owing to the money being pumped in by the Watney Mann Brewery, it was dubbed the Watney Mann Invitation Cup, shortened to the Watney Cup, to the relief of Rowntrees fruit pastille chewers everywhere. The cup only ran for four years but was notable for two reasons – it was the first competition in the world to settle drawn matches by penalty shoot-out and matches were shown live on TV, a rare event in 70s England. In its first season, Manchester United were spanked 4-1 by Derby County in the final, a feat trumped a year later when the Famous Man United got dumped unceremoniously out of the competition at the first round stage by third division Halifax Town. At least a bloke called George Best managed to grab a consolation goal in a 2-1 defeat. The other winners of the cup were Colchester [who beat West Brom 4-3 on penalties], Bristol Rovers [beat Sheffield United 7-6 on penalties] and Stoke [2-0 against Hull].

In the same season, another competition launched with the intention of bringing the Football Associations of England, Scotland and Ireland closer together. Funded by money from oil barons Texaco, the Texaco Cup featured the top teams from the home countries who hadn't qualified for Europe. Wolves beat Hearts 3-2 on aggregate in the first final, with Derby, Ipswich and Newcastle [twice] getting their name on the trophy in subsequent years. The competition wasn't a raging success – Irish teams pulled out in the 73/74 season and competed for their own Texaco Cup. And Texaco themselves pulled out in 1975, although the competition limped on for another six years as the Anglo-Scottish Cup.

Football wasn't quite ready to have its trophies besmirched in those days, but by the 1980s it was ready to start devaluing its cup competitions properly. The League Cup had been established in 1960 to give smaller clubs more revenue. Alan Hardaker, the Football League secretary, devised the competition so that each club had a home and away tie, which would guarantee them a certain amount of income [unlike the FA Cup where, in theory, you could go several seasons without benefiting from a money-spinning home game]. In 1982 the League Cup became the first major English football competition to carry a sponsor's name, when they did a deal with the Milk Marketing Board that saw the competition become known as the Milk Cup. It was the first and only example of responsible advertising attached to the competition. After starting out encouraging us to drink milk, the League Cup promoted betting [Littlewoods 1986], washing machines [Rumbelows 1990], fizzy pop [Coca Cola 1992] and beer [Worthingtons 1998 and Carling 2003].

A year after the League Cup was first milked for sponsorship cash, camera makers Canon became the first company to sponsor the English Football League. In those days, before English football got split into the have loads and the have sweet FAs, a sponsor could expect to get all four league divisions for his cash. Tabloid newspaper *Today* took over the reigns in 1986 for one season, replaced by the Barclays Bankers before the Premiership swished into town and siphoned off the cash like hooky petrol. Carling and Barclays went into the Premier League of sponsorship, whilst Coca Cola, Endsleigh and Nationwide settled for a place at the head of the Football League.

"The contrast is stark," says Phil Carling. "Barclays pay £20m a season to sponsor the Premiership. Coke pay the Football League about £6m a season. The differential is enormous, it's driven by exposure. The Premiership rather sensationally evangelised its product globally. It's now exposed to 180 different countries, which gives sponsors a presence in Asia, Africa and North America. Sponsoring the Premiership can genuinely form part of a global communications strategy. There's not a chance the Football League can offer that."

However, breadth of exposure isn't everything, according to Phil Carling. It's what you are associated with that is important.

"Before they took the decision on where to put their money, Coca Cola did a lot of research," he says. "They found that there was a growing unease about the Premiership. Fans feel disenfranchised by the wealth and elitism and think most of their beloved players are mercenaries. So Coca Cola took an insight that they'd rather be with the fans at places like Rotherham and Barnsley. This sponsorship package allows them to engage with 72 clubs. They've already done some interesting things like the signage at the grounds being done in the colours of the clubs."

As for why you'd put your money into a competition rather than a club, it's all down to the risk factor, according to TNS managing director Mike Harris.

"Brands tend to associate themselves with leagues as it's less risky," he says. "It doesn't matter how a team performs. It takes a brave man to put money behind a team that could end up bottom of its league."

The last island of beauty had always been the FA Cup. The oldest cup competition in the world, the FA Cup was the stuff of dreams. No self-respecting kid of the 60s, 70s, or 80s grew up without wanting to score the winner in The Cup Final.

Now things are different. The Premiership and The Champions League have gone a long way to removing the sheen from the famous old trophy and, in 1995, the FA Cup became the last major competition to accede to sponsorship. Littlewoods were the first to put their names on the cup, followed by insurance company AXA in 1998 which saw teams playing in 'the FA Cup sponsored by AXA.' The FA Cup went bare, naked again for four years, sharing the same partners as the Football Association. But for 2006, direct sponsorship returned, which saw Liverpool and West Ham contest the first FA Cup final sponsored by energy company E.ON.

The last island of beauty had always been the FA Cup

However, the FA Cup does retain a certain standing in the English game and will never lose its name, according to Phil Carling, who struck the deal with Axa when he was commercial director of the FA in 1998.

"We were conscious of protecting the name of the FA Cup," he says. "As much as they wanted to change it, AXA quickly realised it had to be the FA Cup sponsored by AXA. It couldn't be the AXA cup. There's a fine balance between purity of brands and necessity to generate income. If we'd compromised the FA Cup we would have undermined its long term equity and value."

GROUNDS FOR CONCERN?

Twenty years before Mike Harris turned Llansantffraid into Total Network Solutions, the Godfather of commercialisation had attempted a similar move in the Midlands. As Chairman of Coventry City, Jimmy Hill risked the wrath of the fans by examining the idea of changing the club's name to Coventry Talbot, in exchange for truck loads of money from the local car firm.

"We did look at the possibility of becoming Coventry Talbot, but we never got around to it," says Jimmy. "The sum of money they were offering wasn't worth it and the Football League wouldn't have accepted it."

For football clubs, becoming increasingly desperate for cash as attendances dropped and player wages rose, there was an easier route into the commercial bedroom. Rather than radically changing club names, they could simply allow companies to put their names on the dead space on the front of club shirts, in exchange for suitable remuneration. Liverpool were the first league club to go down this route, but it wasn't long before an attempt was made to cut off the new revenue stream. To appease fan anger and an irate BBC who, as a public service broadcaster could not allow advertising, the FA introduced laws that said sponsors' names on kits had to be below a certain size. But it wasn't enough to outfox the Godfather.

Using a trick attempted a couple of years previously by non-league Kettering Town, Hill incorporated a massive T into the design of the 1980 Coventry shirt which got the Talbot message across and stuck two fingers up to his old adversaries on football's governing body.

"We made the T on the front part of the pattern of the shirt to say thank you to Talbot for all the money they'd put into the club," says Jimmy. "Did I chuckle to myself at getting one over on the FA? It's like when you're playing: it's better to win than to lose."

As shirt sponsorship developed it became increasingly bizarre. The big boys might have got away with Hitachi and JVC, but lower down the pyramid the names weren't so glamorous. Crystal Palace players drew childish snickers wherever they went with Virgin writ large on their chests, whilst Wang had a similar effect on Oxford's 1985 Milk Cup heroes. West Brom's shirts in 1984/86 bore a no smoking legend as they were sponsored by the Health Authority and in the 1990s Hull were sponsored by the city's University, openly inviting the chant from opposing fans: "you're just a town full of students!" Then there was Port Vale's natty take on the football shirt-as-sexual-fantasy phenomenon. Whilst some blokes ask their lady friends to don the latest home shirt to spice up life in the bedroom, one suspects the Port Vale shirt of 1983 was given by the men folk of Stoke to their loved ones as the all-time classic put-down. The sponsors that year were Potteries Motor Traction, but the shirt bore the simple legend: PMT.

These days shirt sponsorship is a very healthy wallet-filler for the top clubs. The total value of Premiership shirt sponsorship deals was £70m for the 2006/07 season, ten times what it was when the Premiership began in 1992. Hicksville names like the *Evening Gazette* [Middlesborough] have given way to huge multinationals like Samsung [£50m deal with Chelsea] and AIG [£56.5m deal with Man Utd] as The Premiership has grown into the commercial monster it is today. Businesses spend fortunes putting their names on the front of football shirts. Is it worth it?

"AIG are spending £12m a year on Man Utd, but Pipex wouldn't be spending more than £1m a year on Fulham," says Phil Carling. "It's calculated that the media value generated from press exposure around the world is worth £3–4m a season from shirt sponsorship alone. When you add in things like free tickets, perimeter signage at the grounds and use of some player IP, it all adds up to reasonable value for £1m a season."

The next stage in the money-for-old-rope business plan of football clubs was obvious. A cursory glance around their stadiums had lightbulbs popping over the heads of club chairman the length of the country. They had, almost literally, been sitting on goldmines. The names of stands were sold off to the highest bidder, yielding the fantastic prospect of fans watching their football from such theatres of dreams as the Findus Family Stand [Grimsby Town] and the Bmibaby Family stand [Leicester City].

"Kettering were the first team to have shirt sponsorship with Liverpool following just after that," says the National Football Museum's Mark Bushell. "Stand sponsorship would have appeared not long after that. There had been things done before – Blackpool used to have writing on the roof of their ground so planes could see it. But stand sponsorship as we know it now would have come in at the end of the 70s/start of the 80s. Once upon a time gate money would have been sufficient for many clubs but in this period, with attendances falling and wages rising, clubs needed to find extra ways of making money."

After that, football clubs got cocky and decided that as fans hadn't kicked up too much of a fuss about stand names, they might as well go the whole hog and flog the entire ground's name off. Scarborough started the rot when, on the eve of the 1988/89 season, Chairman Geoffrey Richmond announced that a deal had been struck and the Athletic Ground would henceforth be known as the McCain stadium.

"Scarborough Football Club approached McCain for sponsorship," says Scarborough President John Birley. "But it was McCain who suggested the idea of renaming the stadium. We were worried about the reaction from fans but first and foremost it was a commercial decision. There was a certain amount of disaproval, particularly from older fans – the ground had been called The Athletic Ground since 1898!"

Since then many clubs have decided to cash in their chips, giving fans the pleasure of saying "drink up, we're off to t'BT Cellnet Riverside Stadium," [Middlesborough], "meet outside the Galpharm Stadium," [Huddersfield Town], and "can't wait to visit the Kingston Communications Stadium," [Hull City].

Whilst Bolton Wanderers [Reebok], Leicester City [originally the Walkers Bowl, changed to the Walkers stadium after howls of derision from supporters] and Wigan Athletic [JJB Sports] can all lay claim to some form of credit for cosying up to local firms, 'good old Arsenal' don't have a leg to stand on. The Emirates Stadium? Herbert Chapman's bust must be turning in its grave under the Marble Halls of Highbury.

Drink up, we're off to t'BT Cellnet Riverside stadium

Whilst Arsenal's mega-corporate deal may have helped secure the funding to move to a ground capable of helping them compete with the likes of Manyoo and Chelsea, it can't compete with the shenanigans at York City. Feeling the pinch after relegation from the Football League, the only way for the Minstermen to survive was by selling off the name of Bootham Crescent. A sad story, you may think. But never fear: those nice folk from York came up with the instant cure to your new found malady. Behold their new ground name and pray that one day, you may get to visit: Kit Kat Crescent.

"Kit Kat Crescent was the obvious choice of name for the ground as the product is manufactured in York and like Kit Kat, City's home strip is red and white," York's Managing Director Jason McGill said at the time of the deal.

The home strip is red and white? Give us a break.

"We felt it was important to maintain the word Crescent instead of

Stadium or Park and hope our supporters are pleased with the new name and are proud the club is associated with such a prestigious brand."

Something about this deal makes you think that perhaps, and it is just a perhaps, the words crescent, stadium or park weren't the important issues about this name change. Maybe, and this is just a hunch, it was the shoe-horning in of the words Kit and Kat that upset people.

"I personally, and I feel quite confident that I am speaking for most if not all City fans when I say this, think that we would have much preferred to have kept our stadium as Bootham Crescent," says lifelong City fan Stephen Froud. "Unfortunately after being in administration and having constant financial instability we had to gain every penny we could. This Sponsorship deal was too good to refuse, even though I believe the figure wasn't a substantial amount and if in a stronger position we could have held out for more, we had to take it."

These days clubs have taken sponsorship into the realm of the ridiculous. Grimsby had the back and the front of their shirts sponsored by different people in 2005/06 whilst the same season saw Sheffield Wednesday sell the announcement of time added on to Sheffield City Centre Premier Travel Inn. What's next? Clubs will have to work harder if they're to eek any further drips of revenue out of the game. What can they possibly turn into the next revenue stream? Could we be about to see the arrival of the half time pie sponsorship package? Or what about the half time pee package, with a cheeky post full time whistle stop for gold members?

"It was once proposed at Hartlepool that the backside of the player's shorts would be sponsored by someone who made loo roll," says Jeff Stelling. "You've got to laugh haven't you? I'm not quite sure where it'll end, but I don't think it'll be too long before we see a Domestos United playing in the English football league."

Who said football was going down the pan?

10 Corporate Monster Stadium Names (and some of the teams that play there)

Gaylord Entertainment Center: Nashville Predators
Minute Maid Park: Houston Astros
Kit Kat Crescent: York City
Chevy Chase Bank Field at Byrd Stadium:
   University of Maryland
Pengrowth Saddledome: Calgary Flames
Dunkin' Donuts Center: Boston Bruins
FedEx Field: Washington Redskins
Monster Park: San Francisco 49ers
Tropicana Field: Tampa Bay Devil Rays
Millennium Worldwide stadium: Frickley Athletic

10 names that were really stupid anyway and didn't need any corporate help, thank you very much

Wankdorf Arena: BSC Young Boys, Switzerland
The Dripping Pan: Lewes' ground
The Cock and Bear terrace: Nuneaton
The Scrattin' Shed: Hyde United
Gay Meadow: Shrewsbury Town
Fukuoka Dome: Japan
Butthole Lane: Shepshed Dynamo
La Bombonera [The Chocolate Box]:
   Buenos Aires, Argentina
Palogrande [Big stick]: Once Caldes, Columbia
Ibaraki Prefectural Kashima Soccer Stadium: Japan

> CHAPTER 4
THE REVOLUTION WILL NOT BE TELEVISED

4: THE REVOLUTION WILL NOT BE TELEVISED

When Philo Farnsworth first demonstrated his invention on September 7th 1927, he could scarcely have imagined the impact it would have on the world. On that day in his San Francisco laboratory, television was nothing more than a primitive scanning tube capable of transmitting a single white line on screen. Now it's a global institution, with over 1.7bn sets worldwide and a cultural impact that would make Van Gogh wince. Television is responsible for shrinking the world, bringing global communities together and shaping the lives of children and adults on a daily basis. It's also the single biggest weapon in the war to commercialise football.

Any person, product or sport looking to become famous and successful requires exposure. In the early days, football coverage [results and reports] was confined to local newspapers and spasmodic offerings in the national press. *The Times* first published a report on November 18th 1864 when Old Etonians played Westminster; their first fixture list appeared in 1884 and their first league table in 1892. But things didn't really get going until the birth of the popular press. In 1896 Alfred Harmsworth founded *The Daily Mail*, the first mass circulation newspaper, which was swiftly followed by Arthur Pearson's *The Daily Express* in 1900 and Harmsworth's *The Daily Mirror* in 1904. They all carried football results and reports and whilst football's popularity soared it wasn't enough to grow the game over the long term. Like a boy on a milk crate at the back of the Kop, people wanted to see what was going on.

Football's commercial relationship with moving images began in the late 19th century. Sniffing a potential market bigger than the one in Albert Square, film pioneers Sagar Mitchell and James Kenyon turned up at football grounds with their camera equipment.

"The first moving images we have of football are of the Blackburn v West Brom game in 1898," says Bryony Dixon, curator of silent film at the British Film Institute. "It's only a minute long, as that's all the film you could get in the camera. It was shot by Mitchell & Kenyon, who used to make money by filming crowds at popular events and then charging people to see the footage. The idea was people would pay to see themselves on film. They showed the film in music halls, fairgrounds and church halls. They'd get up to 2,000 people paying pennies to come and watch."

It didn't always work out, though. In 1902, Kenyon and Mitchell shot the first footage of the team who had just ditched the moniker Newton Heath in favour of the snazzier Manchester United, in a game against Burnley. The film was due to be shown later at the Burnley Mechanics Institute, although this was cancelled because Burnley lost 2-0. The good people of Burnley would not be shelling out their hard-earned shillings to watch their side lose twice, even if they might catch a glimpse of themselves on screen.

In the picture house boom of the early 1900s, football became an unlikely favourite on the big screen. There were three main newsreel companies in England – Pathé, Gaumont British News and Topical Budget. They would compete against each other for exclusives, which were shown as part of an evening of 'mixed entertainment' in cinemas until the 1920s, when it became normal for feature length football film to be shown in its own right. It was all good exposure for football, and crucial in giving the game broader appeal.

Newsmen furtively tried to film the match from under their coats

"In the 1890s all you could do was read reports in newspapers," says Bryony Dixon. "Your experience of the football world was the team you saw or read about. Suddenly you could see other teams and other grounds. It's difficult to say as there was no audience figures in those days but the fact that the newsreel companies expanded into the 1920s tells its own story."

Competition between the newsreel companies reached a climax in 1923, when the FA sold the rights for the first FA Cup final at Wembley exclusively to Topical Budget. The 200,000 strong crowd, packed into a stadium that was meant for 127,000 people, included several newsmen furtively trying to film the match with cameras under their coats, like the kindly people who do the filming of the pirate DVDs you buy off the market. Others hovered precariously in zeppelins high above the stadium. On the resulting footage, one newsreel included the following explanation for the rubbish quality of the images:

'Gaumont British News present their edition of the Cup Final. The 'freedom of the press' was not extended to the newsreels this year but Gaumont British News offers you these pictures taken in circumstances of considerable difficulty.'

Clearly something needed to be done. People hiding in glorified hot air balloons above football grounds producing jerky footage that could have passed off as a game between two ant colonies wasn't going to help anyone in the long run. What football needed was something more immediate. Something with better pictures. Something more people could have access to. And, on September 7th 1927, they got it.

A WINDOW ONTO THE WORLD

Football has seen some great battles over the years: Professionalism vs. amateurism, players vs. the clubs over the maximum wage, Newcastle's Kieron Dyer vs. Newcastle's Lee Bowyer. But they all look like handbags at six paces compared to the hissy fit that still rages today over who invented television.

As soon as Marconi invented wireless technology in 1897, inventors fell over themselves like lemmings to try and make best use of it. George Carey and W.E. Sawyer both envisioned something like television, but it wasn't until the 1920s that people began laying their TV cards on the table. On December 2nd 1922 Englishman Edwin Belinn demonstrated a mechanical scanning device at the Sorbonne in Paris. If Roy Walker had been there, he may well have looked Belinn sympathetically in the eye and said: "it's good, Ed, but it's not right."

Next up, Scotsman John Logie Baird entered the fray. On March 25th 1925 he gathered a crowd at Selfridges in London for his first public demonstration of 'television'. But Baird hadn't got it right and, when only silhouettes appeared on screen, the new phenomenon didn't cut quite the dash he'd hoped for. Whilst Baird went back to the drawing board, two Americans stole ahead in the race to invent TV.

The first, Russian-born Vladimir Zworykin, applied for a patent for the electron scanning tube [the main bit of the early TV set] in 1923. With electrical giant Westinghouse behind him, he was the clear favourite to come through with the goods. However, four years after Zworykin applied for the patent but before he'd managed to conjure any moving images, young ex-farm boy Philo Taylor Farnsworth became the first person to successfully demonstrate television, at his laboratory in San Francisco. Debate still rages as to who actually invented television, although eye witnesses to Zworykin's visit to Farnsworth's lab in 1930 claim to have heard him say, "I wish I had invented that."

Whatever, it didn't take too long for the football world to start making use of the new invention. In 1936, a year after the US patents office had declared 'priority of invention awarded to Farnsworth', the first televised pictures of a football match were shown, when delayed coverage of Italy vs. Germany hit screens in Europe. The following year, on September 16th 1937, an exhibition match between Arsenal and Arsenal reserves became the first match to be televised live, and in 1938, the FA Cup Final between Preston and Huddersfield became the first major game to be broadcast live in England.

The BBC got into the groove of screening the FA Cup Final and certain international matches, but they were prohibited by the club chairmen from showing any League games. Chairmen were petrified that the high attendances they were enjoying would drop off if people could simply watch the games on a television set. The football revolution, they declared, would not be televised.

"His fear was a simple one – people wouldn't go to the game," veteran broadcaster Bob Crampsey told *The Scotsman* in 2005, recalling Celtic Chairman Bob Kelly's chagrin at the 1955 Scottish Cup Final being shown on TV. "But one thing we tend to forget was how uncomfortable houses were in the 1950s, especially in Glasgow in the older districts. If you were sitting at home in a leaky tenement you might as well be out in the company of your fellow men. Whereas now you look outside from your centrally-heated home as the snow is falling and decide to give it a miss and watch the game at home instead."

Things began to turn in favour of TV in 1955 when the European Cup was set-up. One of the main stipulations of the new European competition was that it be played in mid week during the evenings, so the working classes might be able to watch on television. In a move replicated nearly 40 years later by BSkyB, young pretenders ITV – a new station themselves at that point – decided to 'go for the footy' in an attempt to get a foothold in British homes.

It wasn't just the TV companies who saw the value of the exposure generated from playing in the new European competition. Sir Matt Busby was a great football manager, but he was also a visionary. He was one of the first people to recognise that, far from being a threat to the clubs' attendances, being on television was like appearing in a window onto the world. It might, just might, help them. And so, in 1956, his Manchester United side entered the European Cup for the first time. As they didn't have any floodlights they had to play their first games at Manchester City's Maine Road ground. By the time they'd drawn Real Madrid in the third round, the local TV company had paid for floodlights and Man U returned to Old Trafford.

Hollywood would have been proud of Matt Busby's efforts

Although they lost on aggregate, after drawing the home leg 2-2, Manchester United gained a great deal by being the first club to embrace television.

"In my opinion TV was certainly beneficial for Manchester United within the UK as Granada's coverage of early European matches would certainly have given the club an extra 'glamour' factor," says Man U Curator Mark Wylie. "I'm not sure how the TV market had developed across Europe in the 1950s. It had certainly grown here at the time of the Coronation in 1953 which is regarded as a major catalyst for TV ownership in the UK. Because European competitions such as the European Champions Cup were pan-European they would have attracted considerably more attention from foreign TV companies than the domestic competitions. They would also have been attractive because the matches were a way for fans to see 'the best teams in Europe' competing against each other. I personally think that coverage of the Munich Air Disaster across Europe made Manchester United a more familiar name throughout the continent than just the appearances in the European Cup. TV companies also like a bit of a 'fairy tale'. The story of Matt Busby rebuilding his shattered team to rise again and eventually 10 years later win the European Cup is one that Hollywood would have been proud of."

It wasn't long after the start of European competition that all top flight English clubs benefited from being in the shop window domestically. On August 22nd 1964, the BBC launched a new highlights programme, *Match of the Day*, with the words: "Welcome to *Match of the Day*, the first of a weekly series on BBC Two. This afternoon we are in Beatleville."

The first featured game was Liverpool-Arsenal at Anfield. The scousers won 3-2, but it looked as if the TV experiment had gone badly wrong. Just 20,000 people tuned in to watch, compared to over 40,000 who'd actually attended the game. It was the opposite of the chairmen's earlier fears: would anyone actually be bothered to watch football on television?

The answer came in 1966, a landmark year for English football on the box as well as in it. The World Cup drew a worldwide audience of 400 million, confirming the presence of a new type of spectator: the armchair football fan. When *MOTD* re-appeared for the 66/67 season, it had moved to a prime time slot on BBC One, to cater for this new phenomenon. The move was rewarded with viewing figures over five million. Effectively football clubs' potential audiences had now gone through the roof – they could have people watching inside and outside the ground. Television was a means of selling the 'product' of football to a much bigger audience than the game had enjoyed previously.

"Programmes like *Match of the Day* and *The Big Match* were hugely important in bringing football to a wider audience," says Jimmy Hill, who presented both programmes during an illustrious TV career. "Audience figures for that period and since then have shown no signs of dropping off. The game lends itself to TV. You can enjoy an evening's entertainment from the comfort of your fireside. TV has made the football audience bigger."

The first live FA Cup Final to be broadcast in glorious technicolour was the 1968 clash between West Brom and Everton, with *Match of the Day* flipping the colour switch the following year. The year after that, ITV introduced the now-essential idea of having a panel of ex-footballers on the show to say nothing about the games they'd just witnessed. It was a glorious time for football on the box: colour TVs, exposure to new markets, no Robbie Earle in an over-sized suit fluffing his words. Yet the relationship between football and television remained uneasy.

In 1974, the BBC was due to film an FA Cup Quarter Final between Burnley and Wrexham at Turf Moor. Despite an agreement between the FA and the television companies to be allowed to screen games, Burnley Chairman Bob Lord refused to allow the BBC cameras into the ground.

"I have never said that I am against the televising of football matches," he said. "But if the TV companies want to come to Turf Moor they have got to compensate us adequately. £10,000 is a reasonable figure to cover this. If the

TV companies are prepared to pay we shall be quite happy to receive them. The ball is now in their court."

If the ball was in their court, the BBC were quite willing to bat it back.

"Our contract is with the Football Association and we do not enter into negotiations with individual clubs," monotoned a spokesperson. "We do discuss with the clubs the question of a disturbance fee but this is only a small amount."

Bob Lord, a butcher by trade and unafraid of the sight of blood, went in for the kill. "The TV companies have been getting their football on the cheap for far too long," he harrumphed. "It's about time they paid for what they got. They wanted to screen the cup-tie at Grimsby and offered each club £87-50 compensation. That's a ridiculous figure. They ought to pay for football the same as the top stars like Morecambe and Wise."

The days of TV companies paying football clubs the same as Morecambe and Wise weren't too far away but, at that point, all Bob got was an FA Cup game that no one outside the ground saw and a ticking off from the FA. The clash between Bob Lord and the FA was a clear indication of the unease that still existed between football and television. The fear of losing 'live' spectators was so great that the Football League didn't allow TV companies to broadcast live games until 1983. They only capitulated then because attendances were falling and they were desperate for cash.

The football world's darkest fears, that television would start dictating terms to them, came to fruition during the 1986 World Cup, when kick-off times were set by television companies, sometimes forcing teams to play in the searing midday Mexican heat.

"It was inhuman," sniffed Argentine striker Jorge Valdano. "They sold a bad football product to the whole world. You have to come for the game and defend it from the outside aggression of commercialism."

Football was at a crossroads. Was it going to let television dictate or was it going to stand up for itself? The answer came at the beginning of the 90s, when football oiled itself up and bent over seductively, whilst TV threw a wad of notes down on the bed.

THE SKY'S THE LIMIT

It's Sunday 16th August 1992. The sun is shining but, in living rooms across the country, people are drawing their curtains and settling into armchairs to watch the beginning of a new era in English football. Before the boy his manager calls Edward Sheringham can score the first live TV goal of the new age, the audience is treated to fireworks, dancing girls and a theme tune by Simple Minds. Welcome to the all-singing, all-dancing always-the-best-game-ever world of The Premiership.

The new league dramatically changed the relationship between football and television. Habitually an uneasy alliance, Sky's billions have smoothed the traditional grumps of football clubs and turned television into one of the biggest contributors to the commercialisation of the game. Had any of the orchestrators of the shift been called Hannibal and a member of the *A-team*, they may well have said: "I love it when a plan comes together." For the blissful new marriage between football and TV was no accident.

The big clubs wanted a bigger share of the television money

"The idea had been around for a long time before it actually came into being," says Premier League Chairman Dave Richards. "The bigger clubs were getting tired of the way things were being run. It was really all about voting, and bigger clubs having a bigger say. So one or two of the clubs got together in the early days about television. The big clubs wanted a bigger share of the television money, so they decided they'd have a look at how they could make more money.

"My first meeting was in November or December 1989. I met three or four of the big chairmen to start talking about having our own league. We decided to look at its feasibility. We got a guy called Rick Parry from Ernst Young to come in and do the feasibility study. So it started as early as 1989. It might have started before that even, but it became serious in 1990. The big clubs felt that they should have a different way of making their own commercial enterprises better. Television was just really coming into its own, broadcasting was starting to change and it evolved."

Before any new league could begin to take shape there were a couple of major hurdles to get over. The first was to make sure a television company was prepared to screen the new league's matches – it would be pointless breaking away from the rest of football for a bigger slice of TV revenue if no one was prepared to screen the games. A meeting in 1990 between the Big Five – Arsenal, Man U, Liverpool, Everton and Tottenham – and ITV grand fromage Greg Dyke soon assuaged those fears.

The second obstacle was cleared more by luck than judgement. To create a new league the clubs at the top of the game needed some kind of backing from one of the game's governing bodies. As the Football League was keen to keep the status quo, this meant getting the traditionally anti-commercial FA on-side.

As luck would have it, the FA made an error of judgement of Graham Taylor-sized proportions, which cleared the decks for the rich clubs to get richer and drove a stake through the heart of English football. In 1990 the Football League had produced a document called *One Game, One Team, One Voice* in which they expressed a vision for the game to be ruled jointly by themselves and the FA, with money being shared around the whole football league structure.

The FA didn't like what they were hearing – they thought the Football League was making a play for power. By this time, the Big Five had had their meeting with Greg Dyke and the idea of a breakaway league was being mooted. The FA decided to back the new division in an attempt to slap the Football League into place once and for all.

"The FA misread the situation," says football journalist and author David Conn. "They thought the Football League were making a grab for power when they issued their *One Game, One Team, One Voice* document. But who was driving that policy? The big clubs."

With TV and the FA onside, the top clubs were free to make their move and in May 1991, the founder members of the Premier League – Arsenal, Aston Villa, Blackburn, Chelsea, Coventry, Crystal Palace, Everton, Ipswich, Leeds, Liverpool, Man City, Man Utd, Middlesborough, Norwich, Notts Forest, Oldham, QPR, Sheffield United, Sheffield Wednesday, Southampton, Spurs and Wimbledon resigned from the Football League.

"We had to give a year's notice to leave the Football League," says Dave Richards. "We had to write to them. There was a tremendous amount of legal work. Of course, there was a mega hooha, and 22 clubs were invited to join."

The 'mega hooha' involved threats of strike action from players and the Football League turning to the courts to try and prevent the formation of the Premier League. But nothing could stop the promise-of-bundles-of-TV-cash-driven juggernaut. With the beastly business of severing 100 year ties out the way, Premiership Fat Cats turned their attention to securing a television deal.

The obvious move was to pair up with ITV. The Big Five had already won the backing of Greg Dyke and rumours were circulating that he'd offered them each £1m to sign up with his station. Then, out of nowhere, Rupert Murdoch slapped a ludicrous amount of money down on the table and changed the course of history.

"At the time BSkyB was on its knees," remembers Dave Richards. "Rupert Murdoch wanted to buy football. He'd been talking to Rick [Parry] and Sir Philip [Carter] and Irving Scholar about buying total football, what they considered total football. They'd been negotiating. ITV in those days were showing Football League football and Sky were wanting to find a product and they picked football. It was a bit of a risk for us because we'd got terrestrial TV going to the masses and you'd got BSkyB with a limited audience on buy channels. But the retainer they offered us was so high we couldn't refuse it. You just could not refuse it. It was £40m. In 1992 that was a lot of money. That was divided between the 22 clubs."

Football's relationship with television had always been uneasy until The Premier League clambered into bed with BSkyB. That deal changed everything. Suddenly television wasn't just advertising the product of football, it was bankrolling it. The first deal saw BSkyB give The Premiership £191m to distribute amongst its clubs over five seasons. The next one, beginning in 1996/97 was worth £670m over four seasons. And the most recent, spread over three seasons from August 2004, was worth a whopping 1.024 billion of your English pounds.

Aside from the cash injection of TV rights money, Sky has helped Premiership clubs net cash in other areas. By beaming games into countries around the world, Sky has helped Premiership clubs sell their 'product' to fans in other countries, ultimately leading to higher merchandise sales. And, because of massively increased TV coverage – there were 10 live games on terrestrial TV in 1983, compared to 60 on satellite in 1992 – sponsorship cash flowing into the game has gone off the scale.

"The Premier League is a global brand," says Dave Richards. "The amount of revenue that it generates is huge. It's mega. All this money has gone into infrastructure, management, players, it's all been used. And clubs do actually use it. The competition and the quality of the game is far better than anywhere else in the world."

Over £1 billion has been spent on stadium redevelopment since the start of The Premiership and the standard of players now on show is phenomenal. English First Division football, let's not forget, used to be rubbish.

"You've got to go back to how stadiums used to be," says Dave Richards. "Look at the quality of stadiums now. The quality of the management in the football clubs to what it used to be. They're now bigger companies. The influx of foreign players lifted our league tremendously. The influx of foreign managers whipped it up and made it better."

The influx of foreign managers whipped it up

Kind-hearted Premiership Fat Cats even have the generosity to filter some of their new-found riches down to the bottom of the game. Never let it be said that the mega rich at the top of English football have short arms and deep pockets. According to Premier League Chairman Dave Richards, "The Premier League gives away £100m a year. That's a lot of money. We give the PFA £12.9m. We give the Football Foundation £20m, we give charities money. Our football foundation pays £375k a year to Supporters Direct. So we do put a bit back."

So there you have it. Shiny new grounds, the best players in the world, help for those who need it, and it's all down to the funny little box that Philo Farnsworth created back in 1927. And those who now make use of it.

"Had a little bit of vision didn't they?" says Dave Richards, referring to TV company BSkyB's cavalier money-throwing exercise at the dawn of the 90s. "They thought it was gonna go and now it's one of the biggest global products you've got."

That, and TV, of course.

DYING FOR IT?

Television has been the single biggest weapon in the commercialisation of football. It has taken football into millions of homes across the globe, attracting new fans into the game and generating more money for clubs. TV rights money has helped build shiny new stadiums and given clubs the cash to get the very best players to fill them. But, like the sneaky phone call that gets interrupted and the phone hurriedly put down, there are warning signs that the football-TV marriage isn't the cuddles-in-the-kitchen success story it first appears.

In September 1998 Rupert Murdoch's BSkyB launched a takeover bid for Manchester United. They knew that the Office of Fair Trading were going to investigate BSkyB's deal with the Premier League, citing the fact that it could be an anti-competitive cartel which acted against the interest of football supporters. Sensing that the gravy train might be about to pull out of Cash Central for the last time, the TV company sought to safeguard its future by buying England's biggest club. The United board accepted the £650m bid. The fans did not.

"I was opposed to it for loads of reasons," says Man U member Bella Abrams. "The main one was fairly political – I didn't want someone like Murdoch taking over my team and potentially making some hideous Sky-run, cheerleaders-style event like he had done with the Super League in Rugby League. In addition to all this, it was an unknown quantity and we had been used to Man Utd being run by the same family for years and letting it be owned by the media was wrong. The takeover was rejected for the right reasons in my opinion – it would have been a monopoly for Sky – a bit like the control Murdoch has with papers and it could only have been bad for Man U and the rest of football."

Thankfully for supporters, the Monopolies and Mergers Commission stuck their considerable snouts into the debate and in 1999 ruled that 'Decisions based on football authorities' perception of the long term interests of the game are more likely to be in the public interest than those based on the commercial interests of broadcasters'. Murdoch and BSkyB were blown a raspberry and the deal was off.

Two years later ITV Digital, having tried unsuccessfully to secure the rights to screen Premiership matches, paid £315m to show Football League. Just as it had done in The Premiership, the TV cash provided a huge fillip for clubs who, playing lower down the pyramid, found money harder to come by than their Premiership buddies. Imagine their chagrin when, just a year into the deal, ITV Digital announced that they were going into administration and had no way of honouring the deal.

"There were rumours of problems with NTL at first and then the whole thing folded," says Shaun Harvey, managing director at Bradford City at the time of the collapse. "Everyone sat waiting for the Football League to resolve the matter but it didn't happen. The timing of the collapse of ITV Digital coincided with our relegation from The Premiership. There was already a reduction in income from not playing in the Premiership. When that added income from ITV Digital was taken away, it was a gap that was too big to bridge. We went into administration. In an administration situation, all the players become available."

How different life is at the very top. Whilst TV inadvertently caused many Football League clubs to struggle frantically to keep the wolves from the door, the big boys had already set up their own TV stations. On 10th August 1998 Manchester United became the first club in the world to have their own TV channel when they launched MUTV. Chelsea, Liverpool and Arsenal followed suit. The bonus for addicts is that they can watch hours and hours of content solely about their favourite club. The downside is the lack of objectivity. When Roy Keane laid into his team mates in an interview with MUTV in 2005, club bigwigs ordered the footage to be shelved. It's hard to imagine ITV or Sky canning such TV gold.

When the Office of Fair Trading launched an investigation into BSkyB's TV deal in 1999, they argued that clubs should be free to negotiate their own deals, increasing the number of games on TV and bringing more money into the sport. The Premiership successfully argued against this by claiming that the current TV deal prevented saturation coverage and ensured that the TV money was shared fairly evenly between the member clubs. Which is funny, as they are the two biggest gripes usually levelled against The Premiership.

In 2004 Sky paid The Premiership over £1 billion across three seasons. In the pre-Premiership days that money would have been distributed throughout the League, helping to keep smaller clubs afloat. Now the big guns get to keep all of it, citing the fact that they earn it, they should keep it.

"The distribution of wealth among football clubs in this country is woefully inadequate," BBC pundit Garth Crooks told *Four Four Two* magazine in 2005. "I would change that straightaway, not only so that the money gets to other clubs in other leagues, but so it's more fairly distributed within The Premiership."

Any company ploughing millions of pounds into anything is going to want a say in how its investment is run. When Sky first teamed up with The Premier League they introduced Monday Night Football to supplement the main Sunday afternoon live slot. Knackers to the away fans, they seem to have thought, who may have to travel hundreds of miles home at 10pm on a Monday night, think of the cash they could make by having two live games a week. These days one of the main reasons cited for falling attendances is the fact that TV has skewed kick off times. You used to know where you were with footy. It kicked off at 3pm on a Saturday afternoon. Now it kicks off virtually any time, leading to the biggest single threat to the future of football: overkill.

"Only time will tell if the amount of football on TV is damaging to the game," says Jimmy Hill. "It doesn't seem to be turning people away at the moment but there's always that danger. The beauty of it is people can start watching the game when they're young. A six-year old might not want to sit through a whole 90 minutes but on TV, they can dip in and out. You could say it's furthering the game's future by introducing it to new 'clients'!"

As Sky's foothold in the game has grown stronger, they've developed relationships with other football associations [notably the Scottish and Spanish] which means they can provide, in addition to Monday Night Football; Tuesday, Wednesday, Thursday, Friday, Saturday and often Sunday Night Football as well. There's a live game on almost every night of the week plus a dedicated football news channel that runs 24 hours a day.

At the beginning of the 2005/06 season, with ten of the 20 Premiership clubs reporting a drop in season ticket sales, The Premier League set up a working party to look into the decline. Sports Minister Richard Caborn was sure where the problem lay – yep, that old chestnut: if it's on telly, people won't go to watch.

"I'm pleased the Premier League have taken this initiative, and the working party are going to have to look at whether clubs are pricing fans out of going to matches," he said. "One also has to question how much football there is on television and whether it's undermining attendances. I believe there is clear evidence that is the case."

Saturation is also damaging to the TV company. Viewing figures for Premiership football on Sky Sports fell by nearly 20% in the 2005/06 season. The British Audience Research Bureau reveals that Sky netted an average of 1.092m viewers in 05/06 compared to 1.205m the previous season.

The solution to these ills, it seems, is simple. It just requires a simple look across the Atlantic.

"The Premiership could learn from the NASL not to be too greedy," says Paul Child, a former Aston Villa striker who made it big in the US North American Soccer League in the 70s. "Marketing is important. The NFL [America's football governing body] does a great job over here of not saturating the market. Every season a team only plays 16 games, eight at home and eight away, so when a game is on, people are dying to see it."

When was the last time you were dying to see a match? Thought not. Press the red button to go inactive.

GAME, TV SET AND MATCH

Football on the box has produced some golden moments over the years. Here's the pick of the bunch

1. Graham Taylor

When Graham Taylor agreed to let a documentary team follow him during England's ill-fated 1994 World Cup qualifying campaign, he could scarcely have envisioned that the ensuing film would produce a catchphrase and a moment of pure TV gold. As he watched England lose in Norway, a baleful Taylor uttered the immortal line: "Do I not like that?" Not content with giving the cantankerous English public this stick with which to beat him, Taylor also produced one of the best ad libs ever. As he watched insufferable refereeing decisions, first not sending Ronald Koeman off for trying to decapitate Paul Merson, then awarding a dodgy free-kick which the lucky-to-be-on-the-pitch Koeman simply stroked into the net, Taylor dissolved in front of the cameras. Patting the linesman on the arse, he said: "Thanks for that. Tell the referee he's just lost me my job." An England manager he never was, but as a clairvoyant he showed great promise. Defeat in Holland did indeed spell the end for the man dubbed Turnip by the press. He resigned in 1993 after failing to get England to the 1994 World Cup finals.

2. Gary Linekar

England's World Cup semi-final against West Germany in 1990 produced more than its fair share of great TV moments. Iconic images of Chris Waddle hanging his head in despair after missing a penalty and Gazza bursting into tears will forever be remembered, but it was Gary Linekar's rubber-faced bench signal that really stood out. With Gazza's tears threatening to waterlog the Turin pitch, Cap'n Gary pointed at his eye, made a face like an old washer woman and told Bobby Robson using the internationally understood power of mime: it's time to get Gazza off the pitch.

3. Bjørge Lillelien

He had them before kick off but, after the referee blew to signal a 2-1 victory for Norway over England at Wembley in 1981, Norwegian commentator Bjørge Lillelien seemed to temporarily misplace his marbles. Showing a Keegan-esque grasp of allowing the situation to get the better of him, he blurted:"Lord Nelson! Lord Beaverbrook! Sir Winston Churchill! Sir Anthony Eden! Clement Attlee! Henry Cooper! Lady Diana! Maggie Thatcher – can you hear me, Maggie Thatcher! Your boys took one hell of a beating! Your boys took one hell of a beating!" The English response wasn't swift but it was damning. Before a game against Norway in 1993, a reporter asked Paul Gascoigne if he had a message for Norway. Gascoigne paused briefly before replying: "Yes. Fuck off Norway."

4. Diego Maradona

As Diego Maradona celebrated maniacally following a goal against Greece in the opening game of the 1994 World Cup, he looked as if he was on drugs. The reason for the crazed look, captured by TV cameras and beamed into millions of homes around the world was: the greatest player of a generation was, indeed, on drugs. The only surprise was that it was ephedrine that caused the big boned star to fail a drugs test, not erstwhile Maradona favourite and grimace-inducing party fave cocaine. Sent home in disgrace, Maradona would have got back to Argentina just in time to see his side crushed by footballing giant Romania in the second round.

5. Billie

Nearly 80 years before Ruud van Nistelrooy bagged a brace for Man United against Millwall, the star of the FA Cup Final was a horse. It was 1927, the first FA Cup Final at Wembley, and people were spilling onto the pitch due to overcrowding. The mounted Old Bill were called in and, in the grainy black and white newsreel images that followed Bolton's 2-0 victory over West Ham, one horse stood out like a beacon: Billie. Set against a sea of black steeds Billie the 'white horse', who was actually grey, became such a cult hero the final became known as The White Horse Final and a new footbridge near the rebuilt Wembley was named White Horse Bridge in 2005 after a fans' poll.

6. David Pleat

No moment encapsulates the sheer joy of a football win like David Pleat's embarrassing jig across the pitch at Man City in 1983, after his Luton side secured the win that kept them in the top division and sent City down.

"The memory of David jumping across the pitch will live with me all my life," recalls goal scorer Raddy Antic, clearly still haunted by the sight of footy elf Pleat's mad dash. "We were a little club, much smaller than Manchester City, and that meant so much for everyone. I remember that day so, so fondly."

7. Waddle & Hoddle

The cover of the single promised a free poster inside and featured a coiffeured Glen and a sans-mullet Chris posing like a Wham cover band complete with vacant stares and hand-on-shoulder familiarity. But that was nothing compared to the horror of the *Top of The Pops* performance of *Diamond Lights*. Some young ladies thought Hoddle looked dead sexy in his white suit, whilst others thought Waddle just looked dead. "I was petrified," Waddle explained, years after the incident. "He was confident. He enjoyed it. He's a positive guy." Sadly, that wasn't the end of Hoddle and Waddle's pop career, although record execs must have known the score, when they released follow-up single *It's Goodbye*. Thank God it was.

8. Diana Ross

Ten years before Janet Jackson 'accidentally' exposed her breast at the Superbowl, Diana Ross committed a sporting boob of Lola Ferrari-esque proportions. It was the opening ceremony of the World Cup in 1994 and America were showing the world how great they are at 'putting on a show'. Diana lined up a penalty which, when the ball nestled in the back of the net, would cause the goal to split open, declaring the World Cup officially open [geddit?] However, Diana fluffed the biggest sitter of her career. The ball sailed over the bar, but the goal split open anyway, revealing those damn yanks as the charlatans they so surely are. Still, Diana's participation that year was greater than England's. Thanks Graham [see number one].

9. Match of the Day

Long before Dennis Waterman sang the "theme toon" on Minder, bosses at the beeb had realised the value of a strong opening ditty. That's why, in 1968, they ditched Arnold Steck's *Drum Majorette* from the opening credits of *Match of the Day* in favour of a specially commissioned piece by Barry Stoller. *Match of the Day*, as it was cunningly titled, was released as a single in 1970 by a group of oiks calling themselves Offside conducted by Mike Vickers. It's this theme toon which still sends shivers down spines on Saturday nights all over the country. Not to be confused with *Match of the Day*, an ode to the programme which appeared on Genesis' 1977 EP *Spot the Pigeon*.

10. A random squirrel

With Juan Pablo Sorrin and Diego Forlan in such fine form for Villareal, the last thing Arsenal needed in 2006's Champions League semi-final was another hairy invader whipping up the crowd. But that's what happened when a grey squirrel stormed onto the pitch and ultimately caused referee Konrad Plautz to stop the game. As the Clock End chanted "there's only one Squirrel!" the feisty rodent goose stepped around the pitch, before disappearing into the West stand. Cue a slew of jokes from Gooners appertaining to the relative Champions League experience of the squirrel and hated neighbours Tottenham.

> CHAPTER 5
THINKING OUTSIDE THE BOX

5:   THINKING OUTSIDE THE BOX

It's 3.45pm on a sunny afternoon in Dronfield, near Sheffield, August 2005. Sheffield FC are playing Mossley AFC in the preliminary qualifying round of the FA Cup. At 1-1, the game is finely poised and after another check of his watch, referee Mr I.D. Knee of Wakefield blows his whistle and sends the teams back to the dressing room on an even keel. The fans warmly applaud the teams off the pitch and then something happens which, to the Premiership eye, must seem totally bizarre. The Mossley fans unpick their flag from the railings and file down to be in line with the goal they'll be attacking in the second half, and some of the Sheffield fans, after a welcome rest at the tea bar, move around the other side of the ground to be near the goal they're shooting into next.

You wouldn't get away with it at The Bridge or Gold Trafford but in non-league football, swapping ends at half time is as much a part of the game as a half time pie or questioning the referee's parentage. There's a certain no-nonsense purity about it: you've paid your money, why on earth would you want to spend half the game squinting up the other end of the pitch to see how your boys are getting on?

Non-league football fans get closer to the action in other ways, too. Your chances of saying hello to Roman Abramovich or Martin Edwards or Peter Hill Wood without a written affidavit are pretty slim, but at non-league level chairmen and players are much more accessible. Rumour has it that at some clubs, the chairman will buy you a beer in the social club whilst at others, the players actually thank fans for travelling away to watch them. You won't find many prawn sandwiches on the terraces of Runcorn or Northwich or Weymouth but you will find families who can afford to go to the match together and a genuine love of the game. That's because non-league football clubs are run on entirely different gravy to some of their more illustrious chums higher up the pyramid. As one poster on a non-league forum put it: "The Premiership's about money, non-league football is about football."

Whilst the non-league isn't as overtly-commercialised as league football [it was impossible, at the time of going to press, to locate a Wakefield and Emley credit card or a Stocksbridge Park Steels holiday villa in Spain] that's not to say that those clubs don't need money. They have stadiums to run and players and support staff to pay just as league clubs do, but they don't have access to cash in the same way. There's precious little TV revenue and many clubs would struggle if they had to rely solely on the bums-on-seats model. Outside the league, football clubs have always had to be more commercially creative.

The tone was set in the 1880s by Sheffield FC, a club who remained proudly amateur in status whilst, all around them, professionalism was spreading like the clap. Timber merchants Joseph Smith and Son had erected a wooden stand on Sheffield's Attercliffe pitch but the club wasn't generating sufficient income to pay for it, so they had to do what, in current marketing speak, would be called 'thinking outside the box'.

After the last smoking concert I was able to pay every account

A letter from the Sheffield FC treasurer to fellow committee member Harry Waters Chambers on February 5th 1885 tells the story:

'Dear Chambers – sorry you could not attend the committee meeting last night as it was principally re. finance. Joseph Smith and Son have written for their first installment, say £18-5s. I have not funds in hand for this but have no doubt we could raise it with another smoking concert. After the last smoking concert I was able to pay every account rendered for this season. I have called a meeting of the sub committee so that they can arrange another one.'

Smoking concerts were like a cross between a school play and an episode of *Phoenix Nights*. Anyone with an ounce of talent was roped in to perform, pungent cigarette, cigar and pipe smoke filled the air and the audience was full of fat blokes who would end up on stage making idiots of themselves.

'Dear Bellhouse,' began a letter from Sheffield FC to Sheffield Rugby Club on February 26th 1885. 'Will any of your rugby team care to attend our smoking concert on Saturday? I enclose you 10 tickets in case they would. Rugby men are notably musical. Will any of your men volunteer to assist in the programme?'

Sadly for the world's oldest football club, their fundraising measures were in vain and on October 26th 1886, Secretary WW Liddell was forced to send this letter to Joseph Smith and Sons.

'I am requested by my committee to ask if you will take back the timber used in the erection of the stand at Attercliffe in part payment of the balance owing to you, and how much will you allow for it?'

Sheffield FC may have had their stand repossessed, but they had shown the way commercially for amateur clubs. In the coming years, leagues were set up which would help further the amateur game commercially. By setting a finite number of games, clubs could plan their budgets accordingly and the element of competition would make the matches more appealing to players and fans. The Northern League [formed 1889] and the Southern League [formed 1894] were forerunners of the modern day Football Conference in that they provided a platform for professional and amateur clubs to compete against each other. In the Southern League, for example, amateur clubs such as Clapton, Ilford and Reading battled for the league title alongside professional outfits Luton Town, Millwall Athletic and Chatham.

I am requested to ask if you will take back the timber

However, it wasn't long before there was a backlash against the commercially-driven professional clubs. In 1905 the Isthmian League was formed as a haven for amateur clubs in the south. The following year professional clubs were kicked out of the Northern League and the year after that the scarily-named Amateur Football Defence Foundation [soon re-named Amateur Football Alliance] was formed to protect and preserve the Corinthian spirit in football. In 1920 the majority of the top Southern League clubs were swallowed up by The Football League, leaving a devoutly semi-professional league behind. The co-habitation between amateur and professional was over.

Non-league football bumbled along for the next 50 years, with clubs' commercial interests stretching no further than match day revenue and whatever their *en dehors de la boîte* thinking could come up with.

"When I first started in 1978 we were one of the biggest clubs in non-league football for fundraising," says Boston United's general manager John Blackwell. "We used to sell thousands of bingo tickets. We'd have people on the road all the time going out to Yorkshire, Cambridgeshire, Norfolk, all over.

We couldn't have managed without it. Not long after I joined Boston a new idea started at Plymouth, then Notts County got hold of it and then we did it. Ours was called the Pilgrim Lottery and it was hugely successful. We were selling 50,000 tickets a week. It was so popular I had to close the door sometimes because I couldn't keep up. The money from that lottery built our ground."

Just down the road a commercial landmark had actually been struck two years previous to John Blackwell's appointment at Boston, when a moustachioed former Wolves legend strode into Southern League Kettering Town, took one look at their bare, naked shirts and said: that's disgusting.

Within a month of his appointment as chief executive of the club, Derek Dougan had found a novel way of covering up Kettering's shirts: he struck a 'four figure' deal with a local rubber specialist. And so, on January 24th 1976, Kettering Town became the first team in the country to advertise a sponsors' name on their shirts, when they ran out for a match against Bath City with 'Kettering Tyres' emblazoned on their chests. It was a landmark day in the commercialisation of football and the FA narrowed their eyes, furrowed their brows and took a very dim view of proceedings at Rockingham Road. Four days after the match they ordered Kettering to remove the slogan from the shirts. Despite Dougan's claims that the FA's 1972 ban on sponsorship had never been put in writing, Kettering's fancy new strip was never seen again. It looked as if football's foray into sponsorship was doomed, but Dougan wasn't to be beaten.

Presumably wearing his best post-foul 'I-never-touched-him-ref' face, Dougan ordered the shirts to be changed to bear the slogan 'Kettering T', claiming the 'T' stood for 'Town' not 'Tyres'. Vexed, the FA wailed and gnashed their teeth for a couple of months before finally deciding to get medieval. They told the Poppies that if the slogan wasn't removed, they'd face a bottom-spanking £1,000 fine. Needless to say, the shirts went bare, naked again and football's dalliance with commercial sponsorship appeared dead in the water once more.

But, like a viagra-chomping Cassanova, Dougan refused to take no for an answer. Looking with green eyes to the continent, where teams such as Bavarian Munchen had enjoyed the benefits of shirt sponsorship for years, Dougan assembled a pro-sponsorship hit squad to tackle the FA. And so, with only Bolton Wanderers and Derby County for protection, he abseiled into FA

HQ and put forward a proposal for shirt sponsorship. On June 3rd 1977, the FA accepted the proposal and shirt sponsorship was declared legal. It was a great victory for Dougan and a massive leap in the commercialization of football but the party poppers and balloons around Dougan's office were made to look a bit silly when Kettering failed to attract a sponsor for the new season.

Although Kettering were showing the rest of English football how it was done, it wasn't representative of the commercial situation at most non-league clubs. The phrase 'beg, borrow and steal' comes out a lot at non-league level because that, without the stealing part, is what you have to do.

"When I first came here there was nothing, maybe one or two little advertising boards around the ground," says John Blackwell. "I'd seen it at other clubs so I went to a local timber merchants and, in return for ten years' free advertising, they gave us enough timber to put boards around the whole ground. Then I got a joiner to put them up, again in return for 10 years' free advertising. The money we generated from the boards was very helpful."

The top non-league clubs were beginning to want more from life than the necessity to blag off local businesses and the opportunity to get turned away from the Football League every season. In 1979, sick of not being invited to the party by the cool gang, the Southern League and the Northern Premier Leagues merged to form the Alliance Premier League. In those days clubs had two chances of getting out of non-league: fat chance and Norfolk and chance. Any time a club finished bottom of the Football League, it was up to the chairman of the league clubs whether to re-elect that team or bring in a Johnny-Come-Lately from the NPL or Southern League. Of course, the Chairman practically always voted their chums back in. It was a closed shop, but the Alliance Premier League was formed with the idea that it would be easier to get a club elected if there was only one top non-league division to elect from. It was a cute piece of thinking that would ultimately bear a whole orchard of fruit including the potentially bad apples of commercialism. But would they spoil the barrel?

CONFERENCE CALLS

It's a warm summer's day in London, 1984. Under the chandeliers of the Café Royal in the West End, members of the Football League are holding their AGM. One of the topics for discussion is whether to elect Maidstone United, the champions of England's top non-league division, into the Football League. Outside the scene is less gentrified. Football fans waving placards and banners are waiting anxiously to see if their presence has made any difference to the vote. It hasn't. As the day wears on, the esteemed members of The Football League choose to ignore Maidstone and their army of fans outside the building and re-elect Chester City to the Fourth Division. Gutted, the Maidstone fans pack up their protest and head back to Kent cursing the Football League for yet again choosing to re-elect, instead of letting some new blood into the league. They're not aware of it, as they clamber into cars, trains and busses to get away from the scene of the crime, but they've just changed the course of football history.

"The fans embarrassed the Football League that day," says Peter Hunter, who was secretary of the Alliance Premier League at the time. "Their chairman Jim Thompson made a big song and dance about it in the press. The publicity was bad but it was the physical protest of the supporters that really shook the Football League into opening negotiations with us."

The Alliance Premier, as the Conference was known until 1986, was run by the Football League for a season when it started in 1979. Football League secretary Alan Hardaker was a supporter of automatic promotion but, after he retired in 1979, his replacement Graham Kelly "cut off everything to do with the Alliance Premier."

"The Football League looked like turkeys waiting for Christmas when we brought up the idea of automatic promotion," says Peter Hunter. "It took a long time to break down. After the protest of the Maidstone fans, a sub committee was set up and we had regular meetings with the Football League to thrash out the criteria for promotion."

Scarborough became the first team to be promoted automatically to the Football League in 1986. The automatic promotion slot was the single biggest fillip to the commercialisation of top flight non-league football, but it wasn't the beginning of the story. From the moment the Alliance Premier League was formed, the goal was to become more professional and better known nationally, to make the league more attractive to fans, players, sponsors and, ultimately, to produce a league that the Football League couldn't ignore.

"The pools company recognised the value of our league straightaway," says present day Conference operations director John Moules. "We featured on the pools coupon from 1979 onwards. Within a year, our results were being shown on *Grandstand*. That was a huge step forward: having our results coming through at the same time as the top division clubs."

Suddenly England's top non-league division became news. Football fans the length of the country began to become familiar with names like Boston, Altrincham and Northwich Victoria. The value of such TV exposure wasn't lost on the slicked-back hair, giant mobile phone brigade in marketing departments across the country. The sharks smelt blood. And an easy route into the nation's living rooms.

In 1984 Gola slipped the Alliance enough cash to ensure that every time James Alexander Gordon read out the scores, he said, "Gola Alliance Premier Division." Two years later, one of the most successful sponsorship deals in history saw Vauxhall Motors take on sponsorship of the division which was then, and still is in some parts, referred to as the GM Vauxhall Conference.

"We were actually in Wakefield on our way to see Gola when the call came through from Vauxhall," remembers Peter Hunter. "Gola were fine about it because Vauxhall offered us much more money, so they understood. It was Vauxhall's US office that caused us to change the name to Conference. We were in negotiations with Vauxhall in Luton and they had to send details of the deal off to the States for ratification. It came back saying 'OK, but we want the name to be Vauxhall Conference.' Faces dropped two feet at the management meeting when we announced it, but money has a habit of making people change their minds. It turned out to be best thing we ever did."

It was the start of a purple patch for England's top non-league division. In the same year as Vauxhall came on board, Scarbrough became the first club to be automatically promoted to the Football League. After years of the old boys' network keeping non-league clubs in their place, it was a victory for progression and it threw open the doors to commercialisation in non-league football like never before.

"Twenty two clubs suddenly had a goal – to get promotion to the Football League," says John Moules. "It was a huge success. Clubs like Wycombe Wanderers, Barnet, Kidderminster, Macclesfield, all became new names in the Football League. From '86 onwards attendances have increased."

The Conference suddenly experienced what the Football League had just over 100 years previous. By introducing an element of competition, the division suddenly became more attractive to players, fans and, in the modern world, sponsors.

"It made a huge difference," recalls Boston's John Blackwell. "It had made a big difference when the results went on the TV. Gola and Unibond became involved in non-league football then. But as soon as you could get promoted automatically to the Football League, even more sponsors became involved with the clubs."

With more money flowing into The Conference from sponsors and increased attendances, crumbling old grounds began to improve and, in 1992, something happened which meant Conference clubs could attract better players.

Play-offs created huge public interest

"When the Premiership came in, it attracted a lot of overseas players," says John Moules. "The knock-on effect is that you now get more high profile players appearing in the Conference at earlier stages in their careers. Academies kick out more players now, a lot of whom appear in The Conference."

In 2001/02 the ever-improving league was rewarded with its first television contract – offering more exposure, attracting more sponsors and bringing more money to clubs through the sale of the rights.

"We felt we had a package to offer so we approached Sky," says John Moules. "We put it out to tender and Sky won the bid. They pay us an annual fee like they do with the Premier League. We share the money equally between the clubs, with additional money going to the clubs whose games are shown."

According to John Blackwell a televised match would see an extra £5k going into the home club's coffers with £3k going to the away club. Not exactly what Arsenal or Man U would be getting for a televised game, but all useful funds for a non-league football club.

Two years after the TV deal, The Conference struck gold again, when they managed to convince the Football League into giving them another automatic promotion slot.

"Play-offs created huge public interest but we couldn't have a play-off," says John Moules. "We couldn't ask the champion club to enter a play-off. We needed another promotion slot, which we started campaigning for almost immediately after the other slot was agreed. We had huge input from the FA, in terms of finance and influence, and in 2003 we got that second promotion place. It's fantastic. It prolongs the season for lots of clubs. Attendances have risen year on year since two up, two down came in."

Now The Conference is fighting fit. Once viewed as the 'dreaded drop' by Football League clubs, The Conference is seen as providing a safe haven for clubs to rehabilitate before attempting to return to the League.

"This year Hereford reached the play-off final at the fourth attempt," says John Moules. "Eight years ago, they came into the Conference on the brink of extinction. For the last three years they've made a healthy profit. Now they're out of administration. They're a viable club and they're ready to go back into the Football League. Every single club that comes down to us goes back to the Football League in a stronger position than they left in."

Although enjoying higher levels of sponsorship and TV coverage than ever before, rising attendances reveal that this embracing of the commercial world has not put fans off. That's because there's one crucial element missing from non-league football that dominates the scene higher up the chain: greed.

"I like conference football because it's quite a laid back affair, but at the same time it's packed with passion," says Halifax Town fan Jamie Guthrie. "On match day you turn up and stand or sit where you want with your friends. It's not like at the Premiership where fans are crammed in and you have to live by strict rules and regulations. The supporters are also more supportive. Pretty much every fan at the ground is passionate, rather than those in the Premiership, who only turn up for the show. I think the Premiership is a sad state where fans are treated not as supporters but as extras. It seems at least that in the Conference, fans are valued. You can openly talk with players and they show emotion and come over to the side to thank the support, like our players did at Grays on Wednesday."

MINOR MIRACLES

Sunday morning is a blissful time on Planet Football, with a plethora of football news, reviews, features and statistics to enjoy over a fry-up. Who's made it into team of the week? What did your favourite player get out of ten? How far are you off the promotion/relegation slots? And just what, in hell's name, goes on in those minor leagues?

A cursory scan of the divisions below the Nationwide Conferences reveals a clutch of names more at home in *Building and Construction News* than the sports sections of national newspapers. Unibond, Jewson, Screwfix, Toolstation, Moore & Co Construction Solicitors are all leagues you could play in at minor league level in the 2005/06 season. As you saw into your sausage and carefully press a couple of beans onto the end of your fork you may think it's a sad indictment of the over-commercial modern day football world. But you'd be wrong, fry-up philosopher.

Clubs playing at minor league level need league sponsorship much more than Arsenal or Man U or even Carlisle or Swansea do. Minor leagues distribute sponsorship cash amongst the clubs, even if it's not in the form of direct payments, which is vital when you're relying on gates of a couple of hundred or less.

"Most of the money goes to the clubs," says Nick Robinson, company secretary of the Ryman-sponsored Isthmian league. "We retain some for things like footballs. For example, we can buy 1,000 footballs and divide them between the clubs, which is cheaper than the clubs buying them individually."

It's not surprising, then, that league sponsorship began in the minor leagues. Years before Nationwide, Vauxhall, Barclays and Coca Cola got in on the act, the Isthmian League sidled up to Rothmans, blotted the pungent cigarette aroma from their minds and said: you smell gorgeous tonight, petal.

"Barry East was the chairman of the Isthmian League," says Tony Williams, who was instrumental in the first-ever deal between a football division and a big company. "He was a big developer in the city at the time. He wanted to look into the idea of someone putting money into the league. The league secretary Ingram Whittingham wrote to different people asking for suggestions. I suggested Jimmy Hill and [ex-England cricketer] Doug Insole get together and draw up a scheme, which they did. I knew Jimmy and I was working with Rothmans at the time, so I put it to the marketing department. Jimmy Hill and Doug Insole produced a suggested deal. We modified it a bit and off we went."

At a restaurant in Mayfair in 1973 Jimmy Hill, Doug Insole and Tony Williams agreed the deal that would make the Isthmian League the first division in England to carry a sponsor's name. How did the clubs take it?

"I was with a club at the time and everyone was very excited about the idea," remembers Nick Robinson. "The whole concept of someone providing money for seemingly nothing was great! Remember that the Isthmian League had for some 75 years not even presented medals or Cups because of the motto of the league *honor sufficit*."

The deal between Isthmian and Rothmans was groundbreaking not just because it was the first, but also because it showed that commercialisation could be a positive force within the game. Each season teams started out with eight sportsmanship points. They lost one point for a booking and four points for a red card. If they finished the season on zero points, they didn't get a share of the Rothmans money.

"It did the game good," says Tony Williams. "I remember Wycombe once going through two seasons and only getting two cautions. Blyth Spartans once went a whole season with no yellow cards. Teams from our leagues did better in the FA Cup because they were more disciplined and referees appreciated the way they approached the games."

The concept of someone providing money for seemingly nothing was great!

The sponsorship deal was such a success that Rothmans quickly moved into other areas. As well as helping the clubs and making the leagues more sporting, the deals helped Rothmans tempt more people to wheeze on their fags.

"We expanded into areas where sales were weak and soon we sponsored the Northern, Western and Hellenic leagues," says Tony Williams. "It was the best sponsorship deal of all time. It broke all records for opening new accounts. We had cigarette machines in all the clubs selling only our brands. It was a fantastic success. We got fantastic coverage out of it. I remember one paper in the north east had 12 mentions of Rothmans on one page."

And what of the fans? Was there a raft of banner waving and season-ticket-ripping at this new onslaught of commercialisation? Not exactly. In fact, our non-league cousins of the early 70s positively lapped it up.

"Supporters were so grateful because we were putting money into non-league football," says Tony Williams. "I remember one meeting in the south west. One bloke stood up at the end and said, 'Thanks for the help. What can we do for you?' I said, 'Well, I don't smoke, but I can see you do.' I could see he had a packet of Embassy at his feet so I said, 'You could smoke one of our brands.' He turned around to the rest of the people and said, 'Let's buy their cigarettes'."

Now you can't move for divisional sponsorship in the minor leagues with Nationwide, Unibond and Ryman adding their monikers to the biggest non-league divisions. For most clubs the extra cash is a godsend but, unfortunately, not all leagues feel the benefit.

"I think we're the only one not to be sponsored," says Richard Tims, chairman of North East Counties League side Sheffield FC. "It's not a spectator sport at our level. You've got to look for other ways to make money. The main ways for football clubs are either individual sugar daddies or sponsorship and I wouldn't say there were many of either knocking about in non-league football. Most clubs now get into the community and try and get government funding for running schemes that basically pay the wages of some of their employees or part time staff and we're no different. Getting involved and being part of the community helps get local businesses involved too."

There are actually two Sheffield FCs. There's the non-league club managed by Dave McCarthy that plays in the North East Counties League. And there's the world's oldest football club brand, which Richard hopes will help secure the future of the club for another 150 years and beyond.

"We're the world's oldest football club," he says. "People want to be associated with the brand. Obviously we haven't got a big marketing department, the only thing that I can offer is the use of Sheffield FC in other people's marketing campaigns – licensing the brand. With all due respect to somebody like Coca Cola, they couldn't hope to put on sales of Coca Cola worldwide by appearing with Sheffield FC. Ours is more of a responsibility sell. We've not had a ground for 144 years, so we're a bit behind. That's where the money will go. We've got more members than supporters. We've already got 600 members but we haven't launched the scheme properly yet. We want to launch the membership scheme worldwide. It doesn't matter if you support Arsenal or Real Madrid, for a couple of quid a month you get to be involved with the world's oldest football club. It's unique. My audience is in millions. It's football fans all over the world."

Talk of Real Madrid and Coca Cola is a far cry from the reality of life for the team that plays in the North East Counties League. Sheffield FC players only get paid travelling expenses and they normally play in front of a couple of hundred people. Still, that's a massive improvement on how it was before Tims got hold of the place. Then they were playing in front of 10-20 people at the cavernous Don Valley stadium, leaking money and staring oblivion in the face.

"We used to play in front of one man and a dog at the Don Valley stadium," he says. "It was awful. The club was losing money every time they stepped out on the pitch. I got involved by chance because FC manager John Pearson, an ex-Sheffield Wednesday player, came to my boardroom looking for a bit of commercial sponsorship. He caught me at the right time. I was a bit disillusioned with my team, Sheffield Wednesday, who I didn't feel were going in the right direction. So I went to have a look at Sheffield FC. Then I discovered it was the world's oldest club. It looked like it didn't have a future and I was brought in by some of the then-directors to stop it going out of business. I set about getting enough sponsors involved to make sure the club could operate at this level, which I'd probably done by 2003. We didn't have enough income to do an international marketing campaign or do things how I wanted to do them, but we had enough funds to run the football club."

Things started to get interesting when Richard got in contact with the FA in 2003 to get an official endorsement of Sheffield FC's oldest club status. By coincidence, Barcelona had been in touch with the FA seeking some historical information and the two parties were put in touch.

"I was flown out to Barcelona," says Richard. "When they received my gift of a picture of the world's oldest football club they were in awe of us. Joan Laporta took me around the Nou Camp, we exchanged shirts on the pitch and he took me to all the places the tourists don't go and everywhere we went people were excited to meet me. I thought this was odd. I thought I should be excited to meet them."

Pricked into action by the response to his club at Barcelona, Richard got in contact with FIFA, who were preparing for their centennial celebrations in Paris in 2004. They invited Tims to Paris to represent the world's oldest football club and he was introduced to FIFA big cheese Sepp Blatter. If his head was spinning at suddenly being invited onto football's top table, it blew off as the night wore on.

"I was invited up to the front and I was sat with Beckenbauer, Platini and all the great and the good of football," says Richard. "And there's me, from some working class suburb of Sheffield! It was quite bizarre. Blatter went on and announced the nominations for the awards and we got put forward with Real Madrid in the club section. We were awarded a FIFA Order of Merit for services to football. Ourselves and Real Madrid are the only two teams to have one. I went on stage with Emilio Butragueno and Alberto Di Stefano, which was unbelievable. It started making me think, heading towards our 150th anniversary in 2007, we have got our part to play. People are interested in the people that developed the beautiful game."

Since Paris, Richard has established the short-term future of the club. After leading a nomadic existence for over 100 years, his wheeling and dealing has allowed Sheffield FC to buy their own ground. Not one to miss a commercial trick, a recent deal with a local financial firm means that the world's oldest football clubs now plays its home games at the Bright Finance Stadium, or the Stadium of Bright, as Tims calls it.

__Ourselves and Real Madrid are the only teams to have one__

"It's taken an awful lot of hard work," he says. "I've put my career on hold to do this. We weren't looking like progressing. I'm not saying we'd have gone bust but we might have been playing at a lower level in a park. Now we've got junior football teams, girls football teams, disability sport and we've got our own ground. We've come an awful long way in a short space of time. So, from looking oblivion in the face seven years ago to owning our own premises and talking to Real Madrid and looking at sponsorship deals with X, Y and Z is beyond anybody's wildest dreams."

With the club now on a secure footing, Richard is thinking massively outside the box in terms of the brand. He returned home from a holiday to South Africa in early 2006 with a plan called *Boots For Africa*, which he hopes will put Sheffield FC on the map, as well as bringing hope to some of the deprived children he saw padding the streets.

"I tried to think how Sheffield FC could affect somebody's life in a township in South Africa. We haven't got any money, so the only thing I could think of was football boots. So I thought 'lets deliver 2007 pairs of cleaned up football boots to Africa.' It started as simple as that and now everyone and his mother wants a piece of the action and we're talking about launching it nationally and internationally."

Alongside the *Boots for Africa* campaign, Richard is now focusing his plans on 2007, when Sheffield FC becomes the first football club in the world to reach 150 years old. If things go according to plan, the celebrations will be fitting and the cash registers over-flowing.

"We offer something that you can't get anywhere else. Obviously if you're a big brand, you could go and sponsor Aston Villa and it would give them so much coverage on TV. We're not going to get on Sky for a Premiership football match, but there might be other ways, certainly in 2007 we'll be able to offer a lot of exposure. If FIFA get behind our celebrations, and the indications are that they will, we're hoping to have an international football match. I'm back out to see Real Madrid in a couple of weeks to talk about an idea for a book and we've got two TV documentaries on the table."

So what happens when the two worlds collide? If the brand takes off as Richard hopes, what effect will it have on the club that plays its football against the likes of Selby Town, Glapwell and Mickleover Sports?

"We don't aspire to be professional," says Richard. "We want to run a football club which plays within its income stream, which would be a nice first these days. We want to play at the highest level possible without being professional. The two founders of Sheffield FC wanted a recreation for the gentleman's sport of cricket in the winter. They didn't need to derive an income from sport. We play for the love of the game and I think there's marketability and commercialism in that area. It doesn't mean we're selling out. To be commercial means we can secure the future of this football club for another 150 years and that's my aim."

From smoking concerts to Rothmans to the Bernabeu: non-league football is on fire.

UPPERS

(Some half-decent players who started their careers in non-league)

1. Maik Taylor [Farnborough 1994–95]

A late developer, 'Iron' Maik Taylor joined non-league Farnbrough aged 23 after a spell as a grease monkey in the army. Eventually he found his way to Birmingham, where his performances earned him the dubious title 'Northern Ireland's Number One,' which looked a lot less dubious after his side's 1-0 victory over England in 2005's World Cup qualifier.

2. Shaun Teale [Southport 1984–86 & 2000–02]

Moustachioed Kevin Richardson look-a-like Shaun Teale began and ended his playing career with Southport in two spells separated by nearly 20 years. In between he starred for Aston Villa and boasted that he'd never missed a penalty, only to miss whilst playing for Motherwell aged 83, only to be saved by ref Father McCurry blowing for a foul by the Dundee United keeper. Ever the professional, big Shaun slotted home the retake, keeping his reputation intact.

3. Stuart Pearce [Wealdstone 1982–83]

'Psycho' began scything down right wingers as a young pup in Wealdstone. He went on to make his name at Forest before shooting to fame as the hard nut who blubbered like a girl after spooning his penalty against West Germany in the 1990 World Cup semi-final. The Sex Pistols fan atoned after slotting home against Spain in a Euro '96 shoot-out, bringing a clenched fist salute and a facial grimace that suggested he was hoping for a stint on the bass if his heroes got back together for the 498th time.

4. Andy Townsend [Welling 1980–84, Weymouth 1984–85]

It hasn't always been Bollinger and foie gras for England's top footballers, you know. Or for Andy Townsend, for that matter. The English-sounding Republic of Ireland international started out on a fiver a week at Welling. After supplementing his wages by bashing buttons on a computer for Greenwich Council, AT was snapped up by Weymouth from whence he graduated to Norwich, Villa and Chelsea. Now part of ITV's good-cop-good-cop routine alongside fellow grin and tonic merchant Ally McCoist, The Townsend shouldn't be mistaken for John Gregory. Although it's easily done.

5. Graham Roberts [Weymouth 1979–80]

Started out as a Southampton trainee, but was forced to kick start his career in non-league at Dorchester [where he scored 34 goals in 79 games] and then at Weymouth. One season with the Terras was enough to convince Spurs boss Keith Burkinshaw to sign him for a then non-league record of £35,000 without even seeing him play. The blind faith was repaid in the '81 FA Cup final when Roberts had his front teeth kicked out by his own player [Chris Hughton] in the opening exchanges. Hard man Roberts refused to go off injured, but he did later call Hughton a bafftard.

6. Jimmy Bullard [Gravesend & Northfleet 1997–98]

A poor woman's Paul Nicholas, Jimmy started his career at double-barrelled barra boys Gravesend & Northfleet before making his name in the 'plucky,' 'brave' and ultimately 'gallant' Wigan team that not only got into the Premiership, but stayed there. After a season of putting up with patronising prefixes he moved to 'crappy' Fulham in 2006.

7. Jason McAteer [Marine, 1991–92]

Nicknamed Trigger after the *Only Fools and Horses* character, Jason made a career of running down the wing [and looking like a queer, according to the Everton fan chant] after being spotted strutting his stuff at Marine. Spells at Bolton and Liverpool ensued, followed by a gruesome commercial involving a naked McAteer lathering himself up with Head and Shoulders. He failed to stay at any club long after he quit the 'Pool', presumably because he managed to annoy everyone so much by continually calling them Dave.

8. Ian Wright [Greenwich Borough 1984–85]

One-time Arsenal record goal scorer Ian Wright Wright Wright started out as a plasterer and labourer who knocked in the goals for Greenwich Borough of a weekend. Palace signed him aged 22, [late for a pro footballer], but he didn't waste any time adapting and ultimately won an MBE for his goals. Somehow the Wright magic didn't translate so well to the international arena but Satch, as he was known at Palace, fared rather better when it came to scoring in a very different kind of box. Sons Shaun, Bradley and Brett Wright-Phillips are all following in his wake on the pro circuit.

9. Les Ferdinand [Hayes 1986–87]

Rio and Anton's cousin started at Southall before hitting the giddy heights of Hayes. From there 'Sir Les' was whisked off to QPR, Besiktas, Newcastle and Spurs before pimping himself to anyone in need of a gentle giant up front. His style was immortalised in the documentary *The Impossible Job*, which featured a forlorn-looking England manager Graham Taylor asking from the touchlines: "Can we not knock it long for Les?" We couldn't and Taylor and Ferdinand quickly disappeared from the international scene.

10. Stan Collymore [Stafford Rangers 1989–90]

Released by Wolves as a yoof, Stanley kick-started his career at Stafford Rangers and was promptly plucked out of non-league by Crystal Palace. Having dropped down the divisions to Southend and done well, he was snaffled up by Forest where he scored bucketloads of goals. Lean spells at Liverpool and everywhere else since have prompted some fans to wonder whether Colly was punching above his weight. Since retiring prematurely at 30, Stan has, allegedly, mostly been shagging strangers in car parks and appearing alongside Sharon Stone in *Basic Instinct 2*.

11. DJ Campbell [Yeading 2003–05]

When Steve 'wor nose has eaten wor face' Bruce signed Campbell for Birmingham in 2005, it completed an amazing journey for the striker:

from non-league to The Premiership in less than a year. Dudley played for Chesham, Stevenage and Billericay before shooting to prominence in Yeading's 2005 FA Cup run. That prompted Brentford to pay five grand for him and, 18 games and 12 goals later, he was a Brummy. Don't expect him to start firing up the wheels of steel, though. The moniker DJ comes from his name, Dudley Junior, rather than a penchant for charging ten grand a night to play Felix Da Housecat records.

Manager: Howard Wilkinson [Boston United 1975–77]
It must be something in the fenland water. In the 1970s not one but two top class managers started their careers at Boston. First Bald Eagle Jim Smith learned the hard way by taking on the duties of running the lottery, digging the drains and concreting the car park as well as guiding the Pilgrims to a 40-game unbeaten run. Then things got done Howard's way, which brought two Northern Premier League titles before Wilkinson legged it to Mossley, Sheffield Wednesday, Leeds and, for two god-awful games, England.

DOWNERS

(Some blinding players who, by the time they got to non-league level were a bit past their sell-by date.)

1. Alex Stepney [Altrincham 1979–80]
One of the greatest keepers of his generation, Stepney kept Man U in the European Cup final at Wembley in 1968. With the game poised at 1-1, Portuguese legend Eusebio out-stripped the defence and unleashed a fierce shot on goal. Stepney saved it and United went on to become European champions for the first time. Ten years later Stepney quit the club and, after whoring himself Stateside, became custodian at Alty. Now available for weddings, christenings and bah mitzvahs as an after dinner speaker.

2. Brian Kilcline [Altrincham 1998]

Kilcline's finest hour came when he captained Coventry to FA Cup glory in 1987. The man, once described as a cross between Billy Connolly and a Viking, wound down his career at Altrincham after spells at Newcastle, Oldham, Swindon, Mansfield and Halifax. After a brief gig as an arm wrestler, 'Killer' settled down to the serious business of renovating homes in *Last of the Summer Wine* country and chilling out on the Midlands barge he now calls home.

3. Julian Dicks [Canvey Island 2001–02]

The last player to score in front of the Kop at Anfield before the seats went in, Julian Dicks is better known for his swashbuckling performances on the left side of West Ham's defence. After a year spent ruining the fun of right wingers in the Football Conference with Canvey, Dicks' dodgy knee forced him to retire in 1996, whereupon he took up the pursuit of ruining a good walk. The knee couldn't take the pro golf circuit either and now Dicks runs the 'Dog and Shepherd' pub in Colchester.

4. Mike Marsh [Kidderminster, Southport, Boston United, Accrington Stanley 1999–2003]

After a solid career with Liverpool, West Ham and Coventry Mike Marsh became something of a Cinderella figure, only he was never allowed to go to the ball. Dropping down to non-league, spells at Kidderminster and Boston brought championship medals, but not the chance to join his new chums back in the Football League. After pocketing an insurance pay-out following a serious knee injury sustained at Southend, Marsh wasn't allowed to play league football again. Having narrowly avoided the midnight pumpkin transformation, Marsh settled for a career as a non-league travelling tinker, seemingly playing for anyone with goalposts.

5. Des Walker [Burton 2001]

They say people don't become bad players overnight, but anyone who saw Des Walker after he left Forest the first time may beg to differ. An absolute legend for Cloughie and England, Walker seemed to lose his powers the minute he strapped on a Sampdoria shirt. Adequate performances at Wednesday and Forest followed, but he never hit the heights again. A Burton fan writes: "He played rightback for us in an evening match against Matlock on a very heavy pitch and after working hard in the thick mud he was beaten and the attack led to a goal. He was substituted shortly after, and as he left the pitch he was heard to mutter that there had to be better ways of earning a living. He never played for us again."

6. John Charles [Hereford 1967–71]
Like Phil Neville, John Charles could play any position. Unlike Phil Neville, he was outstanding in all of them. The Big Welshman was so good he shone for Leeds and Juventus and even helped Wales reach the World Cup quarter finals in 1958. Nicknamed *Il gigante buono* – the gentle giant – because he never got booked or sent off, Charles had a stint as player/manager at Hereford in the 60s before retiring to run a pub on the outskirts of Leeds. Passed away on February 21st 2004.

7. Wilf Mannion [Cambridge 1956–58]
The scorer of England's first-ever World Cup Finals goal [against Chile in 1950], Wilf Mannion was a legend for his country and Middlesborough. Struck down with malaria whilst fighting overseas during the war, 'Winky' was nursed back to help by future Arsenal manager Bertie Mee. A rebellious tyke, he wrote newspaper articles criticising the football establishment and, after retiring from football, netted a job on the assembly line at Vauxhall Motors. He once met the Queen whilst wearing his carpet slippers. Died in April 2000.

8. Kevin Hector [Boston United 1978–79]
After leaving Derby, England international Kevin Hector signed for NASL side Vancouver Whitecaps. When their season finished in September, he went on the lookout for an English team to play for, bizarrely choosing

Northern Premier League champions Boston United. The following season, he filled in his 'winter break' at Burton Albion, before re-signing for Derby County, where he set an all-time appearances record, before heading back to non-league, where he had more clubs than a whaling boat.

9. Steve Bull [Hereford 2000–01]
Often lauded as a tremendously loyal, one-club-man, Steve Bull actually started out at Tipton Town, before being snapped up by West Bromwich Albion. After crossing the Black Country divide for £65,000 in 1986, the 'Tipton Terrier' became a Wolves legend, scoring bagfuls of goals in the fourth, third and second divisions, earning himself an England call along the way. In 2000 he joined Hereford as coach and had a 12 game swansong before netting Bully's special pri…ize: a trip to Buck House, a peck on the cheek from the Queen and an MBE.

10. Tommy Lawton [Kettering 1956–57]
The most expensive player in the country when he moved from Chelsea to third division Notts County for £20,000 in 1947, Tommy Lawton was one of England's greatest strikers. He kicked off his league career stepping into the formidable boots of Dixie Dean and finished it at Arsenal, with some England action in between. Kettering paid the Gunners £1,000 to make him player/manager, which caused such a stink in the Kettering board room that two men resigned. Undeterred, Lawton took the Poppies to the Southern League title in his second season before returning to manage County. Passed away in November 1996.

11. Chris Waddle [Worksop 2000–02]
Christopher Roland Waddle wound down his career with appearances for Worksop, Glapwell and Matlock after making his name as a cultured left-footer on the flanks of his native Newcastle. Classy spells at Spurs, Marseilles and Sheffield Wednesday ensued but all most people remember is the ballooned penalty against the Germans in Italia 90 and the Pizza Hut ad he made poking fun at the misfortune. The mullet lord

currently writes a column in *The Sun* and is still at large for crimes he committed against music in 1987. *Diamond Lights*, indeed.

Manager: Paul Gascoigne [Kettering 2005]

The best England player of a generation by a country mile, Paul Gascoigne's career ended in farce. After failed attempts at keeping the dream alive on the field in places as diverse as Boston and China, Gazza stepped into the hot seat at Kettering Town. Unveiled amidst a fanfare of popping flashbulbs and hysteria, Gascoigne's tenure lasted a full 39 days. In that time, according to club owner Imraan Ladak, there were 37 separate incidents involving Gascoigne and alcohol. Although Gazza refutes the claims, anyone who saw his pitiful interview on Sky Sports after the dismissal got some handy pointers as to who was telling the truth.

> CHAPTER 6
MAGIC AMERICA

6:   MAGIC AMERICA

"Singing la la la la la la
we want to live in Magic America
with all those magic people"

Blur, 'Magic America'

It's a hot summer's day in London, 1966. England are beating West Germany 3-2 at a sun-drenched Wembley in the World Cup final. As Geoff Hurst collects the orange ball and starts running at the German goal, commentator Kenneth Wolstenholme informs the millions watching on TV that some of the crowd have encroached onto the pitch.

"They think it's all over," he says, half-condescending, half wishing it to be true. Then Hurst pulls back his left peg and smashes the ball into the top left hand corner of the goal, and Wolstenholme cries, "it is nooooow!"

Nearly 5,000 miles away in Dallas, Texas, it's just gone 10am and 34-year-old American Lamar Hunt can't believe what he's seeing. It's the first ever live broadcast from England to the US and he's blown away by the noise of the fans and the idea of the nation of England against the nation of Germany. It's unlike anything he's ever seen in American sport and Lamar Hunt decides he wants to bring that kind of excitement to the US.

He's not the only one. As the English weep tears of joy into their Union Jacks – favoured over the cross of St George in those days – American entrepreneurs are frantically making notes across the pond. For both nations July 30th 1966 is a landmark: it's the day England were crowned world champions on the pitch, and America realised they could be champions off it.

"I would say the 1966 World Cup was the single largest stimulant to the start of soccer in America," says Lamar Hunt, who invested heavily in the early days of US soccer. "Potential investors were thinking about starting a league which actually turned out to be two competing leagues which later merged and became the North American Soccer League. The World Cup was instrumental in helping this along. Many, many people watched this telecast in the United States."

English attitudes to America have undergone a sea change over the last decade. When Blur released their album, *Parklife*, two months before the World Cup in USA 1994, the song *Magic America* was a piss-take aimed at the vast army of little Englanders who saw America as the promised land, where there were 'buildings in the sky and the air is sugar free'.

Things are different now. After years of McDonaldisation and the 'liberation' of countries less than keen on it, British public opinion of America is at an all time low. George Dubya Bush has done more to push the British Isles into the arms of Europe than Tony Blair, Jacques

They have a 'World Series' that only they enter

Chirac and Vladimir Putin put together. But there is one small chink of hope for our American friends, and it comes from the unlikeliest of places: the sports field.

England has spent years laughing like drains at the Americans' attempts at sport. Their favourite games are rounders and netball, they have a 'World Series' that only they enter and they have to put on girly shoulder pads and helmets for a simple game of rugby. But what really made us laugh were their attempts to play footy. They were rubbish at it. And they called it soccer. Their best player ever appeared to be John Harkes, an average Sheffield Wednesday midfielder, and their greatest victory was a dodgy 1-0 fluke against England before colour TV, the internet and possibly even the wheel were invented.

What a shock then, when the Yanks turned up at World Cup 2002 and started bitch-slapping everyone. The much fancied Portugal were ripped to bits in the opening group game and talented neighbours Mexico dispatched in the knock-out stages before eventual finalists Ze Germans conjured up a 1-0 defeat. This kind of form has continued post-tournament, forcing the Brits to concede, through gritted teeth: "they're actually getting quite good, you know."

So how have they done it? How has a country with no natural aptitude for the sport turned itself from laughing stock to top ten in the FIFA rankings? The answer is simple: when it comes to the commercialisation of football, America are the world's best – Numero Uno. The champs. Through their brilliance off the pitch, the Americans have finally put in place an infrastructure to make sure they can compete on it.

America has actually been top of the commercialisation pile since the turn of the twentieth century. Almost a hundred years before Llansantffraid prostituted themselves to Total Network Solutions, Bethlehem Steel were ruling the roost Stateside. Huge sums of cash were spunked on over-rated foreigners in the North American Soccer League light years before anyone had even dreamed of The Premiership. Now the megabucks of Malcolm Glazer, Ronald McDonald and Budweiser make a huge contribution to English football, cementing the place of the Americans at the top of the commercialisation league.

They were the first British colony to play football-style games

The galling thing is, it could have been us. We could have been the ones singing "we are top of the league, say we are top of the league!" If only 1966 hadn't happened, England, not America, could have been top of the pile when it comes to sullying the beautiful game with cash. As it is, we remain bit part players, thanks largely to Hursty, Jules Rimet and That Russian Linesman. With 400 million people watching around the world, England widened its nostrils and inhaled the sweet smell of success whilst America, not for the first time, smelled money.

ORIGINS

It should come as no surprise that America is the world leader in the commercialisation of football, as they were pioneers of the game. They were the first British colony to play football-style games, with a form of 'soccer' played in the original Jamestown settlement as early as 1609. Of course, it wasn't really football. Like everywhere else in the world at that time, it was more like fighting with the presence of a ball just adding some legitimacy.

The game evolved in major colleges and universities and, in 1862 in Boston, The Oneida Football Club became the first football club anywhere outside England. It was football Jim, but not as we know it.

In fact it was dangerously close to the game some of us now call egg-chasing. On November 7th 1869 Princeton took on Rutgers in the first college match contested using rules based on the newly-formed English Football

Association's 1863 laws. There were 25 players, a 24 foot wide goal and all parts of the body were allowed to touch the ball [you could punch or hold it but not carry or throw it]. Such is the confusion over the handling issue, this game is also regarded as the first-ever gridiron game, although rumours of players roaming the field in ludicrous hats and over-sized shoulder pads can not be confirmed.

Fortunately this dalliance with rugby/American football was swiftly ironed out. Kindly immigrants brought with them not only cheap labour, but a concept of how the game ought to be played, and football more akin to what we now play began to evolve.

And on the money side, it was far closer to today's financial behemoth than you might expect. For in the 1880s, corporate football sponsorship was born in the good ole US of A.

Unlike Nina Simone, factory bosses in early twentieth Century America weren't 'just souls whose intentions were good'. When they started footy teams, they had more than Georgia on their minds.

"In the 1910s immigrants provided a cheap source of labour for manufacturing," says US football historian Stephen Holroyd. "Factory owners began forming company soccer teams in an attempt to keep their employees occupied and, not coincidentally, too busy having fun to bother with those pesky unions."

The semi-pro status afforded by factory backing allowed the development of local and regional leagues and, when the first national competition was launched in 1885 it was won by the gloriously-titled Our New Thread, the brand name of sewing manufacturer Kearnys, who sponsored the team.

Factory money powered US football in the early 1920s which, until the much later 1970s, was the golden age of American 'soccer'. The American Soccer League [ASL] was founded in 1921 and teams like Bethlehem Steel, Robins Shipyards and J&P Coates had pots of cash, thanks to the huge manufacturing firms that gave them their names. The clubs used the money to do what any self-respecting football club does when they have a few quid spare: they blew it all on mercenary foreign imports. And, to cap the insult to the homegrown players, most of those brought in came from a country whose speciality, at least according to English fans, is producing players who are unsure what cow's arses are, never mind how to hit them with a banjo. Thank you, Scotland.

The Scots queued up like lemmings on a cliff face to sing 'mcla, la, la, la, we'd like to live in mcmagic America'. Tec White went from Motherwell to Fall River Marksmen, Jimmy Young tore himself away from the splendour of Dundee United to sign for Bethlehem Steel and, in 1925, Scottish international Alex McNab stunned the football world by quitting Morton and joining Boston Wonder Workers. Still, The 'Ton' got the last laugh. When McNab pitched up in Massachusetts he received a friendly arm around the shoulder. "That's where we play our games," said the welcoming committee, pointing to the strip of grass they called a pitch. "And that's where you'll be working when you're not playing." A finger pointed to the daunting prospect of the Wonder Works factory. Well, what did he expect? They were paying him $25 a week.

Money was undoubtedly a big factor in the move West. When Tom Muirhead signed for Boston from Glasgow Rangers he reportedly doubled his wages. But it wasn't all about filthy lucre. Whilst some English football bosses, fearful of losing players to the 'Almighty Dollar', dubbed the situation 'the American Menace' and tried to badmouth the playing conditions in the press, some players found that America really was the land of opportunity.

"They not only offered to send me to university," gushed Alec Jackson, talking about his time with Bethlehem Steel. "They presented me with a motor car and took me on many sightseeing tours."

By the end of the decade football's bubble had burst in the US. In the depression that followed the stock market crash of 1929, the manufacturing companies that formed the backbone of the league faultered, and teams like Bethlehem Steel went out of existence.

"In some ways the ASL was ahead of its time, relying on wealthy businesses to support franchises," says Stephen Holroyd. "This proved to be its undoing, as these businesses could no longer afford the luxury of supporting a pro-soccer franchise once the Great Depression hit in 1929. The original ASL was dead by 1932."

Football drifted for the next 30 years. As games like baseball and basketball grew in prominence, 'soccer' took a back seat. Without the clout of manu-facturing cash behind them, teams formed out of ethnic groupings, such as the Ukranian Nationals of Philadelphia and the Philadelphia Americans, but it wasn't top-level football and remained largely ignored by mainstream America.

By 1960 things had changed. Travel and communication had improved and the advent of television had created a new market that needed to be satisfied: the armchair sports fan. Soon enough, it wasn't just players who were saying "la, la, la, la, la we'd like to live in Magic America." It was entire teams.

Seeing the quality of the American Soccer League but wanting to establish the first truly major football league in the US, ex-Philadelphia Phillies owner Bill Cox set up the International Soccer League. It sounded glamorous. European powerhouses such as Sampdoria, Bayern Munich and Glenavon were enticed over to compete against each other in the months when their domestic leagues were shut down.

In reality, most clubs sent over teams of reserves and journeymen for an extended holiday in the States. The inaugural International Soccer League table saw Kilmarnock pip Burnley to top spot, with Bayern Munich pushing up the daisies in fifth [out of six].

But whilst the International Soccer League's lack of star players meant attendances were poor, it wasn't half as bad as life in the low-key American Soccer League.

"The ASL was supposed to be a professional league," moaned Walter Chyzowych, who scored hatfuls of goals for the Ukranian Nationals in the 60s. "But I considered it amateur. It was a higher standard of play, sure. But nobody was making any money. It was a joke. There was no money to be had. I got three dollars for expenses to practise and six dollars on game days. Every two or three years, players would leave because of management problems, coaching problems. You coached yourself, really. Somebody just made out the lineup. The weather was always a problem. Scheduling was never very stable. A lot of teams came in with a lot of enthusiasm and found that they couldn't exist financially."

It was clear that something drastic needed to happen to American football. And, on 30th July 1966, it did.

THE NORTH AMERICAN SOCCER LEAGUE

The North American Soccer League [NASL] is the wet kipper with which the English Premiership should be roundly slapped around the chops. If ever there was a cautionary tale against spending wildly on overseas imports, not getting enough bums on seats and not balancing the books, this is it writ large. At its height it was the greatest league the country had ever seen and boasted the best players in the world [sound familiar?] but as it prepared to enter its 17th season, the NASL was forced to close. There were only two teams left.

The wailing and gnashing of teeth that accompanied the NASL's demise in 1985 was a far cry from the sound of pennies dropping that had accompanied England's 1966 World Cup win. The surprisingly high TV ratings for the tournament, especially for England's victory over West Germany, alerted sports promoters to the fact that there was gold in them there boots.

"I saw, what I perceived to be an opportunity to help build a successful venture," says Lamar Hunt, who invested in the Dallas Tornado Soccer Club in 1967. "I am prone to invest in the entertainment industry and also in businesses related to sports. Even though I had no 'playing experience', I felt soccer could become commercially viable."

Unsurprisingly America's first major football division was born out of pure capitalism. Demand was there – here was a prosperous nation full of citizens with more disposable income than ever before and a burgeoning love of sport. The Super Bowl had just been invented, basketball was on the verge of massive expansion and major league baseball had gone nationwide. The more keen-eyed promoters had already begun to suspect that in terms of equipment and salaries, football could be supplied relatively cheaply compared to other sports. The '66 World Cup viewing figures were the clip around the ear they needed. They could, they figured, make their own stash of cash.

The United States Soccer Football Association [USSFA] was bombarded with applications from promoters seeking sanction to start professional leagues the following summer. As you would expect of a country at the top of the commercial pile, money talked. With three serious contenders in the running to set up the league, The USSFA suddenly upped the stakes, demanding 4% of gate receipts, 10% of TV money and a $25,000 franchise fee from each club. Only one of the contenders, Jack Kent Cooke, could stomach the fees, so he got the nod and the United Soccer Association [USA] was born. The American media was so clueless about football that when USA commissioner Dick Walsh held a press conference to announce his appointment, he had a footy in his lap and theatrically announced: "this is a soccer ball."

Not to be outdone, the two main rivals to USA's bid promptly merged and called themselves the National Professional Soccer League [NPSL]. Without the backing of FIFA, they had to operate as an outlaw league, which meant players who played in the league faced worldwide bans by FIFA. But they did have two distinct advantages: they had a TV contract, which the USA did not, and their season was not determined by the European off-season as the USA's was. Whilst the USA's season ran for only seven weeks from May to July, the NPSL announced that they would play from April to September. And what's more, they said they would start almost immediately.

A footy in his lap, he theatrically announced: 'this is a soccer ball'

To sex things up for an American audience used to high-scoring games like baseball, basketball and American football, the NPSL changed the rules so teams could net six points for a win, three for a draw plus a point for every goal scored up to a maximum of three. So, when Baltimore beat Atlanta Chiefs 1-0 in the first NPSL match on April 16th 1967, they racked up seven points.

The USA was more cautious. They wanted to take their time and get the right players on board, yet they didn't want the NPSL grabbing all the limelight, so they came up with a novel solution: they imported teams from Europe en masse. It wasn't the same as the old ISL, where Kilmarnock would pop over in the summer, humiliate Bayern Munich, then hightail it back to Scotland. No. This time, the European teams played incognito. They played as the franchises they'd been brought over to fill in for. So for one season in 1967 Aberdeen were the Washington Whips, Cagliari were the Washington Mustangs and Sunderland were the Vancouver Royal Canadians. It wasn't totally random, though. Some effort was made to make the transition seamless. The Cleveland Stokers were represented by Stoke City for a season, whilst Los Angeles Wolves had – you've guessed it – Wolves flying their flag.

At the end of the first season both leagues were commercial disasters. Hungry for a quick buck, the guys in charge hadn't really understood the market, or lack of one. They thought that after the high '66 World Cup viewing figures, Americans would be queuing up to watch live 'soccer'. They didn't. By the summer of '67 the NPSL had an average gate of just under

5,000. Those that did turn up were mystified by the bizarre rules of the NPSL and general poor quality of the players. And it was clear that commercialisation was harming the game. On May 15th referee Peter Rhodes showed things had gone too far when he admitted that 11 of the 21 fouls he called in the televised game between Toronto and Pittsburgh were to allow TV company CBS to cut to a commercial break. On one occasion, he even pushed a player down who was trying to get up and carry on before the commercial had finished.

Drastic measures were required and in December 1967 the two leagues merged together to form the North American Soccer League. It was to become the greatest league in American 'soccer' history, boasting some of the greatest players in the world. But it started slowly.

When Wimbledon caused uproar in England by fleeing South London into the all-too-welcoming arms of Milton Keynes, they set a precedent in English football. It was the first time a club had moved cities in an attempt to boost its fortunes, although both Arsenal and Manchester United benefited by moving across London and Manchester in the early part of the 20th Century. A year after Wimbledon's move they won permission to call themselves MK Dons. For most fans, the name Franchise FC would have seemed more appropriate. Although it is seen as a derogatory term in England, where fans build up a bond with clubs over generations of continued support, the use of franchises is central to the way American 'soccer' operates.

"It's really no different from the franchise system in business," explains US 'soccer' historian Stephen Holroyd. "McDonalds, for example, is a brand name company. Individual owners purchase franchises from McDonalds, with the exclusive right to operate them in a certain geographic area. If you think of the National Football League as McDonalds, you get a better idea of how the member clubs operate. The Philadelphia Eagles, for example, have the exclusive right to operate a football team in the city of Philadelphia and 'sell' the NFL's 'product' – football."

The fundamental difference across the Atlantic is that English clubs have grown organically into the somewhat bizarre institutions they are today, but American clubs were businesses from the outset. Their product was football and their customers were supporters and, if there weren't enough of them to sustain the business, then the business would simply move. Following the creation of the NASL, the old NPSL's Chicago franchise moved to Kansas City and the Los Angeles franchise relocated to San Diego in a bid to ensure that no two clubs were competing for the same fans. Can you imagine Man City relocating to the Lake District so they and United weren't 'going for the same fans'? It's this kind of precision, manufactured scenario that marks the US game out from ours. In America, football is a business first. They'd never allow a 'South Yorkshire situation' to develop, where Sheffield United, Sheffield Wednesday, Rotherham, Doncaster, Chesterfield and Barnsley all play within a twenty mile radius of each other. The customer base would be spread too thin.

On the field, the standard of football was surprisingly good. When Malcolm Allison brought his English champions Manchester City over for a friendly in 1968, he was shocked to lose 3-2 to the Atlanta Chiefs.

"They're nothing but a fourth division side," lamented Allison afterwards. "They couldn't possibly beat us again."

But fate conspired against Allison. Man City's next scheduled friendly got called off, and Atlanta promptly challenged them to a rematch. City strode out onto the pitch like men. They were cowering like girls at the final whistle as Atlanta walked off with a 2-1 win in their knapsack.

The debut of the foreign tour was the start of a commercial venture which in those days was designed to help the US teams, although now it's turned full circle and is used by European teams to help 'crack the lucrative US market'.

To prove that City weren't the only team in Manchester they were capable of shoeing twice, Atlanta Chiefs stuffed Man U 3-2 and 2-1. The Famous Man United responded by being gubbed 3-1 by a team called Oakland Clippers. Real Madrid rescued things for the Europeans by duffing up the New York Generals to the tune of 4-1.

The standard of football might have been good, but it doesn't matter if no one's going to watch it. Again attendances were dismal. The average was now below 4,000. With a break-even figure of nearer 20,000, to cover the salaries and stadium rental, nearly every team folded at the end of the season. The future of US football looked bleak.

The 1969 season kicked off with only five teams taking part in the NASL. CBS cancelled its television contract and crowds dipped to practically nothing. There was so much firefighting to be done, it looked as if Red Adair was the only person who could save the NASL. In fact, its saviour was sitting right under its nose.

Phil Woosnam was a university-educated Welshman and former coach of Atlanta. When the NASL clubs turned to him after their meeting in January 1970 and asked him to become their chief executive, he accepted. In his next contact with the clubs, he demanded that salaries and costs be brought under $200,000.

A period of consolidation followed. In 1970 another team folded but two new ones joined, giving the NASL six teams. The following year Woosnam achieved his aim of securing NASL football in New York, which he saw as being essential if the league was to be taken seriously. Initially he approached David Frost [of *Today With Frost* fame] but, when Frost turned him down, he approached Warner Communications, who were only too happy to fund the new team. New York Cosmos was born.

Over the next few years a college draft system was introduced, where teams were awarded the chance to pick the best players from the college teams. In an attempt to keep teams on an even keel, the most rubbish team got first pick, then the second most rubbish team and so on. The upshot was more American players in the league, which seemed to please the fans and attendances grew year-on-year.

CBS cancelled its television contract and crowds dipped

It wasn't all plain sailing. An outbreak of silliness in 1972 saw an offside line introduced 35 yards from goal, which meant you couldn't be offside unless you were over the line. Two years later extreme silliness consumed the NASL when they decided that draws were no good. They were so bad, in fact, they wouldn't even call them draws. So penalty shoot-outs were introduced, the winners of which were awarded tie-wins, worth three points.

Such nonsense didn't seem to harm the league. In fact, it flourished. In '74 the NASL expanded down the west coast, adding four new franchises. The fourth and final one available was grabbed by a chap named Milan Mandaric, who would later become *The Bloke Who Forced Harry Out And Replaced Him With Some Rubbish Foreign Bloke Only To Realise He Was Rubbish Too So He Brought Harry Back To Portsmouth*. The following year five new franchises were added, including the Tampa Bay Rowdies, who would later provide a home for an aging Rodney Marsh.

Having stabilised the league, Woosnam wanted to take it to the next level. To do that, he reasoned that they needed a star player, someone who could give them credibility and ignite the interest of the public. Luckily for him, the Warners-backed New York Cosmos had the financial fandango to realize that dream. And so, in December 1972, New York Cosmos announced that they had struck a deal to bring one of the greatest footballers in the world to the NASL. A fee of $240,000 had been agreed with Manchester United and George Best, in the prime of his career, appeared at a press conference in New York.

"We are very close [to agreeing a deal]," he said. "As far as I am concerned there will be no problem."

But there was a problem. After spending a week in New York being wined and dined by Cosmos chief Clive Toye, Best decided he liked the Big Apple but couldn't eat a whole one.

"I loved the madness of New York for a few days," he later explained. "I just did not relish the prospect of living there full time."

Although Best's move to the Cosmos never materialised, it was a hugely significant event in the commercialisation of US football. It gave other teams the balls to think big, and a spate of big-name foreign signings arrived. The Minutemen tempted Eusebio to Boston, Seattle Sounders snapped up Mike England and St Louis Stars laid out a welcoming bowl of milk for Peter 'the cat' Bonetti. Then, out of the blue, The Greatest Footballer In The World Ever said 'I'd like to live in Magic America.'

THE WONDER YEARS

It's a hot, sunny, humid afternoon in New York, 1976. There are over 65,000 fans packed into the Giants Stadium in East Rutherford, New Jersey, watching the New York Cosmos take on the San Jose Earthquakes. Pelé's on the ball, advancing towards the Earthquakes' goal. Suddenly, out of nowhere, a striker with crazy, bouffant hair races back from his position up front and nicks the ball away from the World's Greatest Player.

"Growing up in England I knew all about Pelé," says Paul Child, ex-San Jose Earthquakes striker. "To play on the same pitch as him was incredible. Although we didn't directly come up against each other because we were both strikers, I'd occasionally run the length of the pitch to get a tackle in to try and take the ball off him. It meant that much."

One of the most intriguing things about the NASL was that it pitched relative unknowns against superstars. Paul Child arrived in the States as a young lad who'd not managed to break into the first team at Aston Villa. He ended up fifth on the all-time NASL scoring charts and bagged a place alongside Pelé in the 'Hall of Fame'.

When Edson Arantes do Nascimento signed for NASL club New York Cosmos on June 3rd 1975, the main question on everyone's lips was: why? Why had the Greatest Player Ever agreed to play out his days in the relative backwater of America's top 'soccer' division?

"I decided to go to the US because I had the opportunity to study sports marketing," Pelé told makers of *The History of Football: The Beautiful Game* DVD. "It was a chance for my kids to learn English. Another important thing was the season only lasted five or six months, so I didn't have the same sort of pressure there was in Europe or Brazil."

It might have cost the Cosmos $4.7m to acquire his services for three years, but the value to the NASL was immeasurable. Overnight, the league became credible and, most importantly, saleable. Attendances rocketed as Americans clamoured to get a glimpse of the great Pelé. Over 35,000 people turned out to see him play in Washington, setting a new league record.

"It just went boom when he arrived," remembers Paul Child. "New York Cosmos were a world class team. They drew massive crowds and the league took a turn upwards."

Suddenly, the Yanks thought they were kings of the football castle. Instead of welcoming European clubs into their homeland, they sent New York Cosmos on the road to showcase the NASL. Results were mixed, with victories in Europe against Gothenberg and Oslo, but a defeat against Haitian minnows Violette. Still, that wasn't really the point. As it had been doing with its films, restaurant chains and culture in general, America was now exporting its football to the world.

"We used to have a competition called the Trans Atlantic Cup," Phil Woosnam told *BC Soccer.net*. "Two teams from our league, the winner of the Soccer Bowl [NASL's annual championship], and one with the best record in the league from number of points gained in a season would play against two top quality teams from overseas. We ran it for six years and in no year did any of those foreign teams win it. That just showed exactly what a quality league the NASL was. The rest of the world was impressed at what was going on. The Cosmos would go on tours pre-season and post-season, and they would be successful wherever they went."

The presence of Pelé was enough to attract the best players in the world to the NASL. Geoff Hurst, Rodney Marsh and Bobby Moore all chose to play their football in America. In 1976 an Elton John-backed Los Angeles Aztecs finally managed to tempt George Best to the NASL.

Attendances increased massively each season and, by the time Pelé played his last ever game against his old club Santos in 1977, 75,000 people turned up to wave bye bye to the master. At the end of the game Pelé swapped shirts with young US protégé Jim McCallister. To some it

Suddenly, the Yanks thought they were kings of the football castle

symbolised perfectly the debate that had begun to kick off about how the league should progress: should they carry on spending massively on ageing foreign stars? Or would the League be sustained better if they invested more in developing homegrown talent?

Those that urged caution lost out, as clubs continued to spend wildly. Even with Pelé gone, American money was good enough to lure Johan Cruyff, Gerd Muller and Trevor Francis to the NASL.

In '79 the NASL finally managed to net a decent TV deal. The coverage generated on ABC resulted in yet more interest in the game, although the constant interruptions for commercial breaks made it frustrating to watch.

By the end of the 1980 season cracks had begun to appear. Clubs were spending too much money chasing the dream [hello, Leeds] and interest in the game was beginning to fade – attendances were dropping and ABC ratings were low. Two of the leagues weaker franchises, Houston Hurricane and Rochester Lancers, folded.

The following year star players put on a passable impersonation of Bob Marley as they headed for the airports humming *Exodus!* When the wages began to shrink, Gerd Muller, Alan Ball, Franz Beckenbauer and Rudi Krol returned to Europe.

Whilst they were riding high, NASL chiefs had slipped another cheeky rule change under the noses of FIFA. To settle 'ties', the NASL scrapped penalty shoot-outs and brought in shoot-outs, where players had five seconds to dribble from the 35 yard offside line and shoot past the keeper.

But, with the power of the NASL on the wane, FIFA decided to stamp its feet. It threatened to make the NASL an outlaw league unless its rule modifications were scrapped. Honourary NASL Chairman Henry Kissinger tried to intervene, sending FIFA a four page letter outlining the case. Unimpressed, FIFA threatened the United States Soccer Federation with expulsion. Eventually, a compromise was reached. The 35 yard line was scrapped and the points system was modified, although shoot-outs remained.

At the end of the season a new problem emerged. Presumably seduced by the introduction of a hairy fluorescent green ball, lots of people started to play and watch football indoors. A Major Indoor Soccer League was formed, which began competing with the NASL for players. Seven NASL clubs folded.

"In one way the New York Cosmos was the beginning of the end," says Paul Child. "They were a bit like Chelsea is now. They could buy anyone. They played all year round because they went on tours. They got huge crowds of 65,000 in the Giants stadium in New York, a city with a high ethnic population, who would turn out to watch soccer. They were backed by Warners as well. They had a lot of money, but other teams couldn't compete. Clubs were paying huge salaries but didn't have the spectator support to fund them."

As the years rolled on, attendances and teams dropped away, and clubs frantically turned to gimmicks to attract fans. The Minnesota Strikers tempted 50,000 through the gate in 1984 by staging a Beach Boys concert before the game. But not all the gimmicks were successful. The New York Cosmos tried and failed to lure Pelé out of retirement. And Montreal Manic talked themselves out of existence. To add some pazazz into their club, they decided to act as Team Canada, pooling together the best Canadian talent to represent the club. What they hadn't taken account of was the fact that Montreal was a pro-French city. In a flash, the 25,000 crowds were lost and the franchise was forced to close.

When only two teams put a deposit down to play in the 1985 season, the NASL did the decent thing and called it quits. After 16 seasons of ribald, rancour and rule change, the greatest football league ever to exist in the United States was forced to close down. What went wrong?

"There were record crowds wherever Pelé played," says Stephen Holroyd. "Unfortunately the powers-that-be at the NASL did not accept this for what it was – people coming to see Pelé, and not necessarily the NASL. Instead they thought they had stumbled upon a formula: ageing stars equals big crowds."

According to the NASL's top brass, they could see what was happening but were powerless to stop it.

"The problem was that the Cosmos brought in Beckenbauer, Neeskens, Chinaglia and so on," Phil Woosnam told *BCSoccer.net*. "There must have been eight or nine who were on high salaries. If a salary cap programme had been established then, we could have brought the Cosmos back under control. But we had no means of controlling how much the Cosmos spent, and that scared the other owners."

Another problem was the small screen. Whilst the English Premiership dines off the back of a fat television contract, the NASL was foraging through the bins.

"Other sports leagues could afford to overpay players because of lucrative television deals," says Holroyd. "The NASL had none. Its clubs survived entirely on gate receipts. Out of these receipts the clubs had to pay exorbitant rental fees to stadiums and didn't even get to keep secondary revenues like parking."

There are too many similarities between the NASL and the Premiership not to feel a little tremour in your pants when surveying the wreckage of the once-great league. The NASL imported mercenary foreigners by the bucketload [Hello, Arsenal], failed to control spending on wages [Sure Rio, here's £120k a week] and allowed one team to become bigger than the league [Whatever you say, Chelsea]. But before you go reaching for your *Rothmans Guide To Scottish Football*, in anticipation of needing something to do on Saturday afternoons post 2010, hold your fire.

These days footballers eyeing a few quick mega bucks before they hang up their boots head out to Qatar. Argentine legend Gabriel Batistuta got $8m for playing two season with Al Arabi Sports Club. It's these kind of deals that ruined the NASL and threatened to ruin The Premiership in the early years. Jurgen Klinsmann and Gianfranco Zola were both the wrong side of thirty when they signed for Spurs ['94] and Chelsea ['96] respectively. But now England's top flight is seen as a place to go at the pinnacle of a career, not the tail end, as it was in the NASL and now is in Qatar. Huge talents like

Christiano Ronaldo and Robin Van Persie came into the English game as teenagers, recognising that is one of the strongest leagues in world football.

"The Premiership is in a somewhat different situation [to the NASL] in that soccer is deeply rooted in England's sporting culture," says US football historian David Litterer. "There's a large and solid fan base, enormous television contracts, and enormous revenue coming in, and long established clubs with an enormous amount of history. The NASL never had any of that. The majority of teams drew between 6,000 and 8,000 fans per game, ticket prices couldn't be as high as the established sports and there was virtually no television revenue. And they had to pay high rents to play in stadiums owned by others."

WORLD CUP WINNERS

It would be easy to think that America's influence on the commercialisation of football died with the NASL. It's certain that the balance of power was shifting, with European commercial activity on the increase and English clubs preparing to go into over-sell. But how do you explain a country with no significant footballing heritage, no dedicated football grounds and no real idea about the game, winning the right to host the 1994 World Cup? The answer lies on track six of Abba's 1976 album *Arrival*: Money, money, money.

For America, hosting the tournament represented the last chance to have a bash at setting up a proper league and establishing the game on the national sports calendar. To FIFA, America was a massive potential market just waiting to be tapped into. It was an obvious marriage of commercial convenience, but before FIFA could get its hands anywhere near the dowry, some pre-nuptial agreements had to be made – the most important of which was the establishment of a fully functioning league in the States.

If you've ever seen an episode of the *A-team* or the *News At Ten*, you'll probably be aware that the Americans love a good fight. They're prepared to travel many miles to get embroiled in a good dust-up, often when there's no earthly reason why they should get involved. What a boon the re-birth of outdoor football must have been. It gave them the chance to have a scrap without the need to travel.

US football veterans Chuck Blazer and Clive Toye had established a new

American Soccer League in 1988 but, as the League grew, arguments raged over how best to take it forward. Some said it should grow organically, starting from grass roots and building up to a Premier League level. Others said that would take too long, and they needed to start with a top division and work down. Proponents of the latter theory won out and the Major Soccer League was born in 1992, although it wasn't until after the World Cup that it really took off.

World Cup '94 was a box-office smash: 3.6m spectators poured through the turnstiles at an average of 67,000 a game. But it wasn't so much the tournament itself that was the real success, more the legacy it left behind.

"The World Cup was critical in establishing Major League Soccer," says David Litterer. "For years various powers were bickering and fighting over attempts to establish a new professional league. That only changed when the US was awarded the cup with the requirement that a new pro league be established. It also pushed the US to get serious about developing their national team program, which really spurred the development of the top US players and provided a greatly expanded talent pool from which the MLS populated its teams."

Following the World Cup, American 'soccer' achieved, for the first time, an operational divisional system. With organisers desperate to succeed where so many others had failed, three different league structures agreed to work together to form an English-style pyramid system, vital for sustaining football in the country. It's impossible to have a Premiership without grass roots football. In the States, Major League Soccer sat at the top of the chain, with the A-league below it acting as a second division and the United States Interregional Soccer League as the basement division.

So why else has MLS been so successful? The main reason is that it learnt from the mistakes of the NASL. Player signing and wages were managed centrally, to stop debts spiralling out of control, and a quota was put on the number of foreigners allowed in a team, to stop homegrown bums spending most of their time collecting splinters on the bench.

"Major League Soccer also has 'franchises'," says David Litterer. "With the difference being that the MLS is actually a single corporation, including all the teams, with the teams run by investors rather than teams being individually owned. This has worked well to keep one team from spending wildly, and forcing others into a destructive spending spree. It has helped keep expenses and salaries down to the point where the league can actually survive. This stability has allowed fans to identify with their teams, now they no longer have to worry if the team will be around next year. MLS is also committed to being part of FIFA and playing the way the rest of the world does."

The other main reason for its success is that, for the first time, US football teams have their own stadiums. Previously 'soccer' games took place in cavernous American Football grounds but MLS chiefs were wise to the fact that if the game was to succeed in the US, this had to change.

"We recognised from day one the need for soccer specific facilities," MLS Chief Operation Officer Mark Abbott told *FC Business* in 2005. "So we had a double task ahead of us. Starting a league was hard enough, but we also had to get into stadium building."

The first-ever major league stadium built specifically for football opened on May 15th 1999, courtesy of funding from our old friend, the guy who got up early to watch the World Cup in 1966, Lamar Hunt.

"I love watching soccer," he says. "It is, as is often said to be, 'the beautiful game'. Obviously, there are all different levels to the game, but when played by high levels of athletes, it is an exceptionally attractive sport and a commercially viable one."

Over 24,000 turned up to the opening of the first specifically built 'soccer' stadium – the Columbus Crew Stadium – in May '99. Since then, the US has gone footy stadium mad. By the end of 2007, all but one of the 12 MLS clubs will be playing in a purpose-built stadium. And it's even bringing in some much-needed sponsorship cash. Home Depot pays $7m a year so that Los Angeles Galaxy and Club Deportivo Chivas can play in the Home Depot stadium.

It seems fitting that a nation obsessed by variants of girls' sports such as rounders and netball should also turn out to be world leaders at girls' football. They won the inaugural Women's Football gold at the Olympics in 1996 and have since gone on to establish themselves as one of the world's best teams. However, when it comes to the commercialisation of the game, US ladies come a poor second to their male counterparts. A women's league, Women's United Soccer Association, was launched in 2001. It closed three years later due to a lack of commercial punch – TV ratings were poor and sponsors said: we'd rather lick our own bums than spend money on that guff.

Things came full circle in 2003. After years of spending money on bringing

European clubs over to the US to promote the game, American clubs now found themselves the recipients of eyelid-batting European clubs desperate to break 'new markets'. The commercially conscious Manchester United were one of the first to recognise the possibilities on offer in the land of opportunity, when they sent a touring team over in 2003 that included all their top stars. The American summer tour is currently part of most major European clubs' summer itinerary.

It's not all one–sided, though. Several American companies have hot-footed it to the UK with dollar signs in their eyes and a supposed love of the beautiful game in their hearts. Those kind chaps at McDonalds pour thousands of pounds into English grass roots football, as they seek to up their corporate responsibility ratings. And Budweiser took on Carling in a battle to be the English footy fan's favourite beer, by taking the piss out of themselves in an advert that harked back to a by-gone age of rule tampering, with ludicrous suggestions such as 'half-time multi-ball' superseded by the notion, 'you do the football, we'll do the beer'.

And there, it seemed, the American influence on the commercialisation of the game ground to a creaking halt. The golden days as top boys were gone. It was time to retreat into the shade and let someone else have a go.

Then suddenly, out of the blue, an old timer yehawed into England on the back of an old mule, turned his bearded face towards the world's most famous football club and said: I'm going to buy that.

Game on.

A VERY PECULIAR PANTOMIME

A pantomime scene unfolded in Manchester in the early months of 2005. Angry chorus members stomped through the streets around Old Trafford holding placards bearing the legend 'not for sale', only for a group of ugly brothers to reply, 'oh yes you are'.

'Oh no we're not!' shouted Shareholders United.

'Oh yes you are!' trilled the Glazers and, eventually, a 76-year old oddment who'd never been to a football match in his life assumed total control of Manchester United.

It was a crushing victory for the Americans in the commercialisation stakes and revenge for the failed attempt back in 1999. Then, Australian-

American Rupert Murdoch had tried to seize control of the Red Devils, only to be slapped back into place by the Monopolies and Merger's Commission. America lay dormant for six years, before ghosting in unmarked to the far post and buying England's flagship club. It was a simple tap-in, and left many United fans wondering: where was the marking?

"I'm a very modest shareholder, I wish I had more so that I could do my best to block what I think is an unwelcome bid," Manchester Central MP Tony Lloyd told the BBC in 2005. "I think most football supporters in this country will see this as being an undesirable move because it's not in the interests of the game of football."

Even the Americans felt a twinge of conscience about the latest branch out from their position on top of football's commercial tree.

"A lot of people are unhappy about what this business model has done to sports in this country with the excessive commercialisation, the runaway salaries and unaffordable tickets," says David Litterer. "The general feeling is this type of thing takes the sport away from the fans by making it only affordable to rich people who get free tickets paid for by corporate expense accounts."

Undeterred, the Glazer juggernaut rolled on. This bloke didn't just want to own Man Utd, he wanted to seriously funk with it. So after sweet-talking all the major shareholders into flogging him enough shares to take control of the club, he pulled off a commercial masterstroke: he acquired more shares [98%] which allowed him to remove Manchester United from the stock exchange, and transfer the majority of the debt he'd incurred during the takeover back to the club. It was a stroke of genius, the like of which hadn't been seen at Old Trafford since the Kung Fu Kid pitched up at a press conference and said "when the sea gulls follow the trawler, it is because they think sardines will be thrown into the sea."

Despite the best efforts of the fans [some painted banners, others burned effigies] to convince us otherwise, the plain truth of the matter is: Manchester United was for sale, and had been since 1991, when they floated on the stock exchange and became a PLC. They were the ones with pound signs flashing before their eyes and they were the ones who, by floating on the market and becoming a money-making PLC machine, were responsible for taking football into the realms of big business. That this same big business has come back to bite them on the arse, in the form of an unwanted takeover, is music to the ears of many English fans.

"Let's not forget that Man Ure made this corporate culture in English football," says Leeds fan Dave Jenkins, barely able to stop his shoulders from shaking with laughter. "When they went PLC and marketed themselves so aggressively they were always targets for people like Glazer because of the media attention. They helped it happen more than anyone else. And it's not as if they didn't have a warning shot. When Murdoch tried to buy them, they should have 'mobilised' themselves, and amassed enough shares to stop something like that happening again. But they didn't."

Whilst the anti-Man Yoo brigade laughed until their socks fell off, hardened Unitedites cried themselves a river so big a brand new team and a vessel of indifference found new waters in which to swim. Renegade fans broke away and formed a new club which they seemingly named after a clothes shop [FCUM] and everyone else did a big bag of nothing. The plan was to hit The Famous Man Utd where it hurt – commercially – but the proposed match and merchandise boycotts failed to materialise and life at Gold Trafford continued pretty much as it had before.

Malcolm Glazer's appearance at Old Trafford opened the commercial floodgates between English football and US commercialisation. In 2005 American businessman Robert Kraft came very close to investing in Liverpool and in August 2006 Cleveland Browns owner Randy Lerner paid £62.6m to become majority shareholder at Aston Villa.

And so, with two of England's biggest clubs casually tucked in its breast pocket and the commercialisation of football crown wedged firmly on its head, what's next for America? Can they really compete on the pitch? Could they actually, gulp, win the World Cup? Paul Child thinks so.

"When I first came to America it was all football fields and baseball diamonds," he says. "Now, everywhere I go, I see soccer pitches. Some of the kids coming through have fantastic skills. It wouldn't surprise me at all to see the Americans win a World Cup."

Then Hursty, Jules Rimet and That Russian Linesman really would have a lot to answer for.

ALL-TIME NASL XI
You could make a fortune on Ebay with this lot...

1. Gordon Banks

They say that in the kingdom of the blind, the one-eyed man is king. The same must also be true of US soccer, which afforded the England World Cup-winner a home long after the accident that left him blind in his right eye had forced him to retire from the English game. Banksy enjoyed two seasons with the Fort Lauderdale Strikers at the end of the 70s, seemingly prompting an English graffiti artist to steal his name twenty years later.

NASL games: 39
NASL goals: 0

2. Carlos Alberto

The captain of Brazil's world-cup winning team of 1970, 'Weller' Alberto was the original Cafu – a rampaging right back who loved nothing better than getting forward then stroking his cross elegantly into the first defender's thigh. Brought honour on his family when he won the Soccer Bowl for New York Cosmos in 1977, then repeated the trick the following year to ensure a generation of Albertos never went without a seat down the local on a Friday night.

NASL games: 145
NASL goals: 8

3. Mike England

An uncompromising central defender, Welshman England was once named in George Best's 'Perfect XI' for footy magazine *Four Four Two*. He played five years for Seattle Sounders, helping to establish them as a force in the NASL, picking up a Soccer Bowl along the way. A constant source of confusion to fans in Wales, who could never work out why the bloke next to them was shouting 'come on England' at Wales games.

NASL games: 116
NASL goals: 7

4. Johan Neeskens

Like Rosencrantz and Guildenstern, Rudi Krol and Johan Neeskens were readily inter-changeable. Both made names for themselves by wearing their shirts firmly outside their shorts in the Total Football But Not Many Trophies era, when Holland were to be marvelled at but not feared, and both made a bit of extra pocket money in the States in the twilight of their careers. Neeskens' commitment was stronger than Krol's, playing six seasons at New York Cosmos compared to Krol's paltry one for the Vancouver Whitecaps.

NASL games: 107
NASL goals: 20

5. Franz Beckenbauer

'The Kaiser' won the World Cup with Germany as both a player and a manager, but in moments of quiet reflection, between mouthfuls of bratwurst and a big slug from his favourite stein, it's surely his 1977 NASL Most Valued Player award that makes the original 'Becks' blush. A commanding presence in *that* New York Cosmos team of 1978, Beckenbauer was one of the best players to play anywhere, never mind the NASL.

NASL games: 132
NASL goals: 23

6. Bobby Moore

Everyone knows Sir Bobby as the only Englishman to lift the World Cup but few realise the San Antonio Thunder and Seattle Sounders star once played against England. King Bob donned the Team America colours in the 1976 Bicentennial tournament that also included Italy and Brazil. Much to the chagrin of the one-time *Escape to Victory* star, England ran out 3-0 winners.

NASL games: 32
NASL goals: 1

7. Johan Cruyff

You know you've done well if something gets named after you as John Montagu, the fourth Earl of Sandwich, would have told you through mouthfuls of a filling placed between two sheets of bread in the eighteenth century. How good must Cruyff have been? He not only had a turn, but an entire style of [total] football dedicated to him. The Los Angeles Aztecs and Washington Diplomats star fell from grace in later years thanks to a certain English commentator's penchant for calling him 'Crife.'

NASL games: 59
NASL goals: 26

8. Eusebio

In an age when nativity scenes are banned in schools for fear of upsetting children of other religions, it seems unlikely that if he were playing today, either of Eusebio's nicknames would have been allowed. In those days, being called 'The Black Pearl' and 'The Black Panther' weren't seen as racist, and didn't deter Eusebio from terrorising the NASL with Boston Minutemen, Torronto Metros-Croatia and Las Vegas Quicksilver.

NASL games: 50
NASL goals: 22

9. Gerd Muller

Who said the Germans couldn't laugh about the war? As far back as 1970 this pesky scamp, with huge thighs and an eye for the goal, earned himself the cheeky nickname "Der Bomber." Having helped West Germany to a slice of World Cup pie, The Bomber hot-footed it to America, where he continued to lash in the goals for the Fort Lauderdale Strikers, before settling down and becoming a type of Adidas trainer.

NASL games: 80
NASL goals: 40

10. Pelé

The greatest player never to be Peter Crouch scored a whopping 1,280 professional goals in his career [he didn't have a robot dance, though] and won the World Cup three times, almost single-handedly. Like cats versus dogs, New York Cosmos starlet Pelé is one half of a late night pub debate as to who was the bestest player of all time. The answer is simple: if you're young and once owned a dog, it's dogs and Maradona. If you're old and prefer pussy, it's cats and Pelé. Unless, of course, you're Pelé, who was a Best man himself.

NASL games: 64
NASL goals: 39

11. George Best

George Best's personal problems were well documented but his abilities on the football pitch acted as a memory serum and, when his liver finally gave out in November 2005, all people could remember was what a hoot he'd been on the soccer field. A European cup winner at Man Yoo, Best played for the Los Angeles Aztecs, Fort Lauderdale Strikers and San Jose Earthquakes before pimping himself out to the likes of Arbroath Vics for a bit of extra beer money.

NASL games: 149
NASL goals: 57

PRAWNS IN THE GAME

> CHAPTER 7
THE EUROPEAN GOLDRUSH

7: THE EUROPEAN GOLDRUSH

Europe: an insane land populated by hairy maidens and chain-smoking savages or the last island of beauty in the civilized world?

For the English it's difficult to tell, as our relationship with our cousins across the pond is shrouded in uncertainty. We used to fight them on the beaches, now we sunbathe on them [the beaches not the people; that would just be rude], we want our children to go on exchanges with them at school but not if it means some freakish foreign kids staying in our homes for a week – and we're getting our heads around this Union idea, but if they try and get their greasy foreign mitts on our pound, we'll bite their dirty fingers off. What to think? To hiss and boo or to welcome with, 'ow you say, ze open arms? If football's anything to go by, we should be building bridges, boats and anything else we can think of to ferry these nice folk across the water *toute de suite*. They are, as they say in the Bank of England, minted.

In 2005 UEFA distributed £289m between the 32 clubs who took part in the Champions League, with eventual winners Liverpool sloping back to Anfield with £21.3m in their back pockets. For those at the very top, the prestige of playing in the Champions League is essential to attracting new players and the cash it generates is a vital part of paying those players' hefty wage demands. For confirmation of the size of the Champions League cash bonanza, examine Arsene Wenger's face in the closing weeks of the 2005/06 season. Faced with the possibility of starting life at the Emirates Stadium without the glamour and, more importantly cash windfall from a Champions League spot, Monsieur Wenger looked a whiter shade of pale.

The biting of nails and indiscreet parping that accompanies the attempt to qualify for the lucrative Champions League group stages is a relatively new phenomenon. Back in the days of Spam, transistor radios and black and white life, it was honour that ruled the roost.

From the Romans and the Vikings through to Hitler and Mussolini, Europe has a long history of war. As recently as 1939, the great and good of Europe conspired to knock seven bells out of each other, for the sake of their nation states. And after 1945, by when the realisation had struck that too much more of this war stuff would be extremely detrimental to the well-being of the world, the perpetrators drummed their fingers impatiently on their desks and shot icy glances at each other when teacher wasn't looking. Then, just ten years after the end of the Second World War, the solution presented itself: the nations of Europe would swap battlefields for football fields in order to find out who was top dog.

The idea of a Europe-wide football tournament had been kicking around the offices of French sports paper *L'Equipe* for a while, but they weren't moved to do anything about it until their counterparts in the English press started getting too big for their boots. When Wolves beat Budapesti Honved 3-2 on December 14th 1954, the

The English press started getting too big for their boots

English press proclaimed them to be the best side in the world. Across the channel, onions were torn from necks and berets were thrown to the ground in disgust.

"We better wait until the Wolves travel to Moscow and Budapest to proclaim their invincibility," haw-he-hawed Gabriel Hanot, editor of *L'Equipe*. "But if the English are so sure about their hegemony in football, this is the time to create a European tournament."

Two days after Wolves' triumph over Honved, Hanot let the world into his mind and exposed his vision for how this new European tournament would shape up. His idea was actually more akin to the oft-mooted European Super League than what would become the European Cup, with 14-16 of Europe's finest slugging it out in a round robin. The games would be played midweek and would start in the evening [which was unusual at that time] so the working classes could watch. And the games would be sponsored by a TV company or a sports paper from the participant club's country.

After consultation with a number of clubs, *L'Equipe* quickly dropped the round robin idea in favour of a straight knockout. In those days, the idea of playing more games was repugnant to clubs, with the high expense of travel. The paper then identified a group of teams they wished to take part, which included Real Madrid, AC Milan and Chelsea, plus a clutch of teams who these days would seem more Intertoto than Champions League: Hibs, Saarbrucken, Stade de Reims.

On March 2nd 1955 *L'Equipe* presented its ideas at a UEFA conference in

Vienna. Amidst a backdrop of yawning and watch checking, the *L'Equipe* delegation explained that they weren't looking to monopolise the organization of the tournament or use it for commercial gain. They were told to go away and come back with something more concrete.

Two days later, the football federations of Austria, Czechoslovakia, Hungary, Italy and Yugoslavia held a meeting to try and revive the Mitropa Cup, Europe's only previous attempt at competitive football. The Mitropa Cup had been big in central Europe in the 1920s, though it had fizzled out after the war. Sensing the thunder being clapped out from under them, *L'Equipe* went into overdrive.

On April 2nd 1955 they called a meeting at the Ambassador Hotel in Paris, inviting the heads of the most powerful clubs in Europe. The clubs decided they wanted to make a European tournament a reality. There were several schools of thought on how to split the revenue but in the end, a proposal by Real Madrid president Santiago Bernabeu was agreed. Flying in the face of the current convention of top clubs cutting themselves an increasing slice of power pie and gate money, Bernabeu said the matchday revenue should be split 50-50. Seeing as Madrid had

Seduced by the magic words 'we'll pay for it', UEFA rubber-stamped it

one of the biggest grounds in Europe, it was a significant gesture which appealed to the idea of collective responsibility rather than the I'm-alright-Jack attitude of today's top clubs.

But the euphoria around the *L'Equipe* office was short-lived. Just eight days after this successful meeting in Paris, UEFA at a meeting in Basel, Switzerland, sanctioned another tournament. Representatives from cities across Europe had met with UEFA officials and suggested that, off the back of the yearly trade fairs they held, they could run a football tournament. Seduced by the magic words 'we'll pay for it', UEFA rubber-stamped the idea and the Inter-Cities Fairs Cup was born.

The wailing and gnashing of teeth of *L'Equipe* and the Mitropa Cup advocates could be heard from Paris to Prague. How had these city halls been allowed to breeze in and walk away with a major European football tournament under their belts? Smelling a groundswell of anger that wasn't to be seen again on the streets of Europe until Marathon became Snickers, FIFA stepped in to try and smooth things over.

At an emergency meeting in London on May 7th, FIFA approved the inception of three football tournaments in Europe: the Inter-Cities Fairs Cup, the Mitropa Cup and the European Champion Club's Cup [as *L'Equipe*'s vision came to be known]. FIFA stipulated that the Champion Club's Cup should be organised by UEFA and that the original name European Cup [proposed by *L'Equipe*] be reserved for a possible tournament between national teams.

Chelsea withdrew from the competition because of incompatibilities with the English league calendar so, on September 4th, 1955 the European Champion Clubs' Cup kicked off without an English representative. The first game was between Sporting CP of Portugal and FK Partizan from Yugoslavia and the first winners of the competition were Real Madrid. But the English influence wasn't too far away.

THE SICK MEN OF EUROPE

In 1955/56 Hibernian became the first British club to enter European competition, with Manchester United becoming the first English entrant the following year, reaching the semi-finals. As time wore on English clubs became more successful, bagging trophy after trophy after Man U opened the floodgates by winning the European Cup in 1968. But it wasn't the multi-million Euro jackpot it is today.

"Clubs made money from winning the Cup," says European Cup winner Phil Neal. "Liverpool progressed in establishing a worldwide brand by appearing in five European Cup Finals."

Bizarre as it may seem in the glitzy, boardroom-oriented world of commercialisation; the first people to run toward Europe splashing wildly across the North Sea chanting 'there's gold in them there hills', were the very tykes who usually find themselves footing the bill at the footy: the fans.

By the beginning of the 80s, hordes of likely young lads from Manchester and Liverpool were blazing a commercial trail of sorts, by returning from European jaunts to watch their sides with more money than they had left with. Or at least, bags full of gear they could shift back home, which would more than cover the cost of the fare.

"I first remember lads coming back with these strange brands we'd never heard of in 1981/82," says Phil Thornton, author of 80s football-fashion-scene book *Casuals*. "You'd see 'em in Ellesse bubble jackets, or Adidas trainers like Trim Trabb which were impossible to get hold of over here. It soon went round that Transalpino trains or even coach trips provided the perfect way to grab all this gear. These lads were scousers who lived by us and basically they just travelled around Austria, Switzerland and Germany, wherever there were ski-wear shops or sports shops and blitzed them. You have to remember that thieving was part and parcel of football supporting then because the size of the mobs made it far easier to steam into places, whether it was jewellers or clothes shops. The security wasn't very good in those days, no electronic tagging or CCTV so it was a piece of piss. Most of the big department stores had got it sussed in the UK by the 80s whereas on the continent they were far more civilised and didn't expect people to actually steal these clothes because they were meant for quite wealthy people who didn't have to steal in the first place. Some only used to do it when there was a European game on that coincided with a bit of zapping but others did it as a full-time job, sending home parcels and getting 'em flogged on. It didn't last long though because the shops were soon onto it and it was all played out by '83, by which time fashion had changed anyway and you couldn't give away Lacoste, Fila and Tacchini!"

Like fashion, European competition seemed to change with the wind. In 1960/61 UEFA introduced the Cup Winner's Cup, a playground for all the winners of domestic cup competitions to scrap it out for supremacy. Ten years later, the outdated Fairs Cup was replaced by the UEFA Cup, which ultimately gobbled up the Cup Winners' Cup in 1999. Incredibly, the Mitropa Cup continued until the 1990s, although you'd be hard pressed to find anyone who remembers it. The top clubs in Central Europe disowned the competition in the 80s, so it was played between lower league sides until it was finally abolished in 1992.

There must have been something in the air that year. In the space of a few months, two seismic changes occurred in the world of football which would change the face of the game forever, elevating a select band of clubs to a plateau it would be impossible for the rest to reach. In August 1992 the top clubs in England kicked off in The Premiership, negotiating a deal with Sky that saw a bigger share of the TV money go to the most powerful clubs. In September, UEFA launched the new Champions League, which took over from the European Champions Clubs' Cup and inadvertently ring-fenced successful clubs' positions in their own domestic leagues. In short, 1992 was the year the rich got richer and the idea of a football community died.

UEFA general secretary Gerhard Aigner came up with the idea to change the European Cup into the Champions League in 1990 in response to requests from the top clubs, according to Thomas Kurth, a competition coordinator for UEFA in 1990.

"Clubs were looking forwards to developing international competition," he says. "In knock-out competitions you live from one day to the next. In a league, you are guaranteed a certain amount of matches. If you lose one game, you have the chance to correct it."

The Champions League was given the green light at the UEFA Extraordinary Congress in 1991, with a pilot league system introduced into the European Cup for the 1991/92 season. Deemed to be a success, the format was ratified and the competition re-branded as the Champions League, complete with logo and specially-commissioned hymn, in time for the 1992/93 season. The competition featured eight teams, all champions in their own countries, and was eventually won by Marseilles. But it was what was going on off the field that was really eye-catching.

During the European Cup years, each club had been responsible for its own TV and commercial rights. When the Champions League kicked off, UEFA issued a new set of commercial regulations which meant each club had to cede its marketing rights to UEFA, in exchange for fixed payments depending on performance in the competition. It soon became clear that losing control of the marketing rights was a bitter pill worth swallowing. An increase in the number of games played by clubs in the competition meant more money at the turnstiles, more TV revenue and more cash from sponsors desperate to benefit from the new, increased exposure. Almost overnight, Europe transformed from being an interesting exercise in garnering prestige to being a passport to Cashville for Europe's top clubs.

"Aside from the central marketing, the Champions League allows for streamlined operations," says Thomas Kurth. "You can offer broadcasters coverage of the whole competition, so it is more attractive to TV companies. It's more attractive to sponsors because they can ensure a presence over an entire season in many territories. And, of course, there are more games so clubs enjoy greater matchday revenue."

In 1998 UEFA funked with the tournament again, throwing open the doors to anyone within a five mile radius of the top of their national division. A complicated system of entry essentially allowed the top nations to send four teams into the 'Champions' League each season, whilst the genuine champions of rubbish places like Iceland had to go through a qualifying process they'd never escape from. The result was a European super league-esque competition, with 32 of the best teams in Europe going at it hammer and tongs – and even more bank notes appearing on the money tree. The following season, UEFA went cash mad when they introduced a second group stage, meaning even more games and even more cash, although they were forced to abandon this wanton greed in 2002 as death by boredom rates soared across Europe. Not that it affected the cash registers too badly.

"Distribution of Champions League money is based on three tranches," says Phil Carling, worldwide head of football for marketing company Octagon. "There's a pool payment to all clubs. There's a payment based on which market you're from. In the current cycle, England is the biggest TV market, so English clubs get a supplement payment. And there are payments depending on how far you go in the competition. In 2006 Arsenal will have got around $60m Euros as they reached the final of the competition. Set against a turnover of around $180m that's a very significant chunk of change."

The Champions League is now the world's biggest annual football competition, with a global audience in excess of four billion people per season. Each year UEFA use money generated by the competition to make 'solidarity payments', to the Football Associations of member states, with more money going to member associations with sides who made it to the group stage of the competition. This money is intended to be used for positive change. In 2003, UEFA stipulated that the money should end up in the hands of clubs with youth training programmes. For small clubs just reaching the preliminary rounds of the competition, Champions League cash can be the difference between rubbish and the dustbin. For instance, Champions League cash has enabled Barry Town to operate a full-time squad in the semi-professional Welsh Premier League. And therein, for some, lies the problem.

In the ten years following the creation of the Champions League, Barry Town won the Welsh Premier League title on seven occasions. The complaint from those who like a bit of parity on their toast is that the Champions League is a virtuous circle. By being in it, you get so much money, your peers in your own country can no longer compete. In England, it seems unthinkable that suddenly Sunderland, Reading, Charlton or Wigan could be the representatives in the Champions League. Chelsea, Manchester United, Arsenal and Liverpool are financially so far ahead of the rest of The Premiership that it is practically impossible to break their stranglehold. In 2005, Liverpool bagged £21.3m, Chelsea £19.5m and Arsenal £16m for their efforts in the Champions League. It doesn't take Carol Vorderman to work out that the longer this monopoly on Champions League places remains, the wider the gap between the clubs grows domestically.

Urgent measures are needed to bridge the widening gap

"Urgent measures are needed to bridge the widening financial gap or clubs such as former European trophy-winners Ipswich Town and Nottingham Forest could disappear within 20 years," UEFA's communications chief William Gaillard told the *Guardian* in 2004. "It's a serious concern for us that in many European countries only a small number of teams can win the domestic league title. This competitive imbalance is not unique in England, but it is quite pronounced there."

The message is clear and simple: if those in charge are not careful, European football will eat itself. By going after pots of cash, clubs are in danger of killing themselves. The more money they get from Europe, the better they do domestically and the more bored the supporters become. It's impossible to imagine Norwich finishing third now, as they did in the first season of The Premiership. Or Forest winning both the League and the European Cup in successive seasons, as they did in 1978 and '79. English football has become snore-inducingly predictable.

What can be done before generations of young would-be football fans bury themselves in computer games like *Championship Manager* looking for the excitement the real thing used to bring? Like Michele Platini, Phil Neal believes the competition should return to being a true champions' cup.

"The European Cup was the best tournament to play in, only second to the World Cup!" he says. "But I think it was better when just the champions from each country played in the competition."

However, you're about as likely to see UEFA turning off the money tap as you are Stoke City representing England in the Champions League. Especially with the emergence in 2000 of an illuminati-type group, who stalk the shadows of Europe in the darkest watches of the night, secretly pulling the strings and making things go bump.

THEY MIGHT BE GIANTS

World domination and the destruction of everyone who isn't you is a fairly self-centred dream. Hitler had it, Saddam Hussein flirted with the idea and all the baddies in Scooby Doo would have achieved it if it wasn't for those pesky kids. To the naked eye it may appear that with Baghdad fallen and the Great Dane still patrolling the streets of Boomerang TV, the world is a safer place, but don't be fooled: across Europe, a new power is rising which urinates on the toes of reason and jabs fingers in the eyes of goodwill. They want more money, more power and more control over the world they inhabit and they call themselves simply: G14.

Not content with the new riches and power afforded to them by the virtuous circle of the Champions League, Europe's top clubs decided that, like Billy Idol, they wanted more, more, more. So, in September 2000, AC Milan, Ajax, Borussia Dortmund, Barcelona, Bayern Munich, Inter Milan, Porto, Juventus, Liverpool, Man Utd, Marseilles, Paris St Germain, PSV Eindhoven and Real Madrid met at a conference centre opposite the Bernabeu stadium in Madrid and agreed a constitution for a new organisation. And, after seemingly naming themselves after a postcode in Glasgow, they set about the serious business of protecting their interests.

"When international club competition was done on a knock-out basis, there were lots of big clubs who'd never played each other, so they didn't have relationships," explains Thomas Kurth, now general manager of G14. "There were no joint interests – they just wanted to knock each other out. When the Champions League came in, clubs suddenly had a common interest. And they played each other more often, so they developed relationships. The first informal discussions happened in the mid 90s. They were driven by the people at the big clubs – Milan, Real Madrid, Bayern Munich. This is a story of persons not organisations. The people realised that if they stood together, they were stronger."

Two years after the formation of G14, four more clubs rocked up at the little G14 house on the prairie, proffered their begging bowls and whispered, "please sirs, can we have some more?" Taking pity on the little mites, Great Uncle G14 beckoned the rag tag collection of also rans and ne'er-do-wells into the warm, poured them a frothy cup of mead and sighed: 'you shall never go without again.' And so it was that Arsenal, Bayer Leverkusen, Lyon and Valencia were anointed to Europe's top table, and the name G14 became ever-so-slightly ridiculous.

So what's the deal with this strangely-monikered gaggle of European football heavyweights? What do they want?

"We want to strengthen clubs' positions and have their interests represented," says Thomas Kurth. "To offer a service point – an office that's not distracted by the daily business of organising matches and running a football club. To coordinate initiatives and provide a platform which the clubs control, which is different to that given to them by the governing bodies."

However, scratch below the surface and it seems one of the main objectives of G14 is to help member clubs stuff more cash in their pockets. Their website lists their main objectives as follows: 'To foster co-operation and unity among member clubs, promote cooperation with FIFA and UEFA, contribute to decisions on the format, organisation, administration and commercial [sic] of international club football, promote the objectives of the member clubs, jointly assess all matters of common interest and, [here's the money shot], support economic development to the benefit of G14 members.'

Who'd have thunk it? One of the key objectives of this axis of evil is to make pots of cash!

"G14 want to guarantee the success of their clubs outside normal business practice," says Dr Adam Brown, former member of the government's Football Task Force. "In the late 80s [Silvio] Berlusconi said AC Milan getting knocked out in the first round of Europe wasn't modern thinking. The chance involved in the game of football does not fit the capitalist model. They're trying to pull the top clubs outside the normal football structure to ensure the rich get richer. The thing is, football is built on people going to games. If you lose that, which you could easily see happening with a European super league, you're in trouble."

The problem with G14 appears to be that they have no concept of the bigger picture. They call themselves 'the voice of the clubs', saying they "represent the heart of European Club Football when it comes to the key issues of European competitions, transfer dealings and commercial considerations." Really? When was the last time G14 rode into battle on behalf Stoke or St Pauli or Toulouse to help them sort out key commercial or transfer issues?

"G14 is a grouping of clubs who play regularly in Europe," says Thomas Kurth. "Each league only has a limited number of clubs who do this. We have been fighting for clubs regarding the international calendar for a while. In the Charleroi case we are fighting for insurance and compensation for players injured whilst on international duty. That is for the benefit of all clubs."

Ah, yes. The Charleroi case. Having already secured a deal with FIFA whereby a share of the prize money from the World Cup will be used to pay compensation to clubs for any injuries suffered by their players in the tournament, à la Michael Owen, G14 are supporting Belgian club Charleroi in their legal battle to get compensation after their player Abdelmajid Oulmers was injured whilst on international duty. This has set G14 on a collision course with UEFA and FIFA, in what promises to be the latest great war to rip through the beautiful game.

There are three elements to football

"You have to look at football from a global point of view," says Thomas Kurth. "There are three elements to football – domestic, international club competition and national teams. They all have legitimacy to exist and that should be reflected by consultation. But that is not currently the case. For instance, in qualifying for Euro 2004 there were 200 matches. Qualifying for 2008 has been increased so there will be 308 matches. That is an increase of more than 50% but it was decided by the governing bodies without consulting the clubs. UEFA found out friendly matches were no longer popular so they've replaced them with competitive games. Qualifying matches will now be played on friendly dates. That means players will be playing for their clubs and three days later they will have to play in a competitive international game. They will play differently with their clubs in the game before an international and they will be at more risk of getting injured but the clubs will have to pay the bill. All this has been done without clubs being consulted."

It's hard not to agree with Thomas' point about there being too many qualifying games, especially in light of Germany's 13-0 thrashing of San Marino and England's virtual training session against Andorra in early qualifying games for Euro 2008.

However, UEFA believe that G14's behind-the-scenes manoeuvring is all part of the plan to clear the decks for a European super-league. In an interview with *The Observer* in 2006, UEFA chief executive Lars-Christer Olsson said: "They will organise a competition for 24 teams, play games in Asia and North America to generate resources. Players would only be released to play for their national teams if their wages were paid and if their release did not conflict with club activities."

Conspiracy theorists might suggest that with the same few clubs winning their domestic divisions each season, a super league is inevitable. With European funding and extra TV revenue for being the most desirable teams to watch, the habitual Champions League clubs are able to stay way, way ahead of their rivals, leading to boring domestic leagues that fans might not turn up to watch in future. The solution? Syphoning the top clubs off into a super league, restoring the element of competition domestically and making top club football even more glamorous. Thomas Kurth, however, disputes this.

"No, we don't want a super league," the G14 boss says. "We have no interest in this. I don't know how many times we have to say this. The top priority of clubs is their domestic league competition. International club competition is also very important. There must be direct representation for clubs. The bodies who organise these competitions do so from an administrative point of view. Clubs should also be included in making the decisions."

The top clubs against the game's governing bodies is an almighty ding dong that will ultimately decide the commercial, practical and moral destiny of world football. FIFA president Sepp Blatter is in no doubt what will happen if G14 emerge victorious:

"The wonderful pyramid of football would crumble because of the prestige and elitism of some," he said in March 2006. "We offer them everything and then we find ourselves attacked. It is unjust. Once you are in a family, there is a minimum of respect that one should observe."

The battle lines have been drawn for the latest [or should that be last?] great battle in the war to commercialise football. UEFA and FIFA or G14? Collective responsibility or individual wealth? The future of Europe or the end of the world?

Watch zis space.

SACRE BLEU!

It's not all money-grubbing, wine-tasting and sunbathing in Europe, you know. There's principles too in That Abroad. Here's a couple of clubs who know the score

St Pauli

Hell in a hand woven basket; what can you say about St Pauli? They run onto the pitch to the sound of AC/DC's *Hell's Bells*. The skull and cross bones is their semi-official emblem. And when they score a goal, Blur's *Song 2* comes through the speakers and the Millerntor stadium turns into a giant mosh pit.

St Pauli first dared to be different in the 1980s, when fascists and Nazis started showing their ugly mugs at German football games. St Pauli's neighbours SV Hamburg were attracting their fair share of skin-headed nutbags, so people started heading to the Millerntor to watch their football in peace. A supporters' office sprang up in 1989 and now the club is populated from ticket office to boardroom with fans from this movement. As a consequence, St Pauli has blossomed into a symbol of what can be good about the game of football, with an active no fascism, no racism and no sexism policy. *Maxim* magazine's adverts were taken down from the ground in 2002 after fans complained they was demeaning to women.

St Pauli don't do conventional, a fact which has turned them into an anti-commerical, anti-hero to football fans around the world. For example, The Birmingham Boys in Brown, a group of Villa and Birmingham supporters, have adopted St Pauli as their second club.

"The commercialisation of football is coming to Germany but St Pauli have put a marker in the ground that they are going to stand against all that," Chris Sanderson, a St Pauli-loving Brummie, told *The Times* in January 2006. "They have the most passionate and friendly and open bunch of supporters you could hope to meet. They have a libertarian attitude and lifestyle — they are a unique force in European football."

It's a wonder they've never turned up on a Carlsberg ad. St Pauli: probably the coolest club in the world.

Barcelona

In these ultra-commercial days, businesses sponsor anything from shirts to stadiums to the announcement of how much time will be added on at the end of a match. But, try as they might, there's one thing big business can't get its filthy mitts on: the front of Barcelona's red and blue shirts.

Not only do the Catalan giants refuse to have their jerseys soiled, they also jab a thumb in the eye of the nay-sayers who pour scorn on the idea of big clubs being owned and run by their supporters. With supporter's trusts spreading like wildfire in the lower echelons of English football, many people believe it is a format that is impossible to roll out into the Premier League. Barcelona disproves this theory.

The club is owned by its 140,000 members who, if they don't like the way the club is being run, can vote the board out. Because of the unique structure, fans are looked after, not squeezed for every last Euro. Season ticket prices for 2006/07 range from £69 to £579 and the value for money factor isn't doing the club any harm on the pitch either: they won the Champions League and Spanish League double in 2005/06 for the first time in their history.

Premier League chairman Dave Richards said that big clubs couldn't involve supporter's trusts because "every now and then you have to dip you hand in your pocket and the ordinary man on the street can't do that." However, Barcelona fans have shown a great maturity in dealing with their financial problems. In 2003 they voted to allow shirt sponsorship for the first time to try and pay off some of their crippling debts. Rumours have flown around since of who might sponsor the club but, as of summer 2006, their shirts are still bare, naked.

"The club's healthy financial situation means that we have been able to ease off in our pursuit of a shirt sponsor," Barca president Joan Laporta told the club's website in October 2005. "We have always had the idea of shirt sponsorship in mind, but there are a series of conditions. It has to be the most expensive shirt sponsorship deal in the world, and the sponsor has to have as prestigious a name as FC Barcelona does."

> CHAPTER 8
A-Z OF EVIL

8:   A-Z OF EVIL

A is for.........Agents

Unlike weeping Toms, Hanks and Cruise, football agents are always cast in the role of villain of the piece. The levels of disdain they cause are so pantomime, even the meekest football fan is likely to boo, hiss and give a big Styrofoam thumbs-down at the very mention of the word *agent*. But is the reputation as football's parasite really deserved?

Agents cigar-chomped into the game following the legalisation of professional football in 1885. In those black 'n white days, agents knew which side their bread was buttered on. Power was with the clubs and so they served the clubs – scouting and helping to find new players. As time went on, the influence and use of agents dwindled as clubs developed their own scouting networks. Then Jimmy Hill popped up, retain-and-transfer and the maximum wage were abolished and things started to change.

Realising that men with cigars and sovereign rings were better at negotiating contracts than they were, players increasingly turned to people from outside the game to help them in matters fiscal. Agents, sniffing the power change on the wind, dusted off their Gucci sunglasses and prepared to come out of hibernation. Only this time they'd be batting for the players.

The change of allegiance has proved to be a masterstroke. Since Jean-Marc Bosman cut a huge slice of power pie and handed it to footballers everywhere, wages have gone through the rafters. And the chief beneficiaries, after the players themselves, are the agents. Think about it – every time a multi-million pound transfer is struck, 15% goes in the agent's back pocket. But before you tell the boss to stick it and put a card in your pork pie hat bearing the legend 'agent', beware – they don't let any old Tom, Dick or Harriet grab the 15% these days. There are regulations and exams and everything.

"You have to be FIFA registered to operate on behalf of a club or player in any transfer," says player agent Gethin Evans. "To act as a licensed players' agent, you are required to pass a strict exam set by FIFA via The Football Association. This exam is conducted on a case study format and includes questions on the FIFA Statutes and Regulations relating to domestic and global contractual and administrative issues. Only 5% of people pass. Any club or player found guilty of dealing with unlicensed agents will be subject to sanctions from the FA or FIFA."

So what do agents actually do for their cash? According to some ex-players, agents are an important buffer zone between them and their managers. They can't, they allege, negotiate like Alan Sugar one minute and then expect their boss to turn around and pick them for the first team the next. And who on God's green earth, if it wasn't for the agents, would be on hand to help dress the players – or locate the perfect pooch?

We receive calls asking if we can find a certain kind of dog

"One day could be spent on behalf a player negotiating a new contract with a club, the next day could be agreeing a mutual contract termination on behalf of a client," says Gethin. "This is an extraordinarily dynamic environment. The sayings 'it's a funny old game' and 'a week is a long time in football' are so very true. One phone call and any scenario can be turned on its head, so we always have to be ready to react in the best interests of our client. During transfer periods we deal with vitally important financial issues but otherwise we receive phone calls asking if we can find a player a certain kind of dog breed or a good tailor outside London for a fitting. Every imaginable situation can and will arise at any point 24 hours a day, 365 days a year. Dealing with the worries and questions from parents is another regular issue. Our experience is vital to players and their families, as we have seen it all before."

However, just as surely as one man's trash is another man's treasure, not everyone buys into the idea that agents are salt of the earth geezers. In fact, says Mike Newell, they're really not very nice at all.

"The FA must play a much bigger role than they are doing, agents are the scourge of the game," the Luton boss harrumphed in 2005. "I've seen the money agents make at Championship level and I can only imagine what they make at the top level. So many players have come and gone who have been absolutely no good to the game or the clubs who bought them. But the agents will have made money once again and the game in this country will have suffered. Millions of pounds have gone out of the game that will not be seen again. If the governing bodies don't eradicate some of the things that are happening, it will kill the game."

B is for..........Berlusconi

Some people like to sip from the cup of power now and again but for Silvio Berlusconi, it seems nothing less than a constant drip feed will suffice. Imagine the Frankenstein offspring of Rupert Murdoch and Tony Blair and some would say you were getting close to Signor Berlusconi. Not content with owning the Italian media, Signor B bought Italy's most esteemed club – AC Milan – in 1986 and then, after trumping up a political party named after one of Milan's chants [Forza Italia], he promptly romped home in the elections of 1994 bagging himself the prefix: Prime Minister.

As surely as *Stella* was written by early 90s dance wizards Jam and Spoon, controversy follows hot on the heels of a man wielding such a powerful axe. His various regimes have been dogged by consistent allegations of corruption, leading some folk to infer that the Busy B is as bent as a nine lira note. He certainly seems to be in a would-have-to-negotiate-very-hard-to-lose situation when it comes to his two big loves: footy and TV.

When the rights to screen free-to-air football came up for auction in 2005 the two main candidates were RAI, the state broadcaster who cede *defacto* control to the Prime Minister [then Berlusconi] and Mediaset, an independent company owned by...that man Berlusconi. The smell of fish gets stronger when you note that the Chairman of Lega Calcio, Italy's top division, was Adriano Galliano who also happened to be deputy and acting chairman of AC Milan, the club owned by....gosh, Mr Berlusconi.

Things took a turn for the worse in January 2006 in a row over pay-TV rights. In 1999 the idea of collective television rights was abandoned in Italy, leaving clubs free to negotiate their own pay TV deals. This led to the bizarre scenario of the Milan-owning Mediaset group gobbling up the rights to show Juventus games. When it was proposed that the law governing TV rights be reformed in Parliament it was blocked by, you guessed it, Forza Italia.

"We'll withdraw our interest from the championship," salivated Sampdoria president Riccardo Garrone in early 2006. "We won't play against the three big teams, Juventus, AC Milan and Inter Milan, or we will send out our youth team to play to make it uninteresting. If a solution doesn't arrive as soon as possible, there will be severe consequences."

Psychic or sinister? Four months later, Berlusconi lost his position as Prime Minister. The king is dead. Long live the king.

C is for.........Clowns

Clowns have always been evil on Planet Football. First there was Jan Tomaszewski, the Polish goalkeeper labelled a clown by Brian Clough, before turning in a performance so evil it kept England out of the 1974 World Cup finals. Then there was Bruce Grobbelaar, the clown whose bandy legs won Liverpool the 1984 European Cup but whose evil moustache should have been picked up on earlier. Anyone with a penchant for such hirsute apparel must be more than a little suspicious. After starring in a video discussing match-fixing, Grobbelaar was charged with conspiracy, though later cleared. He sued *The Sun* who had exposed him and won damages of £85,00, later slashed by the House of Lords to £1, the lowest libel damages possible under English law.

And then again there's the world's most famous clown Ronald McDonald. And who'd have thunk it? He's the only one to subvert the clown-as-evil doctrine. Since sticking his big red wig and thin-for-a-clown body into English football in 1995, Ronald's company – the modestly named McDonalds – has pumped millions into the game. The Premiership has been sponsored and 10,000 qualified football coaches have been produced thanks to McDonalds' cash. Sir Geoff Hurst, Pat Jennings and Kenny Dalglish have all been McDonalds' ambassadors and even England's then Head Coach Sven Goran Eriksson was impressed when he attended a McDonalds' event in April 2006.

"The McDonalds' coaching programme is an important part of developing and improving grassroots coaching across the country," he said. "This type of initiative plays a big part in getting youngsters involved in football and making the most of their ability."

So there you have it. McDonalds: absolutely, definitely 100% not evil.

Just don't think about the food.

D is for.........Developers

Like Jaws and chums circling a bleeding body in the sea, property developers home in on football clubs with a hungry look in their eyes. It's easy to see why. Football grounds are often in prime city or town centre retail spots and could feasibly be turned into mountains of cash with the right development.

But who in their right mind would let these vile sharks anywhere near a football club? Desperate folk, that's who.

There's two main ways for property developers to sink their substantial jaws into a football ground. The first is to convince an idiot in charge of the club that it's the solution to all his problems to sell up and use the money made from the nice town centre development to wipe out the club's debts and build a shiny new out-of-town ground.

This is what happened at strapped-for-cash Brighton & Hove Albion in July 1995, when directors Bill Archer, Greg Stanley and David Bellotti sold the

It looked as if Brighton might go to the wall

Goldstone ground to Chartwell Land property developers. With no viable alternative in Brighton and the developers asking a fortune to rent the ground back to Albion, for two seasons Brighton were forced to play home games 70 miles up the road at Gillingham's Priestfield Stadium. Obviously gates fell – to a record low average of 2,328 – and, not for the first time in the turbulent 90s, it looked as if Brighton might go to the wall.

In February 1997 Brighton hosted the first Fans United day, when supporters of other clubs turned up to witness Albion's 5-0 demolition of Hartlepool as a show of solidarity against the way the Albion fans were being treated. After mediation from the FA, a consortium finally ousted the hated Bellotti from power in September 1997, although Archer clung on as a shareholder until 2002. The new board helped get Albion back to Brighton at the temporary Withdean Stadium for the 1999/2000 season, and two years later they submitted plans to build a new ground at Falmer, on the outskirts of the city. The Powers That Be refused to give a verdict on the new ground and the uncertainty caused managers to leave the club to yo-yo between divisions until, finally, in late 2005 the Office of the Deputy Prime Minister gave its blessing for Brighton & Hove Albion to build a new, permanent home at Falmer. The exile that had begun with the Goldstone being sold off to property developers was finally over.

"Never mind over the moon, we're over Jupiter," said Brighton Chairman Dick Knight on hearing the decision. "This is the greatest home win ever in the club's history. There's been a lot of hard work gone into this project over the course of the last seven years and we've really been through the mill."

The second way for developers to sink their fangs into football is much less subtle. They simply wait for a club to fall to its knees under the financial burden, then pop up announcing themselves as the truth, the way and the light before promptly pulling the rug out from under the club. That's what happened at Wrexham.

In March 2002 Cheshire-based property tycoons Mark Guterman and Alex Hamilton bought the club and acquired the freehold for the Racecourse Ground, which they transferred to Hamilton's holding company. Having changed the terms of the club's lease, so that instead of paying nothing they were required to pay £30,000 a year, Hamilton gave the club 12 months notice saying they'd either have to quit or pay him loadsamoney to prevent the ground becoming a retail park.

The fans formed a trust and set about trying to save the club but it was the Leagle Eagles who would ultimately put the kybosh on the evil developers. At a High Court ruling, Alistair Norris QC ruled that Guterman was in breach of his duties as chairman and director of the club, when he bought the Racecourse Ground for his and Hamilton's own benefit. The key evidence was a written statement by Guterman and Hamilton, in which they had set out their aims for what they called 'the Wrexham Project'.

'The management and control of the football club is to be on an equal control basis,' the note read. 'With the main or sole objective to realise the maximum potential gain from the property assets of the football club for the benefit of [Mr Hamilton] and [Mr Guterman].'

As if that wasn't enough, Hamilton and Guterman also steered Wrexham into administration in December 2004, after rebuffing several offers to sell the club. The move saw Wrexham docked ten points which contributed to them being relegated to the bottom tier of English football for the 2005/06 season. With the clock ticking towards extinction – the club would have been booted out of the League if they'd hadn't come out of administration by June 2006 – Wrexham were saved at the eleventh hour when administrators did a deal with local car salesman Neville Dickens to buy the club. The Dragons had lived to breathe fire another day, and football scored another victory against the evil property developers.

E is for.........Edwards

Since slipping on the cloak of power at Man Utd in the mid 60s, the Edwards family have been prone to sporadic outbreaks of 'not very nice' behaviour. First there was the rights issue in 1978, which allegedly allowed Chairman Louis to cream off extra dividends to bail out the family's ailing meat business. After Louis' death in 1980, son Martin took over and eleven years later he effectively paved the way for the Malcolm Glazer takeover when he floated Man Utd on the Stock Exchange.

"Martin Edwards sold the family silver to make himself a rich man," says Jules Spencer, former chairman of the Independent Manchester United Supporters Association. "If he hadn't floated the club, we might not have ended up in the position where we got taken over by Malcolm Glazer."

This is the same Martin Edwards who also accepted a bid from Rupert Murdoch in 1998. For £623m he was prepared to sell the club into the hands of the hated media baron, legitimising an unhealthy *entente cordiale* between England's biggest football club and media company BSkyB. Thankfully the Monopolies and Mergers Commission stepped in and ruled the move illegal.

To top it off, Edwards reportedly sold off huge blocks of his shares to the tune of £93m, whilst maintaining the position of chief executive [accompanied by generous chief executive's salary]. So, whilst the club his family has been involved with since the 60s now finds itself in considerable debt thanks to the takeover Martin Edwards helped facilitate, the man himself could afford to buy Shevchenko, Henry and Ronaldinho and still have enough left over for a little plot of land on Evil Island, an idyllic evil hideaway somewhere in the middle of the Evil sea, between the peninsulars of Not Very Nice and Really Rather Deplorable.

F is for.........FA

When it was formed in the Freemason's Tavern on London's Great Queen Street in 1863, the Football Association was an admirable conglomerate of toffs and often-do-wells whose first serious task was to fashion a set of rules so that every football club would sing from the same hymn sheet. The FA was the bastion of fair play, outraged by the new commercialisation sweeping through the game. It vehemently opposed the idea of professionalism although it eventually accepted the idea, reasonably concluding that it's better to try and control an enemy you can see than one you can't. And in 1896 they introduced Rule 34, to prevent football clubs from being run like normal businesses.

But time hasn't been kind to the FA. As the organisation has grown older, a level of incompetence has crept which suggests senility may have taken hold. In the early 1980s it allowed Tottenham's lawyers to bypass Rule 34 completely, by setting up a holding company to make Tottenham's flotation on the stock market more appealing to the city. The following decade it allowed the breakaway of the top 22 clubs in England and the formation of The Premiership – the most money-oriented, commercial behemoth it is possible to imagine.

Nowadays it frequently makes buffoonery seem an art form

Nowadays it frequently makes buffoonery seem like an art form. The attempt to woo Luis Felipe Scolari into becoming England manager in April 2006, only to be forced into backtracking and appointing no one's favourite Steve Mclaren, was farcical. Nor does it seem to hold any real control over the powerful players, managers and owners at the top clubs and an organisation that once blanched at the amount of cash flooding into the game has taken to spending money as if its water – £2m a year in rent on its glass house in Soho Square, £4.5m a year in wages to maligned ex-England boss Sven Goran Eriksson up to July 2006 and a total £757m on the new Wembley stadium.

The FA is meant to be the game's regulatory body, the knight in shining armour who keeps things fair and on an even keel. In reality it's more like a bunch of old men in blazers who cow tow to the big clubs – the mega rich monsters that the FA's *Blueprint For The Future Of Football* helped to create.

So what are the chances of it rediscovering its original ethos and helping to combat commercialisation and bring the game back to its purer form?

Sweet FA.

G is for.........Galahs

Australia is an evil place populated by sharks, crocs, snakes, spiders and ex-convicts. Fortunately, English football's associations with the place have been minimal. There was predator-inventing right winger Craig Johnstone's dazzling performances for Liverpool in the 80s, Mark 'and Lard' Viduka and Harry Kewell's presence in Leeds' chasing-the-dream team of the 2000s and that game at Upton Park where we let them win 3-1 in 2003. And that's where the story would have ended, if it hadn't been for then Wembley chairman Ken Bates taking a look at a firm of Australian contractors and saying: bless my barnacles, this looks like the perfect outfit for Wembley.

The Australians wheedled their way into the job after sending a two and a half page letter to the not-at-all evil or incompetent Bob Stubbs [chief executive] and Ken Bates [chairman] claiming they could build the new Wembley stadium for a fixed price of £326.5m. Sniffing a bargain bigger than a tin of No Frills beans, Batesy and Stubbsy jumped on the deal before skipping off to pastures new, confident they'd pulled off a coup.

They hadn't. The stadium which was meant to host the 2006 FA Cup final was so far behind schedule that the FA, in a startling echo of their sudden cosying up to Steve Mclaren over the England job after flying out to meet 'Big Phil' Scolari the previous week, suddenly had to go back to second choice Millennium stadium and say 'prepare thyselves for a cup final'. More importantly, the cost of the project had spiralled to a whopping £757 million, making Wembley the most expensive football stadium in the world. Ever.

But Bates remains confident he made the right move.

"If we hadn't done that," he told *The Guardian* in May 2006, "Wembley would still be a shell and the FA would be bust. We secured a world-class contractor, which had produced the Olympic stadium in Sydney, for a price no British builder would touch. That's my legacy. The FA should be thanking me."

Whether the FA's thankyou card is sitting proudly atop Mr Bates' mantle-piece or 'got lost in the post' is uncertain, but one thing is for sure: if *Home and Away's* Alf Stewart had been consulted on the project he would have no doubt 'run those hoons out of town' long before they went £430.5m over budget. Flaming galahs.

H is for.........Hornby

The conspiracy theory amongst older, more traditional fans runs like this: when The Premiership came in, clubs took the opportunity to upgrade their grounds which meant they could legitimately charge more for admission. Actually, what they were really doing was coercing a new, more affluent group of fans into the game. By pricing some of the old hooligans out and making grounds all-seater, football clubs fancied they could attract a class of fan who would spend more on tickets, shirts and other merchandise. But just raising the prices and attracting better players into The Premiership wasn't enough. What the Fat Cats needed was something more arty, something with a cultural pull that would drag the *Guardian*-reading muesli-eaters through the turnstiles. And, in 1992, they got it.

It's pretty certain that when slap-headed Arsenal fan Nick Hornby sat down to write *Fever Pitch* he just wanted to write a good book about football. One best-selling novel and critically-acclaimed film later, he was sitting on a phenomenon. Suddenly here was an advert for the New Labour New Football Premiership that did more to attract new fans than the dancing girls and Simple Minds theme tune on Sky ever would. This was the best marketing campaign ever. This was art. But it didn't go down so well in parts of the Clock End, who began naming the new fans they saw at Highbury after the man they fingered as the culprit.

"Hornbys are the plastic twats who turned up after 1992 with their cameras and their dyed hair," said one 'poster' on an Arsenal forum. "They don't know any of the songs and they're always telling you to sit down. You get them at all big grounds but at Arsenal we call them Hornbys."

Of course thousands of people enjoyed *Fever Pitch* and even more benefited from the new bonhomie at football grounds but, in one small corner of the new Emirates stadium, there will be a section of support that regards Nick Hornby and his new-fan army as forever evil.

I is for.........In-ger-land

Every major tournament that rolls around is a chance for budding entrepreneurs to get fat off the green and pleasant land of In-ger-land. Slap a St George's cross on anything pre-World Cup or European Championships and you'll make yourself a nice pile. Sweat bands, figurines and beach towels have all had their time in the sun but, since the 2002 World Cup, the accessory of choice has been the car flag. A quick Google search reveals a plethora of sites and suppliers, all keen to furnish you with the highest-quality England flag, with prices ranging from £1.99 to £5.99. Judging by the number of flags fluttering proudly atop the cars of England in the weeks running up to the 2006 finals, someone somewhere is making a lot of money out of In-ger-land. And who would have believed it? One such money-making machine is the non-commercial-turned-amnesiac institution that is the FA.

Each major tournament is a chance for the game's regulatory body to get its hands on some cold, hard cash. In the weeks leading up to the tournament in Germany, the first page you arrived at on the FA's website was a link though to the FA shop. Once inside, you were invited to buy the new World Cup training range, the new England away shirt, footballs, tumblers, key rings, teddy bears, mugs or, for £9.99, an Official England Supporters Pack which included a flag, a car flag, a whistle, a kick and trick ball, a flying disc, a captain's armband, a team sheet selector and, that old favourite, an inflatable hand.

"The England brand is already huge – it would have been colossal if we'd won," Professor Ellis Cashmore, Lecturer in Football Culture at the University of Staffordshire, said after England's 2002 World Cup exit. "Before the defeat, the FA will have been rubbing its hands in anticipation of the number of extra England shirts, mugs and flags that were set to fly out of the shops."

Mugs? That'd be us.

J is for.........Jean-Marc Bosman

When no-mark Belgian footballer Jean-Marc Bosman goose-stepped into the European Court of Justice in 1995, his only thought was to try and secure the transfer he wanted from RC Liege to French outfit Dunkerque. To achieve this, his legal team had to challenge football's governance, insisting that as an EU citizen he should be free to move between clubs as he pleased, as his contract was up. The court agreed and their ruling changed the face of football forever.

Jean-Marc Bosman is, in himself, not inherently evil. A leaf through his record doesn't reveal anything about drowning puppies in bags or being rude to old ladies. However, the football practice that bears his name, the idea of leaving a club 'on a Bosman', is so evil that it should not be approached without armour. And a gun.

When Jean-Marc won his court case he didn't so much stick two fingers up at the old world order as run into the kitchen, steal granny's entire power pie [dish and all] and distribute it to every footballer in the world. Footballers, feasting on the pie like vultures on a carcass, took the opportunity to hold guns to their clubs' heads and demand salaries that look more like telephone numbers than money you'd expect to find in your current account.

Bosman's evil rating went up in 2005 when he came out in support of transfer weasel Ashley Cole, who not-very-secretly and not-very-legally met with Chelsea big wigs in a London hotel to discuss a transfer from Arsenal.

"It's outrageous," blustered JMB. "If Ashley wanted me to come to London to support him publicly, I would be happy to do that. This is a restraint of trade and I am fully behind Ashley. If I worked in a bank and wanted to change to another bank I would be allowed to go and speak to them. It's crazy that footballers in England cannot do that."

Hush now, Penfold. Your work is done.

K is for.........Kenyon

If ever there was a person who seems to embody the greed of post-Premiership football, it's slap-headed cash gremlin Peter Kenyon. The rich man's Iain Duncan-Smith, Kenyon is widely credited with turning Manchester United into the corporate mega-brand they are today. During his six-year reign at the club, Kenyon put the gold into Gold Trafford, tying up sponsorship deals with Nike and Vodaphone worth a combined £283m. But when the Cossack came a-calling, lifelong United fan Kenyon dropped his breaches, slapped his bare, naked thighs and said: Man Who? I love Chelsea, me.

After reportedly having his salary doubled to over £1m-a-year, Kenyon was happy to join Roman's Russian Revolution. His new fans weren't so keen, though. During a match against Leeds in 2004, the Matthew Harding stand started a chant that spread like wildfire around the stadium: "stand up, if you hate Kenyon!"

Perhaps the Chelski fans objected to Kenyon calling them customers. Perhaps it's because he seeks ways of 'monetising' the game. Perhaps it's because he openly plotted to remove popular manager Claudio Ranieri. Perhaps it's because he says things like "the champions this year will come from a small group of one." Or perhaps there's just something about him that makes people want to punch him in the face.

"I'm getting fucked off with this idiot's comments and I would think I'm one of a majority of supporters with this feeling," said a Chelsea fan on a message board after the 'champions coming from a small group of one' quip. "Being hated because we are winning is natural, being detested because some cocky twat in a suit loves the limelight is wrong. Peter, shut up or get the fuck away from Chelsea. Your arrogance is doing us nothing but harm."

L is for...........Littlewoods

Although they were usurped when the National Lottery big pointy fingered its way into the nation's consciousness, there was a time when Littlewoods were the biggest peddlers in the land of one particular evil: gambling. When he handed out 4,000 pools coupons at Old Trafford in 1923, future Everton chairman John Moores would not in his wildest dreams have imagined how big his new venture would become. Soon he had a company, Littlewoods, and an idea that was practically a licence to print money – all he had to do was print the coupons, pay the winners a dividend and he could keep the rest. For years he dangled treasure in front of blind, stupid and desperate folk, taking shillings off them in return for a bunch of Xs marking the spot. Then in 1959 the Football League stamped its feet, pointed at the fixtures and said: 'they're ours!' The ensuing court battle upheld that view, and Littlewoods were forced to pay for printing the fixtures.

Anyone wanting to print league fixtures has to pay a charge

Fast forward 46 years. A Watford fanzine, aptly titled *Blind, Desperate and Stupid*, has been hit with threatening legal letters from a company called DataCo, which is owned by the Premier and Football Leagues. The reason for the hullabaloo? BDAS dared to print Watford's 2005/06 fixtures.

Since the Football League successfully sued Littlewoods, anyone wanting to print league fixtures has had to pay a charge. DataCo is the company detailed to enforce the charge and in 2005 the going rate was £266 + VAT per club. That's a lot of money to non-profit making organisations, as most fanzines are. As special dispensation for this, DataCo allowed every club to nominate one fanzine each, which would only have to pay a nominal charge to print the fixtures. Many dismiss this as inadequate: what good is a fanzine if it is cosying up to the club? At BDAS, they simply get around the problem by flagging up forthcoming fixtures, without mentioning the dates.

"Why can't you see the rest of the fixtures?" the site asks. "Because we're not allowed to show you them. Never forget, people, that football is just a means to make money."

M is for.........Mastercard

It's amazing what you can get away with these days. You'd have thought, in this age of ultra-regulation, cameras on every street corner and technological sophistication that it would be difficult to say boo to a goose without a virtual park warden popping up and placing you under house arrest. But there's still room to manoeuvre in the grey areas of life. In February 2006 crooks pulled off the biggest heist ever when they wobbled away from a Securitas depot in Kent with £53m in their pockets. At the same time, Mastercard International were pulling off the biggest coup in sporting history: by partnering up with FIFA they had ensured that any fan wanting to buy tickets for the 2006 World Cup would either have to use a German banker's draft or a Mastercard.

For Mastercard it was a master stroke, creating a monopoly for an event that was sure to have millions of potential customers worldwide. It wasn't so good for the fans, though. In the UK alone Mastercard has only 24 million users compared to Visa's 42 million. By creating the monopoly Mastercard clearly hoped to make inroads into those figures. But was it fair to force people into subscribing to their cards, just because they might want to see a football match? The European Commission thought not.

After a campaign by *Which?* highlighting the unfairness of the situation, the European Commission had a word in FIFA's shell-like, and in May 2006 it became possible for fans to buy tickets using bank accounts in their own country. As a double slap in the face, Visa announced that they had won the rights to partner FIFA for the 2010 and 2014 World Cups. Ouch.

N is for.........Nike

Seen by many as more evil than Evil Knievel, Dr Evil and Evil Edna put together, Nike are, for them, the undisputed kings of the Evil Empire. Middle class kids with dreadlocks throw stones at Niketown in London whenever there's a protest and the web is littered with sites campaigning for Nike to stop abusing its Asian workers in sweatshops. But it's Nike's shadowy involvement in the higher echelons of football that has rocketed them off this particular Richter scale.

In 1996 the Brazilian Football Confederation [CBF] signed a contract with Nike that was reputedly worth £200m. It seemed like a good deal: the CBF were skint and that kind of money could do a lot of good for the Brazilian game. The sportswear giants also signed a personal deal with Ronaldo, worth around £10m a year.

The following year Ronaldo, who was playing for Barcelona at the time, was offered a new deal by the Catalan club. Negotiations broke down amidst allegations that Barcelona and Nike could not agree on how to divvy up the £30m payments needed to keep Ronaldo in Spain. So the player moved to Inter Milan, also sponsored by Nike.

In 1998 Brazil met France in the World Cup Final in Paris. Star striker Ronaldo was taken ill under bizarre circumstances on the day of the game – apparently fitting uncontrollably – and was omitted from the team initially announced by manager Mario Zagallo. However, when the teams came out on the pitch, Ronaldo was amongst them. Ronaldo claimed he'd felt ill but declared himself fit after being checked over by doctors. Others weren't so sure. When the Brazil team arrived home, a Brazilian flag at Rio de Janeiro airport had been altered so the slogan 'order and progress' was replaced by the word 'Nike'.

"It's clear that something happened that we don't know about," former Brazil star Romario told *Globo News*, as the drama unfolded. "And even if they told me what it was, it would be unethical for me to say it here."

A year after the World Cup Final defeat in Paris, Ronaldo played in a special centenary game between Nike-sponsored Barcelona and Nike-sponsored Brazil. Again he was injured and again he took to the field. Around the same time, the terms of the CBF's deal with Nike were leaked to the press. The details were startling: every year, for ten years, Brazil were contracted to play in up to five games organised by Nike, and were obligated to field at least eight first team players.

It was too much for the football-loving Brazilians. In 2001 an inquiry was set up under the presidency of congressman Aldo Rebelo, to investigate the perceived corruption in the Brazilian game, including the deal with Nike.

"The deal was very good for Nike but very bad for Brazil," Rebelo thundered. "The CBF sold the team. They betrayed the nation. They may not have had that intention, but that's what they did. Disney didn't sell Mickey Mouse, but the CBF sold the national team to Nike."

On the first day of the inquiry Ronaldo was called upon to explain the finer points of his contract with Nike, but he refused.

"The contract with Nike is an international contract and has a secrecy clause and unfortunately I can't say anything about it," he told the congress. "The only agreement I have with Nike is to wear their brand of footwear. It's the only thing that Nike have requested of me until now."

Undeterred, the congressmen pressed on. They wanted to know what had really happened that day in Paris. Why had their star player been declared unfit then fit again? Why had they lost?

"We lost because we didn't win," Ronaldo said, before explaining that he felt healthy enough to play in the game. But the congress wouldn't let up. They asked him who had been detailed to mark Zinedine Zidane, whose brace won the cup for France.

"I don't remember," Ronaldo told the politicians. "But whoever it was didn't do it very well."

There were howls of laughter from the floor but in the end, the serious business of finding out what had gone wrong at the World Cup drew a blank. The congress concluded that Nike were not to blame for the defeat or the presence of Ronaldo on the pitch.

In 2001 Nike unveiled a nine foot bronze statue of Ronaldo next to the Ronaldo Sports Field at Nike HQ in Beaverton, Oregon.

"I am really excited to see the statue," Ronaldo told Nike employees through a translator. "I am thankful to Nike for staying with me through the hard times. They have supported me every step of the way."

Bless their evil little cotton socks.

O is for.........Oligarch

When Roman Abramovich paid £140m for Chelsea in July 2003 no one knew quite how to react. Chelsea fans were ecstatic, they were £80m in debt and going nowhere fast, but the rest of football held its breath. The little-known Russian oligarch was worth billions of pounds it was said, but would he really spend it on Chelsea?

The answer wasn't long in coming. Launching a shock and awe-style spending spree, he spent £111.4m in his first three months at Stamford Bridge. In the next three years he lavished another £195m, taking his total spend on players to over £300m.

The result was a squad which was the envy of The Premiership and a Premiership which was the envy of no one. Since aligning his *nouveau galacticos* with the considerable managerial talents of José Mourinho, Roman

Abramovich has guided Chelsea to two league titles out of two, with both title 'races' over a considerable distance from the final hurdle.

The air of predictability which now chokes The Premiership has descended twice before, first in Liverpool in the 70s and 80s, then in Manchester in the 90s, but on both occasions it was attributable to the best endeavours of those clubs. Now that the funding has come from outside, as it did to some extent when Jack Walker bankrolled Blackburn to the title in 1995, it doesn't sit so well. People dismiss Chelsea's achievements with a shrug of the shoulders and a scowl. "Just bought the title haven't they?"

No they haven't. Roman has. Chelsea Football Club recorded losses totalling over £200m pounds in the first two years of Abramovich's tenure. It's Roman's Roubles that have turned The Premiership into a snore fest and for that he must sit in the corner wearing the evil hat.

"Chelsea have just signed Michael Ballack on £130,000 a week, even though they lost £140m last year and £87.8m the year before," UEFA chief executive Lars-Christer Olsson told *The Observer* in May 2006. "Fans don't understand how that is possible. Such deficit financing is very bad for football. What happens if the benefactor who is providing all this money decides to walk away?"

P is for.........Phoenix

The Phoenix League proposal has been mooted several times since 1992, when England's top clubs swooped on football's cash reserves in the middle of the night, ring-fenced them and ran off giggling back to their ivory towers.

The idea is simple enough – clubs with Premiership pretensions who can't get there by conventional means back a widening of the top flight into a two-tier system.

The nearest the Phoenix has come to flying so far was 2001, when the likes of Man City, Sheffield Wednesday and Wolves all banged on the walls of their Football League prison cells and demanded to be let out to play with the Premiership big boys plus Rangers and Celtic.

Possibly realising that Premiership Fat Cats would sooner give up milk and licking their own balls than their stranglehold over the power and money of English football, Football League chiefs put the kybosh on the idea themselves during a meeting in Nottingham in November 2001.

"As far as I am concerned, the Phoenix League is a dead duck," Football

League chief executive David Burns said at the time. "I am willing to put money on it that none of those clubs resign. Unless someone has got a commercial plan which has got an associated broadcasting contract with it, which is as good as or better, than the one we've got with ITV Digital, then it won't happen."

Burns' faith in the ITV Digital contact came back to haunt him when the company collapsed in early 2002 and couldn't honour its contract. He resigned a few months later.

Q is for.........Qatar

Money is important in all football but no one seems to bow down and worship at the altar of Dirty Cash quite like the Qataris. Home to the world's third largest natural gas supply, money actually grows on trees in Qatar. There are orchards of the stuff everywhere and, seeing as they like a game of fitba as much as the next man, they decided to merge their passions together.

Its Olympic Committee handed each club a £5.5m war chest

Clapping their hands over their eyes in order to ignore the evidence of the North American Soccer League, Qataris believed that, by investing in top foreign players, the standard of their own boys would improve and they'd qualify for the 2006 World Cup. Therefore, in 2003, its Olympic Committee handed each club a £5.5m war chest to tempt quality overseas players to the small Middle Eastern state. Gabriel Batistuta, Franck Leboeuf, Romario, Stefan Effenberg and Ali Bernarbia all promptly arrived, stifling smirks behind the backs of their hands as they attempted to sound as if they weren't just there for the money.

"I saw a big challenge in Qatar and that was the main reason behind opting for this offer," Batistuta said at the time, before diving Scrooge McDuck-style into a large vat of cash. "I would like to give my best and score as many goals as possible for my new team."

After a record-breaking 25 goal haul in his first season for Al-Arabi, a knee injury cut short Batigol's £5m stay in Qatar in 2005. To compound the misery, Qatar's hopes of reaching Germany 06 were dashed when they finished a dismal third in qualifying behind Iran, led by 98-year-old Ali Daei, and a country named after Katie Price's more boobular alter ego.

R is for.........Reynolds

When George Reynolds way-ayed into town in 1999 he was heralded as the saviour of Darlington FC. He paid off the clubs debts, rumoured to be around £5m, and unveiled ambitious plans to move the club up the Football League ladder, which included building a new state-of-the-art ground to replace the crumbling Feethams.

Clues about the Reynolds psyche appeared in 2003 when, after spending £30m on building Darlington a new ground, the chairman didn't seek to get any back by auctioning the ground name off as most clubs do now to get some extra cash. He simply named it after himself.

"We didn't build this for the Third Division," he tub-thumped. "We built this for the Premier Division. We will get there sooner or later."

The Reynolds Arena opened in August 2003. It was the beginning of what was meant to be the realisation of Reynolds' dreams but the 03/04 campaign soon turned into run-to-mummy nightmares. After 11,000 ghouls pitched up to see the first game against Kidderminster Harriers, high on the I-was-there euphoria of Being There, crowds soon dropped off to an average of nearer 3,000: a respectable enough figure for the basement division, but one which looks a bit silly in a ground that holds 27,000.

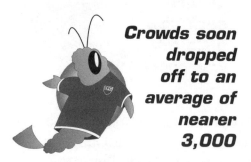

Crowds soon dropped off to an average of nearer 3,000

Building the Reynolds Arena cost Darlington dear. On the pitch the team struggled, with fans blaming Reynolds for spending too much on the stadium and not enough on the side. There were more rows than an episode of *Coronation Street* as Reynolds fought fierce verbal battles with the local press, fans, the council and seemingly anyone in Darlington with a pulse. Financially, the new ground was a burden that even Reynolds found too much to bear and, two days before Christmas 2003, he put the club into administration.

"It's very sad news," Reynolds hark the herald angel sang. "We've tried very hard, built the stadium and worked untold hours. Whilst the administrators resolve the footballing issues I will endeavour to develop other commercial interests for the benefit of the club. My message to the fans is this: if the fans and the business people in the town get behind us we will dance through this."

However, the only dancing Reynolds did was towards the exit door. A couple of weeks after the trip to Administrationville, he resigned from the club.

"I've decided that I should take a back seat," he explained via the power of written word on the club's website. "I intend to continue to offer my support to the administrators in respect of any matters which may arise in the future. I would like to take the opportunity to wish the club well and I firmly believe that the new stadium will be an asset for the community for many years to come."

George the clairvoyant was right. The club were able to make cash out of flogging off the stadium name to Willamson Motors in 2005 and radio frequency 96.6 TFM in November 2005. The stadium also proved to be an asset for new owners the Sterling consortium, who slapped in a bankruptcy application against Reynolds in 2004, claiming he owed them the £4m they'd had to pay to finish off work on the ground. The following year Reynolds' calamitous fall was complete when, penniless after selling his assets to clear debts, he was sentenced to three years in prison for tax evasion.

"I accept you are a ruined man living in much-reduced circumstances," said Judge Guy Whitburn QC. "Your investment in the stadium project cost you your fortune but it was not quite as altruistic as you make out. This was a very serious cheat of the Revenue in a sum in excess of £400,000."

Suddenly, the PR shot of George in comic prison regalia he'd had taken whilst Darlo chairman didn't look quite so funny.

S is for.........Shepherd

When The Powers That Be dole out prefixes they usually home in on a person's most obvious characteristic – 'Gorgeous' George Wagner in the 1950s, 'Marvellous' Marvin Haggler in the 80s – but when they got to 'Fat' Freddy Shepherd they must have got confused. Whilst it is true the Newcastle big wig is rather portly, his most obvious trait is that he is monumentally stupid.

How else can you describe a man who once called female Geordies dogs? Actually, if you peel behind the blubber of Fat Freddy you soon begin to see there is another way of pigeon-holing the barcodes' top boy: it starts with'e' and ends with 'l' and it's not eel.

Whilst relaxing in the salubrious confines of a brothel, Newcastle chairman Freddy Shepherd and deputy chairman Douglas Hall called Toon legend Alan Shearer the 'Mary Poppins of football' in front of undercover *News of the World* reporter Mazher Mahmood. Not ones to pull back once the foot was heading rapidly towards the mouth, the pair went on to mock Toon fans for spending extortionate amounts of money on merchandise and, for good measure, finished off by calling the Toon's female fans 'dogs'. After trying to blag the public that they were contractually unable to resign, the vile pair resigned two weeks after the *NOTW* sting, only to reinstate themselves to the board ten months later.

As if bragging about ripping off fans and questioning the beauty of the fair Tyneside lasses were not enough, Shepherd sealed his invite to the evil dinner party by relieving his beloved Toon of hatfuls of cash. Between 1997 and 2005, le grand Shepherd took £8.3m pounds out of the club in a combination of share dividends and an annual salary that by 2005 had reached £552, 954.

Toon fans must be barking mad.

T is for..........Tobacco companies

Cartophily sounds like something perverted politicians get up to in brothels, but in actual fact the grandiose name refers to the rather more mundane hobby of collecting cigarette cards.

In the 1880s plain card was used to stiffen the backs of fag packets but by 1885, the year English football went professional, tobacco companies had realised the added value that could be generated by using that space and the first printed cigarette cards were made in America. The idea worked on the same principle as magazines which give away free gifts today, in this instance it was the collectability of the cards that were meant to coerce fag smokers into smoking one brand instead of another.

In 1887 English manufacturers began issuing their own cards but it wasn't until the start of the next century that the craze for collecting them really took off, with thousands of cards being issued by over 300 tobacco companies. As most smokers were blokes, sporting heroes figured high on the list of would-be card stars and the warped relationship between football [it's healthy doncha know] and cigarettes [they kill you doncha know] was born.

After tempting people into the murderous habit of smoking by giving them images of footballers on little pieces of card, tobacco companies decided to really go in for the kill, enlisting the help of black and white football legends such as Sir Stanley Matthews and Fulham chairman Tommy Trinder to actively promote the evil weed. In the 1970s Rothmans went one further when they sponsored the Isthmian League and several other non-league divisions, installing dispensers that belched out only Rothmans brands at the grounds of all the clubs in their leagues and driving up sales as they went.

However, the bastardised link between sport and cancer sticks was finally severed in 1997 when New Labour's health secretary Frank Dobson announced that sponsorship in all sports by tobacco companies would be banned.

"We recognise that some sports, like some smokers, are heavily dependent on tobacco sponsorship," Dobson bru-ha-ha-ed, pleased as punch his scriptwriters had given him something approaching a double entendre to play with. "We will therefore give them time and help to

According to Oxfam, sportswear workers earn £51 a month

reduce their dependency on the weed. The tobacco industry kills around 120,000 of its customers every year. So it has to recruit 120,000 new smokers to its ranks each year to make up for the casualties."

For fags and football it was the end of the road, save for the odd mobile phone incident.

U is for.........Umbro

Sometime between England beating Poland to top their World Cup qualifying group and striding out for their first match against Paraguay at the 2006 World Cup, someone had to manufacture the kit for Becks & Co to wear. On face value that someone was Umbro, who had an eight-year £15m deal with England to supply the kit. In reality, it was made by workers in a factory in China, where the workers have rights and are represented by a union of sorts. They are the lucky ones.

For many people working in factories in Asia and South America work is hard and pay is low. According to Oxfam Australia, Indonesian sportswear workers earn £51 a month – 32p an hour – whilst a list of abuses in a *Labour Behind The Label* report included reports of Indonesian workers being harassed and intimidated for joining in union activities, people working for 16 hours a day sewing sportswear and people in China earning as little as £7 a month during the low season.

Sweatshops are an ugly stain on the sporting landscape but are by no means a problem exclusive to Umbro. Nike, Adidas, Puma and Kappa have all been shown up for the practice of turning huge profits but paying little to workers, who are often forced to work long hours in appalling conditions. Although many of the big sportswear brands have improved their attitude to sweatshops over the last 15 years, the problem still persists.

"All the big sportswear companies will have merchandise that has been made in sweatshops whether they know it or not," says *Labour Behind The Label*'s Sam Maher. "The problem is that work gets subcontracted out, so it is harder to monitor. Working conditions have improved in first tier factories monitored closely by the big sportswear companies. This is as much down to the fact that they were worried about counterfeiting than it was about labour rights. The problems come further down the chain, when work is subcontracted out to second and third tier factories. Sportswear has roughly stayed at the same price for the last 15 years so to make bigger profits, companies squeeze the supply side. The bigger brands are improving but smaller companies like Fila still refuse to even acknowledge the problem exists."

V is for.........Vice Chairman

The most famous vice chairman in football, David Dein is accused by his detractors as being the chairman of football's biggest vice: greed. Whilst there's no doubt that others such as Peter Kenyon, Martin Edwards and Freddy Shepherd like to stick their snouts in the trough, no one seems to have sucked and slurped on the pie of power for as long or as loudly as Arsenal's vice chairman.

David Barry Dein began his march to the pie stall in 1983, when he paid £292,000 for a 16.6% share of Arsenal. The following year he was made vice chairman of the Gunners and two years later he was voted onto the board of the Football League Management Committee. Powerful positions kept throwing themselves at him. He won a place on the FA Council, before being promoted to vice chairman of the FA in 2000, and bagging a place on UEFA's executive committee.

Over the years Dein has been one of English football's great movers and shakers. In the early 90s he moved and shook so much that England's top clubs broke away from the Football League to form The Premiership. A decade later he was instrumental in manoeuvring Arsenal into the illuminati-esque G14. The problem was, the fatter this Fat Cat got, the more suspiciously the rest of football eyed his milk.

Mumblings of discontent had been whispered for years about Dein's increasing power within the game and his role as Arsenal's figurehead. Politely, it was called a conflict of interest but what people really meant was: 'ere, that bloke's cheating!

The first person to openly suggest an ill wind was blowing from the Marble Halls of Highbury to the ivory towers in Soho Square was Sir Alex Ferguson, when disciplinary hearings for Thierry Henry and Patrick Vieira were delayed at the height of the Arsenal-Man U title race in 2001. Two years later, after an encounter between the Gunners and Red Devils had turned so violent it was dubbed The Battle of Old Trafford, two Arsenal players were disciplined by the FA compared to United's five. Taggart smelt a rat.

"I think it's obvious they [Arsenal] have been doing deals [with the FA] for years," the Scotsman thundered in November 2002. "Look at the number of times they've got off with charges outside of the 50-odd sending-offs they have had under [Arsène] Wenger. I think they have been up 10 times before the FA and have got off with eight of those. It's remarkable, very remarkable."

Three years later, Chelsea boss José Mourinho took up the Dein-bashing baton. Eyeing a fixture list that saw Arsenal play five post-Champions League Premiership fixtures at home, whilst Chelsea played five away, he turned up the collar of his coat, his favourite a-winter coat, and said:

"A person who works in the club should not work in the FA. The FA is the FA and the club is the club. I don't think we are so ugly as to be treated like devils and I don't think Mr Wenger and Mr David Dein and so on are so beautiful to be treated like angels. After Champions League games Chelsea always have to play away from home and Arsenal are always at home. You have nothing to write about that? Or is José Mourinho the only one who can look at the fixtures and find something very strange?"

The wheels really came off the power wagon for Dein in 2006. First, his attempt to land Big Phil Scolari as the replacement for Sven Goran Eriksson as England manager was embarrassing in the extreme. It was leaked in the press that England had secured the Brazilian's services, only for him to turn around the following day and rule himself out of the race, citing media intrusion. Eventually Steve Mclaren got the gig, but not after massive involvement from Dein, who some thought had stuck his oar in to prevent the FA trying to prize Arsène Wenger away from Arsenal.

"I don't know how much power David Dein has but he obviously has a great influence at the FA," over-looked candidate Sam Allardyce harrumphed. "One minute he had nothing to do with it, the next he was on the top table interviewing candidates. You'd have to ask them how that came about."

The final straw came on the eve of FA elections in June 2006. During a special investigation, *Newsnight* alleged that Arsenal had made illegal financial payments to Belgian club Beveren, who had been acting as a feeder club for the Gunners. Although both sides claimed the deal was above board and Belgian prosecutors declared Arsenal had no case to answer, the scandal was one pointed finger too far for Dein. The day after the *Newsnight* programme, he was ousted from the FA Board and replaced by Man Utd's David Gill.

W is for.........World Cup Willies

One of the great things about World Cups used to be exploring new places and immersing yourself in the local culture. Not any more. At least, not inside the stadiums. Such is the commercial straightjacket afforded by official sponsorship these days, that Budweiser's £21.6m deal with FIFA ensured that the only beer available in beer-loving German football grounds during the World Cup was American-owned Budweiser. A similar deal with McDonalds meant that burger and fries were easier to obtain than more traditional German fayre.

However, never ones to take insults against their cuisine and beer guzzling lying down, Ze Germans hit back. Residents in the tiny town of Trebgast organised a 'FIFA-free zone' where fans could watch games, drink German beer and scoff sauerkraut to their heart's content.

"It's our idea, but it's not a war against FIFA," oom-pa-pa-ed organiser

Wolfgang Shenker. "We like football and we're happy about it in Germany, but we don't like the marketing and wanted to give craftsmen and small brewers a chance to present their specialties."

The mind boggles.

X is for.........X-rated

There's no crime more X-rated in football than match-fixing and, as sure as seagulls follow the trawler, as football becomes more commercialised there are more people willing to 'bend the rules' to get what they want.

Unsurprisingly, the first target for the heavies of dodgy betting syndicates wishing to influence the outcome of a game is the man in the middle. What better way to ensure the result you want than having the ref on the payroll? In 2005 German whistler Robert Hoyzer was banned for life for fixing four Bundesliga matches for a Croatian betting ring whilst in Brazil another ref, Edílson Pereira de Carvalho, pocketed £2,300 for foul play in the Juventude-Figueirense game. He was later found to have fixed 10 other games and was banned for life.

However, the Brazilians and the Germans are nothing compared to our friends from Italy. In 1980, Juventus and AC Milan were demoted to the second division for a betting and match-fixing scam; a scandal that threatened to de-rail their preparations for the 1982 World Cup as star striker Paolo Rossi copped a two year ban for his part in the scam. Lightening struck twice when, just before the 2006 World Cup, prosecutors fingered 41 people with regards to 19 matches they believed to have been suspect in the 2004/5 season. Juventus and AC Milan were again under the spotlight, with newspapers reporting a taped conversation in which Juventus general manager Luciano Moggi tried to cherry pick favourable referees for Juve games. The entire Juventus board resigned as the threat of another demotion hung over the club.

In the week following Italy's World Cup win in Germany, a guilty verdict was returned and harsh penalties meted out, although these were cut drastically on appeal. Still, AC Milan were ordered to start the 2006/7 season on -8 points, with Lazio starting on -11 and Fiorentina on -19. But the worst punishment was reserved for Juventus, who were stripped of two league titles, relegated to Serie B and forced to start the new season on -17 points. What a mistake-a-to-make-a.

Y is for.........Yen

There's nothing more galling for fans of Man U, Chelsea, Arsenal and Liverpool who haven't been able to get tickets for the match than turning on the telly to see Japanese tourists sitting in the stands frantically photographing anything that moves. It's not the tourists' fault. Their yen is as good as the next man's. The problem lies with one of the most evil forces on Planet Football: ticket touts.

Ticket touts have been around for years but it wasn't until the Premiership arrived in 1992 that their star went into the ascendancy. Suddenly demand for football rocketed whilst conventional supply of tickets was restricted by soaring prices and the commitments of having to join a membership scheme or buy a season ticket. Enter the touts, sourcing tickets that ought to have been in the hands of the fans and selling them on to the fans at vastly inflated prices. For the glamour clubs, tourists are one of the touts' main customers, as they're often only in the county for a short while and are willing to pay a higher price for the once-in-a-lifetime chance to see the famous Man Utd/Arsenal/Liverpool/Chelsea.

Touts are traditionally burly bald men with a menacing eye and a penchant for patrolling around football grounds furtively asking people if they'd like to buy a ticket for the match. The reason for the shifty demeanour? In 1999 the Football [Offences and Disorder] Act amended the 1994 Criminal Justice and Public Order Act so that anyone caught touting tickets at football could be fined £5,000. The touts, showing a hitherto unsuspected level of intelligence, simply moved their business online.

These days there isn't a nose big enough to pay through for the chance to go to an important sporting event. When Arsenal reached the final of the Champions League in 2006, internet touts were offering tickets from £800 to £1,500 for the 90 minutes entertainment. Touts put the same ludicrous mark-up on tickets for just about every event. It's no wonder they're living in the lap of luxury. In 2006 the *Evening Standard* exposed one tout, Terence Shepherd, whose online ticket shop had plundered so much cash he was living in a £1.5m house in Blackheath.

Enough was enough for The Powers That Be, who pledged to stamp out the touts for the 2006/7 season. New laws being considered include issuing online touts with winding up orders, hitting on-site touts with ASBOS and giving police the power to seize the touts' assets.

One suspects, though, that shutting down the touts for good will be easier said than done.

Z is for.......... Zahavi

If agents are evil [and we've established at the beginning of this chapter that they are], then logic would suggest that Pini Zahavi must be super evil. For he is a super-agent, the lord of all 15% men [as agents are frequently known] and the person who has helped facilitate Roman Abramovich's buying of a football empire.

Like all good football agents, Zahavi has the gift of the gab. The Israeli was on holiday in England in 1979 to watch his favourite team, Liverpool, when he ran into 'Pool chairman Peter Robinson at Heathrow airport. Zahavi opened a dialogue and within a couple of months he'd convinced Robinson to sign Israeli defender Avi Cohen. The path to super-agentville had begun.

Zahavi spent the next two decades building up contacts and carving out a career for himself as a football agent then, in 2002, he hit the big time. He brokered the record-breaking £30m deal that took Rio Ferdinand from Leeds to Man Utd, pocketing a massive wedge of cash and alerting the world to his super powers. The following year, he must have thought his numbers had come up on the lottery when his 'mate' Roman Abramovich bought Chelsea. Unsurprisingly, the new Chelsea boss turned to Zahavi and said: Get me a new team.

Zahavi brought in world class player after world class player and even brokered the deal that brought cash gremlin Peter Kenyon to the Bridge. Together, Abramovich and Zahavi re-wrote the transfer history books, with a relentless period of transfer activity that saw £300m change hands in three years. The influx of world class players was bad for the rest of The Premiership but great for Chelsea. The fella with the cape and the big A on his chest wasn't grumbling, either: any % of loads is a fucking lot of money.

> CHAPTER 9
PAWNS IN THE GAME

9   PAWNS IN THE GAME

Football supporters have always been pawns in the game of football. From the Egberts of the 19th Century, to the right Herberts who brawled on the terraces in the 70s and 80s to the present day Cuthberts with their prawn sandwiches, football fans have been pieces on a chess board, manoeuvred around by clubs and players at will. Players toy with fans' emotions, kissing the badge one minute then disappearing out the door the next in search of greener grass. And clubs do as they please, trying to squeeze as much cash as they can out of their devoted followers, whether it be on exorbitant ticket prices or that club-endorsed mouse mat you never knew you needed. But, as Alan Hansen might have said if he'd mixed his metaphors and was half-dreaming about chess when he poured scorn on Man United's young guns in 1995, "you win nothing without pawns."

Football fans are the cornerstone on which the commercialisation of football has been built. They provide the demand, and the all-important pounds sterling, for it to exist. But it hasn't always been so. If the toffs who founded the game had got their way, no one would have been watching football at all.

"As with payment for playing, spectatorism was almost certainly not envisaged by early public school and university participants," says football historian Dr Graham Curry. "Indeed, it was almost seen as repugnant and unhealthy. H.H. Almond, Headmaster of Loretto School in Scotland in the mid-1800s even said that 'spectating is the greatest of all football dangers'. He continued 'no idle spectator should be allowed to stand looking on at school sides'. Football and similar team games were certainly considered as instilling the positive values of leadership, perseverance and teamwork into young men, whilst spectatorism only promoted idleness."

However, people soon embraced the idea of idly standing in a field watching grown men kick a bag of wind around. The first noteworthy football crowd appeared in March 1867 when 3,000 turned up at Bramall Lane to watch the final of the world's first organised football tournament, the Youdan Cup, between Sheffield sides Hallam and Norfolk. The game marked the arrival of the first pawns in the game of football: the Egberts. Rich, educated and dedicated to the beautiful game, it wasn't long before some enterprising tykes realised that these strange folk who stood around watching football could be pumped for some serious cash.

"When football was an amateur game dominated by the wealthy upper middle class," says National Football Museum's Mark Bushell, "they'd think nothing of having gilded bronze clocks with football figures or ornate ceramics with football figures on their mantlepieces."

These strange folk... could be pumped for some serious cash

By 1873, with rugby looming like a weird fat-bloke-and-oval-ball ghoul in the background, attitudes towards football spectators started to change. Instead of blathering on about the importance of not being idle, the toffs realised that it was more important that their game won the rugby-football popularity contest than it was to try and hold back a tide that wouldn't be kept back. The Cup Final that year was deliberately scheduled at 11am so that afterwards players and spectators could watch the nearby University Boat Race.

"The Association code had not established itself in preference to the Rugby form and, as such, required fairly blatant popularisation," says Graham Curry. "Such popularising efforts, aimed as they were at increasing spectator numbers, might still be construed as a notable departure from one of the main principles of amateurism, that is, participation rather than spectating."

Football fans grew rapidly in numbers over the coming years as the working classes gradually eased the upper classes out of the game. Just 1,500 turned out to see Wanderers play Old Etonians in the FA Cup final of 1876 but ten years later Blackburn Rovers and West Bromwich Albion drew a crowd of around 15,000. By this time, professionalism had become legal, and the role of the football fan as finance provider became more crucial to the game – even though they had slimmer wallets than their predecessors.

"When the working class oiks got hold of the game, they didn't have the money to spend on clocks or figurines, so manufacturers looked to cheaper merchandise like cigarette cards," says Mark Bushell. "Right from the first day of professionalism in 1885, clubs have had to organise themselves like businesses and look at their profits and losses. That's why women, who until that point had been allowed in for free, were kicked out and forced to pay when professionalism came in. Clubs needed to make money in order to pay the players."

That's pretty much how the relationship between fans, players and clubs has remained to this day. Players charge for their services and clubs transfer the burden of that cost to the fans. It's a simple enough equation, although it did come under threat just after the First World War from a hitherto unsuspected enemy: ladies.

During the First World War the men of Britain disappeared off to tackle The Bosh, meaning ladies could think and act outside their meagre little lady boxes for the first time. One of the areas into which they channelled their new found chutzpah was football, organising games between the munitions factories they worked for and raising money for War charities. When the War finished, the men returned to find their pretty little wall flowers had turned into handy footballers.

On April 30th 1920 a Preston-based team called Dick Kerr's Ladies [from the Dick Kerr munitions factory] played the first ever international game between two women's teams when they hosted a French representative side. If the FA's bushy eyebrows were raised when a crowd of 25,000 people turned up to see Dick Kerr's chicks win 2-0, they went into furrowed overdrive when on Boxing Day that year 53,000 turned up to watch them beat St Helens 4-0 at Goodison Park. Jowells were wobbled, saliva hung from the side of mouths and, a year after the insolence, the FA issued a ban that prevented women playing on Football League grounds.

"Complaints have been made as to football being played by women," blustered an FA statement. "The FA feel impelled to express their strong opinion that the game of football is quite unsuitable for females and ought not to be encouraged."

Even in those days, when women were meant to know their place and not get ideas above their kitchen, it seems a little far fetched to prevent them playing football on moral grounds. It's far more likely that the FA saw the increasing popularity of women's football as a commercial threat to the men's game. If 53,000 people would turn up to watch Dick Kerr's Ladies, they might not bother to watch Preston or Burnley or Bolton. So it was nipped in the bud.

The 1930s and 40s represented a boom time in English football, with more fans attending matches than at any time before or since. The three highest attendances ever occurred during this period, with Man U holding the record after packing 83,260 fans in for the game against Arsenal on January 17th 1948. With bums-on-seats being the main source of income in those days, it follows that these were great days for the clubs. But they were also brilliant times for the fans.

"I've been going to Hillsborough since I was a toddler," says Premier League Chairman Dave Richards. "In the early days they used to lift me over the turnstile and pass me down to the front of the kop. I used to sit on the wall with hundreds of kids and the policeman would come by and give us all sweets. That's how different it was. They'd pass you back to get back to your dad at the end."

However, the days of the football family; when fans would look after each other on the vast terraces, would not last forever. It wouldn't be long before a new, altogether more sinister ethos took hold of the nation's football fans, ushering in the most terrifying era in the history of the game.

THE DAWN OF THE HERBERTS

The origins of the term 'hooligan' are uncertain. Some say it comes from an Irish hoodlum named Patrick Hooligan, others that it originates from an Islington street gang named 'Hooley' whilst another claim is that the name first appeared in a London police report in 1898. What most people can agree is that hooligans are generally associated with football and are the type of folk who have the propensity to gather in groups and kick the living shit out of each other.

Football hooligans tend to be real 'Herberts', Jack-the-lad types who like beers, 'babs and brasses when they're not fighting at the match. Despite their aggressive behaviour, football hooligans are still pawns in the game of football, so dedicated to their clubs that they are prepared to travel the length and breadth of the country supporting and fighting for their heroes. The only difference between them and pawns from other eras of the game is that the Herbert years cost clubs a lot of money, whereas the Egbert and Cuthbert years made clubs bagfuls of cash.

Although widely believed to be a late 20th Century disease, football hooliganism has been around in some form pretty much from the word go. In the early days, groups of 'roughs' would hurl obscenities and pelt the referee with missiles, a problem exacerbated when two local teams played each other. In 1906 in Glasgow, 6,000 fans were involved in a riot that kicked off between Rangers and Celtic fans. The World Wars put a check on things – why fight each other when there's an enemy to duff up? – but by the 1950s, fighting at football had started to come back into vogue. Between 1946 and 1960 there was an average of 13 incidents a season involving disorderly football fans. This figure doubled in the eight years that followed as TV, which did so much to promote the game itself, helped spread its disease also.

Football violence really kicked off in the 60s

Football violence really kicked off in the 60s, as television images of riots at the footy helped to glamorise the good old fashioned punch-up and turn it into something more mystical. One of the first games to whet the appetites of would-be hooligans was the Tottenham-Sunderland clash of 1961. The televised clash descended into a riot, prompting *The Guardian* to note later that in terms of hooliganism the match had "provided... encouragement to others."

Football hooligans dominated the nation's terraces from the 1960s to the 1980s. Although, as with any era, there were other types of football fan present at matches, these were the years of the Herbert, when the areas behind the goals became young male-only zones and, due to the fear of violence, many families, women and older people simply stopped going. This was still a time when bums-on-seats was the most important source of income, so the hooligans' commercial impact on clubs in terms of lost revenue was enormous. In 1977 an aggregate of 27m watched league football but by 1982 it had fallen to just 18.8m. Clubs like Middlesborough, Charlton and Bolton, although in the lower tiers of English football at the time, struggled to average 5,000 fans a game. A lot of bums were missing from the seats of English football, meaning a lot of cash was missing from the registers.

It wasn't just the hooligans' fault. Attendances had been in decline since the Second World War as access to travel, TV and other leisure pursuits opened up. But, by the mid-1980s the 'English disease' had become chronic.

In the 1984/85 season alone, 500 seats were ripped out at a cup match between Man City and Coventry, Clive Walker had to dodge police horses to set up the winning goal in the Sunderland-Chelsea Milk Cup semi-final and 81 people were injured in a night of sickening violence as Millwall invaded Luton.

"Seats were torn out of the stand and hurled onto the pitch," journalist and Millwall fan James Murray said after the match. "They became weapons for the invading fans who hurled them again at police. The scenes before me were ones of open bloody warfare. As I watched policemen led off the pitch, dazed and bleeding, and a superintendent lying in the centre circle writhing in agony, I was reminded of the Brixton riots. As a life-long Millwall supporter I could only stand in disbelief as I watched the riots and I felt like crying. Children around me clung to their parents in fear; women and pensioners vowed never to go to a football match again."

Yet still the violence didn't stop. On May 11th a boy was killed and nearly 100 police injured as Leeds fans rioted at St Andrews. And, just 18 days later the biggest hooligan-related tragedy of them all unfolded. On 29th May 1985 60,000 fans of Liverpool and Juventus gathered at the rickety Heysel stadium in Brussels to watch what should have been one of the best European cup finals for years. Instead, 39 fans were trampled to death after fighting broke out between the two sets of supporters, and a wall in sector Z collapsed, causing widespread panic. As a result of the tragedy, English football clubs were banned from Europe for five years, costing the players valuable European experience and the clubs much-needed extra gate revenue.

"The European ban did untold damage to English football," says Phil Carling. "We didn't win the Champions League again until 1999. Technically, we'd fallen a long way behind. It was a nadir for English football. Being out of Europe contributed to the general malaise about football in this country."

But it took another, even greater tragedy, to change the way football was organised, marketed and consumed. Four years after Heysel, another disaster took place which would change the face of the commercialisation of football forever.

CUTHBERTS: THE NEW HERBERTS

April 15th 1989 was meant to be a day of celebration. The two finest footballing sides in England met at Sheffield Wednesday's Hillsborough stadium for a match to determine who would contest the FA Cup Final. Forest or Liverpool? Clough or Dalglish? It was a mouthwatering prospect as the fans gathered near the stadium in the baking hot afternoon sun. Yet, just six minutes after kick off the referee was forced to abandon the game as people started spilling onto the pitch. At that moment the thought that had hit home with the Liverpool fans twenty minutes previous was suddenly writ large on TV screens across the world: something had gone very, very wrong.

"I knew I was really in trouble, in great danger, and remember thinking 'I hope my mum hasn't heard about this' because she'd only have worried," Liverpool fan Damian Kavanagh wrote on the Hillsborough Justice Campaign website. "There were people lying on the floor with others over them trying to revive them with mouth-to-mouth being given by those who knew how to do it. Some people had been sick. I saw one man whose trousers had been soiled."

The Hillsborough disaster was a watershed moment for English football. In total 96 Liverpool fans died from crushing caused by severe over-crowding in the Leppings Lane end. If football was going to carry on, things were going to have to be done differently.

"I think that will go down in history as the time football had to change," says Premier League Chairman Dave Richards. "It was a tragic event. It was the catalyst for change. Out of it came all-seater stadiums. Lord Justice Taylor was a man before his time. He was a great man. His vision of things changed the history of football – how people were treated, being sat down, having proper toilets, about attitudes of people. It really changed. Don't forget those were bad days, when people used to fight in the streets, throw bottles onto the pitch, swear and curse."

A month after the tragedy, the Home Office launched an inquiry under the leadership of Lord Justice Taylor. The inquiry lasted 31 days and culminated in the two Taylor Reports, which were published in 1990. The first sought to clarify the causes of the Hillsborough disaster and the second made recommendations as to the future path football should tread. Its main thrust was that the top clubs in England and Scotland should phase out terraces and bring in all-seater stadiums but it also noted, with a Nostradamus-like grasp of what might happen in the future, that 'it should be possible to plan a price structure which suits the cheapest seats to the pockets of those presently paying to stand. At Ibrox, for example, seating is £6, standing £4.'

Two years after Hillsborough, The Football League published a document called *One Game, One Team, One Voice*. In it they set out a vision for the future of football, which would see the game ruled jointly by the FA and the Football League from top to bottom with any TV money shared out around the whole game.

Which way would the game turn?

The FA followed this with a document of its own, the *Blueprint For The Future Of Football*. In between the two documents the Big Five – Arsenal, Liverpool, Man Utd, Everton and Spurs – had met with ITV boss Greg Dyke to see if he would back a new breakaway league. He said he would and, when the FA's Blueprint came out, it also backed the breakaway league and urged that football should move upmarket and chase 'more affluent middle class consumers.' Whatever happened to the guardian angels of the game who used to rail against commercialisation? They got scared; seeing the Football League's *One Game, One Team, One Voice* mandate as a direct challenge to their position at the head of English football.

The game was at a crossroads with Lord Justice Taylor and the Football League on one side encouraging the idea of a strong football community and the FA on the other recommending a journey into money. Which way would the game turn? Community or self-interest? Business or pleasure?

Football's bigwigs chose to fart in the face of Lord Justice Taylor, the Football League and community-minded football fans when they chose the path marked M.O.N.E.Y.

Using the £160m of public money they'd been allocated by the Football Trust, the Fat Cats began converting their grounds into all-seater stadiums as requested, whilst slipping in little extras like corporate entertainment and conference facilities, which would allow them to generate more cash. In 1992 the top clubs went into commercial overdrive when they formed The

Premiership, netting themselves a huge TV deal which didn't have to be shared with the rest of football. From that point on, with power running like Linford Christie through their minds, the top clubs started to get a bit giddy. Not content with sacks of TV money, non-matchday cash from corporate hospitality events and increased merchandise sales, they decided to go the whole hog and put ticket prices up.

In 1991, the final season before The Premiership began, Arsenal's team sheet was dominated by names like Bould, Adams and Smith; you could stand up for six quid and the dearest ticket in the stands was £15. Fifteen years later, Gallic flair had replaced the hands-in-the-air back four and ticket prices ranged from £32 to £66. For many loyal pawns the post-Premiership price hike was cheque mate.

"After Hillsborough and Bradford ground safety became government policy and police control got to a stage that casual fans were put off attending games," says Phil Thornton, author of *Casuals*. "The idea of having to buy season tickets and paying inflated seat prices made it impossible for thousands of ordinary fans to follow their teams. Obviously the football is far better these days and you could argue that The Premiership has led to the British game being the best in the world but it's come at a cost. When you see crowds at the San Siro or Delle Alpi you realise just how much has disappeared from the British game. There was a lot of violence and skullduggery attached to being a football fan and you were always treated with utter contempt by the clubs and the police but that's what made it so much fun. When I see all these new England fans who've never been to a match in their lives, it makes me nostalgic for the good old bad old days again."

Many fans can remember a time when it was a couple of quid to get into the footy, now it's the equivalent of 50p a minute at some Premiership grounds. The dramatic hike in price has prevented many of the old Herberts from going to the match and ushered in an era of more family-oriented, affluent fans: The Cuthberts. You only have to look at the make up of England fans at the World Cup to see the stark change in personnel at football. Germany 2006 was all fan fests and showing the world what great fans we were. Italia '90 was a fight fest and an exercise in showing the world how hard we were. Whilst Rimini was buried under a hail of flying bottles, chairs and Union Jacks, Gelsenkirchen marvelled at the silly wigs and smiles of the Cuthberts who arrived wrapped in flags of St George.

At home, the change in personnel has been a godsend for the club's bank managers, as the new fans have higher disposable incomes than the Herberts and are more likely to spend their cash inside the grounds on merchandise and food than frittering it away in the pub and steaming into the ground ten minutes before kick off. Team managers are probably less impressed, as a combination of being sat down and being more reserved has seen atmospheres inside grounds become a pale imitation of their former selves. As Roy Keane famously put it after a Champions League clash with Dynamo Kiev in 2000: "Sometimes you wonder, do they understand the game of football? We're 1-0 up, then there are one or two stray passes and they're

---

The Top 10 English league attendances...Ever!

83,260	Manchester Utd v Arsenal (Div 1, 17 Jan 1948)
82,905	Chelsea v Arsenal (Div 1, 12 Oct 1935)
79,491	Manchester City v Arsenal (Div 1, 23 Feb 1935)
78,299	Everton v Liverpool (Div 1, 18 Sept 1948)
77,696	Chelsea v Blackpool (Div 1, 16 Oct 1948)
76,839	Everton v Preston (Div 1, 28 Aug 1954)
75,952	Chelsea v Arsenal (Div 1, 9 Oct 1937)
75,322	Everton v Wolves (Div 1, 27 Dec 1954)
75,043	Chelsea v Wolves (Div 1, 9 Apr 1954)
74,918	Manchester City v Arsenal (Div 1, 10 Apr 1937)

source: Football League website

---

getting on players' backs. It's just not on. At the end of the day they need to get behind the team. Away from home our fans are fantastic, I'd call them the hardcore fans. But at home they have a few drinks and probably the prawn sandwiches, and they don't realise what's going on out on the pitch. I don't think some of the people who come to Old Trafford can spell 'football', never mind understand it."

For many people, a drop in atmosphere is a small price to pay for the improvements the game has seen since 1992. Increased revenues have heralded the arrival in England of some of the world's finest players. Think back: who would you rather be watching – Bracewell, Crosby and Harper or

Henry, Ballack and Alonso? And, since the hike in ticket prices, incidents of hooliganism have fallen dramatically at football grounds.

The reason for this is threefold. First, some of the new fans, The Cuthberts, tend to be more middle class, family-oriented people who have trouble saying boo to their Christmas goose never mind giving it 'come and have a go if you think you're hard enough' on a Saturday afternoon. Second, all-seater grounds are less conducive to fighting than the old terraces, where gangs of lads used to 'mob up' before, during and after games. And third the Herberts who used to love a dust-up on a Saturday afternoon got old and can't be bothered with it all any more.

"The main phenomenon to hit football fans over the last decade is ageing," says author and football journalist David Conn. "OK, some of the old fans have been priced out. Some have dropped out. But look at any crowd and you'll notice the amount of old baldies with thick necks and replica shirts. I believe hooliganism was to do with the age of people at football. Football grounds used to be full of 17-19 year olds. Teenagers fight. To say they've got rid of hooliganism is a laugh. What they've got rid of is access to football for teenage lads. There's still plenty of old hooligans who go, they just can't be arsed to fight anymore."

Clubs have used elasticity of demand to ramp prices up

With hooliganism on the wane and facilities at football grounds improving, the make-up of the crowds began to change in the early 90s. Women and children appeared back inside football grounds, safe in the knowledge that they were more likely to encounter a prawn sandwich than a knuckle sandwich.

"The Taylor Report said it was a necessity for clubs to demolish terracing and become all-seater stadiums," says Phil Carling. "At least clubs had the vision to think 'if we're going to do this, let's do it right'. So they put in things like female toilets. Previously there had been no incentive for blokes to come with their girlfriends or families. So clubs decided to make it a decent experience. That changed the profile of who went to the match. Previously it was just young men. Suddenly women and families felt safe and had the facilities to go to football. It's difficult to beat the crap out of the person sat next to you if you're sat down. The downside of the new functionality is it's a bloody expensive sport. Clubs have used elasticity of demand to ramp prices up to the ultimate stretching point."

Aye, there's the rub: the prices, the filthy lucre, the dirty cash. Was this changing of the guard at football a sinister plot by The Powers That Be to get rid of the troublesome old fans and bring in a new, more affluent breed? Or was it just natural evolution? The FA's *Blueprint For The Future Of Football* points to the dramatic culling of one set of pawns to pave the way for another. The document had, remember, urged clubs to go after 'more affluent middle class consumers'.

However, Phil Carling, who was working in the commercial department at Arsenal when the Taylor Report came out, disputes this.

"I don't believe football set out to attract a more affluent type of fan," he says. "There was never any conspiracy or objective to try and get a new type of person to the ground. In fact, at Arsenal there was uproar when it was suggested we build 50 executive boxes as it wasn't believed we would fill them. There wasn't even a realisation of the potential corporate market then, never mind a deliberate attempt to go for it. I created the first package of meal and a ticket at Arsenal and I struggled to get 100 tickets out of the box office."

Whether it was a deliberate ploy or not, the fact remains that to be a football fan in the 21st Century, you need plenty of wonga and a nice bright biro to mark off the games you want to attend when the fixture list comes out. Because unless you're minted or a complete addict, you won't be going to them all.

"I must stress straight away that I'm an Everton fan," says 27-year-old James Cooper. "But when I was a kid I used to go to Goodison one week and Anfield the next, as my mate was a red. It was only three or four quid to get in either ground so we used to alternate and still have a bit of money left over for other stuff. These days my match-going has plummeted dramatically due to two things. First is the price – I live in London now and all the grounds down here charge forty to fifty quid to get in. And second is the general dirth of quality outside the top four now that Sky and the Premier league have colluded to ensure that the rich get richer and the rest have to play shite negative football in an attempt to avoid the dreaded drop and all the financial woes that it brings."

Viewed through commercial eyes, the way in which the football puppet masters rebuilt the game post-Hillsborough was genius. Not only did they usher in a new breed of fan with more money to spend; they also oversaw the introduction of a new, upper echelon of fans with even more dirty cash to splash – The Corporates.

Corporate boxes have existed at football since Hursty scored that hat-trick and Bobby lifted the World Cup, but the pursuance of the mega-rich only really kicked in post-Hillsborough. Handed pots of free readies to rebuild their creaking grounds, clubs opted to stick in more corporate hospitality and conference facilities, turning a bigger proportion of the ground over to the suits.

Now The Corporates have taken over at the top level. In 2006 Manchester United opened new areas of Old Trafford called Quadrants, a third of which were given over to corporate seats linked to top-of-the-range dining facilities. At the World Cup, only 8% of tickets were made available to real fans, whilst The Corporates bagged a staggering 837,000 seats. And then there's Arsenal.

Forced into leaving the beautiful Highbury stadium in search of higher match day revenue, the Gunners came up with the Emirates stadium at Ashburton Grove – a corporate spaceship designed to suck cash out of the prawn sandwich brigade.

A key feature of the ground is the Club Level tier, which runs around the stadium and provides 'dedicated entrances separate from general admission ticket holders', according to the promotional brochure, and is surrounded by 'an enviable range of first-class bars, restaurants and lounges'. There are 6,700 seats available on the Club Level tier and they range from £4,750 a season to a mere £2,500. And if they're not snooty enough for you, you can get your hands on one of the 150 executive boxes for £76,375 a season.

"Our gate income in the new stadium will probably be the highest in the world," boasted Arsenal's managing director Keith Edelman, presumably trying to put himself in the shop window for the next Carlsberg advert. "That will be because we will have 60,000 fans and we have higher priced tickets and more premium tickets than any other club in the UK."

Once upon a time such a boast would have been seen as ill thought-out and a massive own goal, but these days its par for the course. Football fans have always been pawns in the game but now they're prawns, devoured by the game's Fat Cats and openly pumped for as much cash as is humanly possible.

"The Arsenal development is a monument to corporate football," says David Conn. "You're walking through Islington which is a nice, quirky part of London and suddenly you see Emirates written in massive letters on this thing. It looks like a spaceship has landed from the planet Emirates. There's no community use for that stadium. It's a place for millionaires to kick a ball around making money for the people who run the club. It cost £800m to build. They were going to build a community centre but the council said they didn't have to, so they gave £1m to local sport. It should be so different. The whole thing should be about involving more people in sport. The football boom has been in spectating. If you take the Arsenal stadium as an example, it's there to make you eat, drink and consume. It's the ultimate endorsement of what football is now."

The opening of the Emirates Stadium in 2006 was a grim landmark in the history of English football. It was the first time a ground had been built specifically for the prawn sandwich brigade and it was the first time one of England's biggest clubs had allowed a corporation such a big say in its identity. Where now? Was this the beginning of the end?

Or is there another way?

PRAWNS IN THE GAME

> CHAPTER 10
SWIMMING AGAINST THE TIDE

10: SWIMMING AGAINST THE TIDE

It's July 23rd 2005, AFC Wimbledon v FC United of Manchester, Kingsmeadow, Surrey. The early afternoon sun has been replaced by the kind of fine drizzle that soaks you to the bone, but neither that, nor the one nil deficit, can dampen the enthusiasm of the 1,000 fans who've made the four hour trip from Manchester. They're jumping up and down as if they're in the European Cup final and singing:

> *"Under the boardwalk!*
> *Watching FC*
> *There'll be no knobheads in jester hats*
> *Watching Sky TV!"*

Sung to the tune of The Drifters' *Under the boardwalk*, it could just as easily be adopted as an anthem by any fan objecting to the money-oriented, Sky-tinted world of The Premiership. Looking around the away terrace at Kingsmeadow, the recently-departed missionaries of Manchester United don't seem to be missing the prawn sandwiches too much. Dressed in short sleeves, the followers of 'Little United' ignore the drizzle and break into another song. "You can stick your fucking franchise up your arse!" The fans of AFC Wimbledon respond with a song none too complimentary about Malcolm Glazer. This is it: the second coming of football, the first game between two teams created 'by the fans, for the fans'. The lunatics have taken over the asylum.

Like a chav baby with parents swathed in burberry and gold, the first fans' football clubs were born out of adversity. AFC Wimbledon formed in the summer of 2002 after an FA commission allowed Wimbledon to move 70 miles up the road to Milton Keynes. The club carried on farcically as Wimbledon for one season, before they were allowed to change their name to MK Dons. Three years after the formation of AFC Wimbledon, FC United of Manchester was created by a group of Manchester United fans unhappy at Malcolm Glazer's takeover of the club. Both sets of fans managed to magic up new clubs in a matter of weeks before the start of a new football season and, although both groups were shocked when their darkest fears about their old clubs turned to reality, they didn't receive a Spanish-inquisition-style surprise either. In both cases, warning shots had been fired across the bows long before the ships started to sink.

Things started going wrong for Wimbledon in the 1991/92 season, when they moved away from their Plough Lane home and began a ground-share with Crystal Palace.

"It was sold to us as a temporary move," says Kris Stewart, former Chairman of the Independent Wimbledon Supporters Association, now Chairman of AFC Wimbledon. "Sam Hamman said Plough Lane wasn't suitable to be turned into an all-seater stadium, so the idea was we'd move out, sell the ground and look for somewhere else close by. Then all these stories started appearing about us trying to move to Dublin. Then it was Basingstoke, Gatwick, Glasgow and Belfast. We kept being told there was no suitable site in our home borough of Merton."

Nostrils flared in Manchester when, in 1998, Rupert Murdoch, that large camembert of the media world, slapped £623.4m on the table in the United mega store and said, this looks like somewhere I could hang my hat.

"That's when the idea of a new club was first mooted," says Jules Spencer, board member of FC United of Manchester and former Chairman of the Independent Manchester United Supporters Association. "In the end it wasn't necessary because Murdoch's bid was defeated. *The Red Issue* fanzine rekindled the idea in 2004 when Malcolm Glazer came on the scene."

Then it was Basingstoke, Gatwick, Glasgow and Belfast

Even the cutest, fluffiest of animals will bare its teeth and fight when it's backed into a corner, and so it proved with the Wombles of Wimbledon and the northern monkeys of Manchester. They may not have been pursued by gangs of jodper-clad toffs on horses and packs of woefully-underfed hounds, but the danger they faced was just as real and just as imminent.

In 1997 Wimbledon Chairman Sam Hamman sold 80% of his shares to Norwegian businessmen Bjorn Rune Gjelsten and Kjell-Inge Rokke. Three years later, he sold the remaining shares to Gjelsten and soon after Norwegian lawyer Charles Koppel became Chairman. With the club haemorhaging money by playing every home game 'away' at Selhurst Park, the Norwegians set about trying to find a new home although, suspiciously, none of the new options appeared to be anywhere near the club's Merton home.

In May 2001 it emerged that Wimbledon and QPR were looking to merge. *The Sun* broke the story and Dons fans were, understandably, miffed.

"True, they will feel that we have gone far down the road without discussing it with them," Koppel wheezed at the time. "But the reality is we are still at a very early stage. We will not take any decision without consulting our supporters."

How those fans must have laughed three months later when they munched their cornflakes and opened the morning's post.

"All season ticket holders got a letter from chairman Charles Koppel saying we were moving to Milton Keynes," says Kris Stewart. "I was shocked but not surprised – we'd been hearing rumours about Milton Keynes for a while. We'd been pushing the club for answers but they never gave us any."

As luck would have it, Wimbledon were due to play Brentford in a friendly at Griffin Park the day after the Chairman's letter. The Independent Wimbledon Supporters Association organised a protest. A couple of hundred Wimbledon fans turned up with banners and made their feelings known.

"It was quite funny actually," says Kris. "Brentford were managed by Steve Coppell at the time. When we started singing 'we want Koppel out' it caused a lot of confusion."

The protests continued and the majority of the football world, everyone in fact "except Koppel and David Mellor" according to Kris Stewart, was united behind Wimbledon. The club should not and could not be moved 70 miles away from its home, fans and community. When Wimbledon applied to the Football League to set up home in Milton Keynes on August 16th 2001, the proposal was unanimously rejected.

Like a big bag of girls, Wimbledon cried and mewled and crawled to the court of arbitration, saying the Football League hadn't undertaken proper procedure. The court of arbitration agreed, and duly ruled that the Football League decision was wrong. Instead of taking the decision again, The Football League referred the task to a three man FA Committee consisting of Alan Turvey [FA council member, member of FA disciplinary and membership committees and chairman of the Ryman League], Steven Stride [Operations Director at Aston Villa] and Raj Parker [partner at international law firm Freshfields Bruckhaus Deringer].

Wimbledon fans cranked the protests up a notch, hiring a plane to fly over Vicarage Road when they were away at Watford towing a message that read: 'Dons fans say Koppel out.' They also set about trying to discredit Wimbledon's argument for moving. The club were saying that without their own ground, they made no revenues at home matches except the admission prices and would go into liquidation if the situation continued. The fans set out to prove that a 20,000 seater stadium could be built on the Plough Lane site.

"The club feigned interest in Plough Lane a few times," says Kris. "They paid lip service to it but, at the same time, Charles Koppel went to a residents meeting in the area and encouraged local people to oppose plans for a new ground. Why didn't he want us to move back home? 'Cos he'a cunt."

In Manchester feelings were running just as high. The United fans have a sketchy history when it comes to protests. The Monopolies and Mergers Commission had ridden to their rescue in '98 to see off Rupert Murdoch but a similar wave of protest in '92 about the stock market float was met with a collective putting of fingers in ears on the United board and a headlong dive into murky waters of the London Stock Exchange. This time they were determined to win.

Protests, like the fatally flawed 'not for sale' effort, seemed to spring up around the ground on an almost daily basis. Anti-Glazer fans canvassed the board, to make sure they were in no doubt how the fans felt. They undertook flash mob events near the premises of Nike and Vodaphone, two of United's main sponsors, to alert them to the ire of the fans. Trips were made to London to try and garner political support for the anti-Glazer faction.

"We were absolutely confident of beating Glazer," says Jules Spencer. "We didn't think his business plan would work and we didn't think the PLC would agree to anything that the supporters were so obviously against."

But nice guys don't come first. The hopes of the fans were crushed under the wheels of commercialism – at United, where the money and marketing skill of the Glazers won out and at Wimbledon, where the club was sold down the river to Milton Keynes where, it was argued, they could earn enough money to survive. This thinking conveniently ignored the fact that by making the move, they were actually killing the club. Wimbledon playing in Milton Keynes is not Wimbledon any more.

People remember where they were when Death poked his skeletal face through the curtains at John F. Kennedy, John Lennon and Kurt Cobain. They also tend to remember where they were when he pitched up at their football club.

"I was on the forecourt at Old Trafford in front of the TV cameras," says Jules. "I thought 'Christ – it's happened'. I cried. I remember thinking about my son, who was six months old at the time. I've had loads of great times at Old Trafford and have so many great memories. But he's not going to have that. I remember thinking 'I'm not going to be able to take my son to Old Trafford'. It was devastating. There were thousands of us in the same boat. We all had a hard decision to make – do you stay and fight it from within or do you sack it all off?"

Do you stay and fight it from within or do you sack it all off?

Kris Stewart was outside the FA Headquarters in Soho Square when the news officially broke. The three man FA committee had been considering the case of Wimbledon vs. Milton Keynes for two weeks. Kris had given his evidence to the panel and, even though Charles Koppel had hired a high-powered QC, making it a rather one-sided affair, Kris Stewart still didn't expect to lose.

"I thought they'd postpone the decision," he says. "During the hearing I was asked if I'd prefer Wimbledon to die or move to Milton Keynes? I said I saw both things as death. The panel then disappeared off the face of the earth. There were loads of rumours flying around, then one night a journalist from the *Evening Standard* called me. He said, 'You've lost. They're off to Milton Keynes'. I felt sick. The bottom fell out of my world."

Next day Kris and some of his fellow fans held a vigil outside the FA Headquarters in Soho Square.

"I'd been made redundant the day before, so I had plenty of time on my hands. There was no formal announcement, everyone just seemed to know. Eventually we went into the FA building, against their wishes, and forced them to make a comment. They confirmed what we already knew. The commission found in favour of a group of people and their bank accounts rather than football."

The Wimbledon fans went for a drink in the Pillar of Hercules pub around the corner, before heading back to south London in a fleet of black cabs. There they piled into the Fox and Grapes on Wimbledon Common, one of the many pubs where the great Wimbledon team was rumoured to have gone for a beer the night before the 1988 Cup Final. The mood was mixed. Some were down, some were angry, but by the time they left the pub that night enough people had agreed what needed to be done: they'd become the first set of fans in England to form their own club.

The resolve to start a new club up in Manchester was rubber-stamped over a curry. Just after the Glazer deal was struck, a group of United fans, mainly drawn from fan groups and fanzines, were in the Dilda curry house in Rusholme, Manchester's 'curry mile'. Emotions were running high, with some in favour of trying to bring down the Glazer administration from the inside, but eventually it was decided even if there were only a few hundred who refused to go back, they'd have to start a new club for them, or else those fans would be lost to the game forever.

When 800 supporters turned up at a Methodist Hall in central Manchester it gave the protagonists of a new club heart and, when over 2,000 turned up to another supporter's evening at the Apollo Theatre, they knew they had to act. Fast. They only had six weeks before the new season started and they didn't want to lose momentum by hanging around until the following season.

A phone call was put in to AFC Wimbledon, who were 'tremendously helpful', and a steering group was set up to move the club forward. They drew up a business plan, sought pledges of money from United fans, secured FA affiliation and convinced the North West Counties Football League to accept them.

"We asked for money from United supporters," says Jules. "Some gave us the 600 quid they would have spent on a season ticket at Old Trafford. We raised £100,000 in five weeks, which meant we could sustain the club for at least a season."

With an agreement struck with Bury to play their home games at Gigg Lane, FC United of Manchester then set about slotting the final pieces of the jigsaw into place – a manager and some players.

"The name Karl Marginson kept coming up," says Jules. "He's a United fan and knows football inside out at this level. We wanted someone who would buy into it and know what the club is all about."

After holding trials and attracting players from other clubs with the promise of taking part in something historic, FC United of Manchester were ready to run out in their red, white and black kit, with no sponsor.

"That was deliberate," says Jules. "We wanted to keep the shirt pure, like Barcelona. Commercialisation is not evil in itself. It's greed that's the problem with the top clubs. We sell shirts, but we don't over do it. We don't do duvets. And even if we did, the money would go back into the football club."

Two days after the FA Commission's decision to allow Wimbledon to move to Milton Keynes, it was the AGM of the Independent Wimbledon Supporters Association. Stung into action by the events of the last few days, around 1,000 people turned up to the Wimbledon Common Centre.

"People were literally hanging from the rafters," says Kris Stewart. "There were TV cameras there. TV cameras! It was a passionate meeting. We said we were thinking of going ahead with a new club. Some thought we were giving up on the club. We'd been fighting Wimbledon FC for over a year and I was fed up with it. I just wanted to watch football."

Over the next six weeks, the new Wimbledon – now officially called AFC Wimbledon after negotiations with the London FA [who refused to allow them to be called FC Wimbledon] – raised money through donations from fans and businesses, installed Terry Eames as manager, assembled a squad of players, convinced the Combined Counties League to accept them and negotiated a deal to play at Kingstonian's Kingsmeadown ground, about a mile and half from Wimbledon Common.

The new Dons' first game was a friendly away at Sutton United. Over 4,500 people packed into Gander Green Lane on Wednesday July 10th to see the birth of the country's first fans club.

"I was on the pitch, on the phone to Radio Five Live when an announcement came over the tanoy that we were delaying kick off because everyone couldn't get in the ground," says Kris. "It was a carnival atmosphere. People were trying to shoehorn AFC into the old Wimbledon songs. We were thrashed 4-0 but we invaded the pitch at the end and danced around like madmen. People were chanting my name and it made the hairs on the back of my neck stand up."

When he saw the birth of England's second fans' club, away at Leigh RMI on July 16th 2005, Jules Spencer experienced something similar.

"We drew nil-nil, but it was an amazing moment," he says. "It was very emotional. The supporters had taken control of the football club. We all knew that that was our team. The club is owned by the supporters. They dictate the direction of the football club."

AFC Wimbledon and FC United of Manchester have demonstrated that there is another way; that it is possible to swim against the tide of corporate sponsorship and extortionate ticket prices and drag a beautiful game out of the crazy world of modern football. Unlike their friends in the Football League and Premiership, AFC Wimbledon and FC United make it affordable for people to turn up and watch. It's £150 for an adult season ticket on the terraces at Kingsmeadow and £25 for under-16s, whilst a father can take his son to Gigg Lane for under a tenner to watch FCUM. The same gig at Old Trafford would set the same father-son combo back between £31.50 and £54.

The best part about belonging to a fans' club is you know the money you put in will go back into the club and you actually get a say in the way the club is run. The board at AFC Wimbledon, elected by members of the Dons Trust, reports back to the fans on a regular basis and holds open meetings two or three times a year. It's a transparency that is reciprocated at FCUM.

"A board has been elected but they can easily be de-selected by the fans if they're not happy with the way the club is being run," says Jules Spencer. "All major decisions are taken by the supporters and it's one vote per member. If a rich sugar daddy turns up with a million quid, he gets one vote, the same as a bloke who's put a fiver in."

But isn't it all a bit, well, rubbish?

The new fans club model has been a big hit with, you guessed it, the fans. Wimbledon average nearly 3,000 in the Ryman Premier and FC United are pulling in 3,500-4,000 a match, roughly twice the amount of their landlords who play six leagues higher up the pyramid. But isn't it all a bit, well, rubbish?

"Sometimes the football is a bit crap," says Kris Stewart. "But I watched plenty of dire games when we were professional. I'm glad to be away from all the hype and the crap at the top level – players earning £120 grand a week and a Champions League full of also-rans. It feels like there's more honesty down here. It's a lot more straightforward."

The future for both fans' clubs looks bright. FC United is aiming to get two promotions in two seasons, which would take them into the Unibond League, and then re-assess from there. AFC Wimbledon, already promoted a couple of times, want to fulfill their dream of seeing the name Wimbledon in the Football League once more.

But as they journey onwards and hopefully upwards, it's hard for the fans' clubs not to cock a snook at the past. Both sides play in kits reminiscent of their old selves, FC United in red, white and black, and AFC Wimbledon's royal blue kit, designed by the fans, features an old Wimbledon club badge. But that's where the love affair ends.

"I hate even saying the name MK Dons," says Kris Stewart. "It annoys me when it's written down. Those wankers don't have the right to use the word Dons. They should take their filthy hands off the word. I don't recognise them as a football club. They are a franchise. That's the polite word. They're vermin. Scum. I'd hate to play them. It would be horrible. I don't want us to have to acknowledge them. It would be much better if they just died."

"I can't put into words what I think of Malcolm Glazer," says Jules Spencer. "Sometimes I don't care. I can't summon the energy to hate him any more. Other times I detest everything he represents. In many ways the takeover was a symptom of a greater ill. If Martin Edwards hadn't floated the club, we might not be in this position. But then every time I see his three sons at the match, my stomach churns and I want to cry."

Whilst Kris Stewart doesn't recognize MK Dons as a football club, Jules Spencer sees FC United as an extension of Man Utd.

"They're Big United, we're Little United," he says. "We sing a song about there being two Uniteds but the soul is one. I still jump up and down in the pub when we [Man Utd] score. But I'll never go back to Old Trafford whilst Glazer is there. Even if he died tomorrow – what's changed? Kids still wouldn't be able to afford to go. I'd want to see more supporter ownership before I went back to Old Trafford. Is it a comedown watching FC United? No. The standard of football is surprisingly high. There's some really handy footballers around. And a winning goal is a winning goal, whether it's in the Nou Camp or on a park."

THE ROAD TO POWER PIE

Football supporters haven't just breezed in off the terraces and helped themselves to a slice of ma's homemade power pie. For the best part of 150 years they were serfs in the game of football. Clubs traditionally held the power, feeding off fans to pay players a meagre salary. Things changed in the 60s, when Jimmy Hill and George Eastham smashed the maximum wage and retain-and-transfer stranglehold of the clubs, giving players a session at the trough. Then came The Premiership, with its flashy new stadiums, TV deals and players from overseas. More money was pouring into the game than ever before, yet still the burden of cost was transferred to the fans. Forced to pay spiralling admission fees to see their heroes, seduced into showing their 'loyalty' by buying souvenirs from the club but given no voice in how their clubs or football in general should be run, supporters have been the whipping boys of football since commercialisation took a hold in 1885. Or at least, they had until Brian Lomax came on the scene.

The first notion that football fans ought to start standing up for themselves occurred at the Brewer's Arms pub in Northampton in November 1991. Brian Lomax and his friends were holding an inquest after what had been a strange day – Northampton Town had failed to issue a programme for the match against Burnley and there were rumours the players hadn't been paid. Before they left the pub that night they agreed that something had to be done. The only question was: What?

It didn't take Brian too long to come up with the answer – it was staring him in the face. He was the managing director of a housing trust which helped the homeless and people with special needs find accommodation. Because the organisation he wanted to form to help Northampton Town would be used for the benefit of a public or private company [ie NTFC], he couldn't register it as a charity. But there was nothing to stop him setting up an organisation exactly like the one he was already working for – a trust.

And so in January 1992 the world's first football supporters' trust was born. Over 600 people turned up to the 250-capacity Exeter Rooms in Northampton for a public meeting about the state of the club. No one from the club was going to come but, at the last minute, manager Theo Foley turned up with a club employee.

"We were explaining that the club was in trouble," says Brian Lomax.

"Theo Foley, who was sat on a table at the front of the hall near me, leaned across to his colleague and said 'don't tell them the fucking figures'. But some people in the crowd knew the figures. When everyone heard we were £1.6m in debt, they were shocked. The proposal to form a trust was passed unanimously."

Up to that point, the only serious mobilisation of fans had revolved around supporters' clubs and associations – sad collections of men who paid a small yearly subscription fee to become the proud owner of a wallet-sized membership card, a newsletter they'd never read and the right to brag that they were the club's most dedicated supporters. Like the small kid at school, supporters' clubs were roundly picked on and abused.

"At Southend the supporters' club built the ground but never received a single share or any influence in the club," says Brian. "At Northampton, the floodlights were paid for by the supporters' club. Apparently they were given blazer badges and the right to have a drink in the sponsors' lounge once a year. That's no longer acceptable. Supporters' money is as good as anyone else's. If people invest their emotions and raise money for a club, they have the right to hold shares. A trust is a legal personality with a right to acquire and own shares in a club, with a view to gaining power and influence in order to make sure the club is run properly. Supporters' clubs are benign organisations with no rights to own shares."

Supporters' money is as good as anyone else's

Brian outlines the broad aims of a supporters' trust as follows: to support the club, to ensure good corporate governance at that club, to promote the right of supporters as active members of the club, to promote the right of supporters to be elected to the board and to build up a shareholding in the club which will provide a financial back-up on the board for that director.

After a meeting at Abington Park Hotel, Brian was elected chairman of the Northampton Town Supporters' Trust. A player's representative was at the meeting, as was someone from the council, but Trust members weren't sure exactly how the club and the world at large would react to this new phenomenon. They didn't have to wait long.

The Trust's first activity was to hold a bucket collection at the ground, during the game against York City in January 1992. It was a make or break time. Would the fans take to them? What would the club do?

"The campaign took off like a plane with a pilot that day," says Brian. "The Chairman threw us out in front of the TV cameras. We said 'don't you want the money?' and he said 'give it to the dog's home'. Everybody gave us money and we raised £15,000 in a month."

The Trust continued with a two-pronged attack. It continued the bucket collections at every home game, to raise funds with which to help save the club. And it held secret meetings with the club's creditors with the aim of bringing a winding-up order against them. It eventually managed to persuade Abbeyfield Press Limited, the club's programme producers, to bring a petition against the club. The Trust had been advised that this was the best way to get rid of the Chairman, Michael McRitchie, although not all Northampton fans thought it was a good idea.

"Some supporters didn't like that at all," says Brian. "They said, 'you're going to kill the club'. We said, 'no we're not. We're going to save it'. The club was in a mess. One day I was in the club bar and players came marching through one after the other carrying big bags of cash. Bobby Barnes looked like Father Christmas, he had a sack of pound coins over his shoulder. None of that was ever recorded."

Three months after the Trust had been thrown out of the County Ground in front of the TV cameras, Michael McRitchie called in the administrators to run the club. It was claimed by some that he thought it would buy him some breathing space, and that he could walk away from the debt and then breeze back in when the problem was solved and take over the club again.

The administrator had other ideas. He called a meeting at his office in Birmingham with two members of the Trust, two former directors, McRitchie and his wife. The administrator took a vote on whether McRitchie should remain as Chairman. McRitchie lost 4-2.

"He gave a very gracious speech," says Brian. "He wished us well and said he was sorry to be leaving. 'The first thing you'll have to do,' he said, 'is to sack the players'."

He was right. To cut costs the administrator sacked eight players and management staff and installed Phil Chard as player/manager. As a result of the shake-up at the club two Trust members, including Brian Lomax, were invited onto the board of Northampton Town. They were the first elected supporters' directors on the board of an English club.

"It was fascinating," says Brian. "The other directors had prejudices about supporters. They thought we'd be straight down the pub telling our mates what was happening at the club. But we proved quite quickly that we could be trusted."

Northampton Town came out of administration in 1994. The number of supporters on the board was reduced to one, although that one place has been guaranteed by Northampton Council until at least 2019. The same year they moved into the shiny new Sixfields stadium, built and owned by Northampton Borough Council with the aid of a £1m grant from the Football Trust, and more than a little help from the Northampton Town Supporters' Trust.

"If the Trust had not existed it would have been politically unacceptable to provide a football ground from public funds for an unreformed club recently guilty of gross mismanagement," says Brain. "Councillors have frequently stated that the stadium would not have been built were it not for the Supporters' Trust."

Northampton Town paid off their debt in August 1998, six months ahead of schedule. The following year, feeling he 'ought to let someone else have a go', Brian Lomax resigned his place on the board. But his thumbs weren't allowed to remain idle for long.

STICKING TO THE TASK

Supporters haven't been the only people to swash their buckles at the onslaught of commercialisation. In 1998 the Government set up the ominously-titled Football Task Force, whose mission was to don balaclavas and investigate and recommend new measures to deal with the public's concerns on issues of racism, ticket prices, access of the disabled and the increasing commercialisation in the game.

"The game of football has changed dramatically over the last decade," Sports Minister Tony Banks table-thumped, at the announcement of the Football Task Force at Charlton Athletic's Valley ground in January '98. "Following the Hillsborough tragedy it was essential for football to think afresh about the safety and comfort of the spectators coming to watch our national game. The depth of top quality stadia in this country shows that we are well on the way to meeting that challenge. But we should not assume that this is the only challenge facing the sport. That is why the Government has decided to establish a Football Task Force to ensure that those in a position of power have an opportunity to hear the views and suggestions from all quarters of the game. Many clubs are taking action to stamp out racism – but more needs to be done. There are questions, not just of access for minority groups like the disabled, but how clubs can avoid alienating the less well off from the sport that they love. Let's really make football Britain's family game. There are many ways that clubs can achieve this and I hope that the group will highlight some of the good things already going on within the game."

Gap-toothed Tory David Mellor chaired this government-led football hit squad, which drew representatives from a wide range of football bodies: the Football Trust, FA, Premier League, Football League, Football Supporters Association, PFA, Commission for Racial Equality, Local Government Association, English Sports Council, National Federation of Football Supporters Clubs, National Association of Disabled Supporters Clubs, League Manager's Association, Football League Referees and Linesmen, and football academic Dr Rogan Taylor were all invited to the party.

A working group was put in place to do the legwork – going out to the regions and meeting people from all different football backgrounds, listening to what they had to say, and compiling their findings. Reports were then submitted to Mellor's barmy army who would promptly pass on recommendations to the Sports Minister, who non-too-handily had about as much legislative power to enforce the suggestions as Wurzel Gummage.

"It was like banging your head against a brick wall," says Dr Adam Brown, senior research fellow at Manchester Institute For Popular Culture, whose previous work on England fans abroad had won him a place on the Task Force working committee. "There's a real problem here with the way football is being run. It needs independent regulators. Labour recognised the problem when they were in opposition but when they came to power they restricted the enquiry, for example by not allowing us to look into issues like broadcasting. Ultimately they chose to side with the football establishment. I was disappointed with the FA. This was their opportunity to bring back power from the Premier League. They didn't do it. The only good thing that came out of it was Supporters Direct."

As a result of the work of the Football Task Force a member of the Football

Trust, Phil French, and MP Andy Burnham [who had worked as an administrator on The Football Task Force] wanted to set up an organisation to help promote supporters trusts. They approached three people and asked them to put together a business plan to secure the funding to get an organisation off the ground – Jonathan Michie from London University, Trevor Watkins from Bournemouth Supporters' Trust and Brian Lomax, the man who started the 'trust movement' in 1992.

When the government came up with the cash, Supporters Direct was born. Its aim was, and still is, to help supporters become more involved in the running of their clubs, to promote clubs as community and civic institutions and promote the health of the game as a whole. In Spring 2000, Supporters Direct set up HQ at Birkbeck College, London. At this point there was a grand total of six supporters trusts in the UK, most of which had had some informal help from Brian Lomax. Now it was time to get formal.

"We were inundated with enquiries," says Brian Lomax, the inaugural Chairman of Supporters Direct. "In the first two years we were constantly on the road addressing meetings. We'd get more than the Prime Minister in some places, two to three thousand people would turn up, especially if the club was in crisis."

Supporters Direct has done more to give football fans a voice than any other organisation in the world. Its aim is to help set up each supporters' trust as an Industrial and Provident Society [IPS], to help fans attain representation on the board and to help fans increase their power by owning shares in a club. It helps out with legal and financial advice, speakers for meetings, media campaigns, training and any other support a group of fans needs to get off their collective backsides and make something happen at their club.

"I've been delighted and surprised at the response," says Brian. "At first we were only hearing from fans of clubs on the brink of closure. Now we've got trusts at every Scottish Premier League club and more than half of the English Premiership, including Arsenal and Manchester United, simply because fans felt they were entitled to have a say in their football club."

The success rate has been phenomenal. There are now over 140 supporters' trusts in the UK, 61 of which hold equity in their clubs and 39 of which have supporter representation at board level. Three league clubs are now completely owned and run by their supporters [Brentford, Chesterfield, and Stockport County], with nine non-league clubs in the same boat. Supporters' trusts have been responsible for saving 13 clubs from going out of business and have brought over £10 million into the game. Fan power, eh? "The tide is definitely starting to turn," says Brian Lomax. "I won't be satisfied until it's the norm. I want to see the day when 90% of clubs have active supporters' trusts and anyone who doesn't have one is seen as peculiar. I can see fans on the boards of all Football League clubs. It'll be a slower process with the Premiership, because of the astronomical amounts of money required to acquire a shareholding. My view is that every club would benefit from having at least one elected representative from their supporters on the board."

WHAT NEXT?

Having helped secure the futures of many of England's football clubs, Supporters Direct is now swivelling its neck in the direction of pastures new. It's been asked to share its experiences with UEFA and is starting a project in Northern Ireland. Its influence is even starting to spread into other sports. Supporters at some rugby union clubs have shown an interest, whilst in 2006 Lancashire became the first cricket club to have a supporters' trust. But what of the future of the beautiful game?

Most people seem to agree that supporters being involved in running clubs is a good thing. They are often the life blood of a club, remaining loyal way past the lifespan of players, managers and directors. And, as Football Supporters Federation deputy chairman Alan Bloore points out, they often have a lot to offer their clubs in terms of expertise.

"Whether it's with a trust or not, we'd like to see a proper process of consultation with fans at all clubs," he says. "We're not all cloth caps and whippets. Supporters have expertise in every field, a wide base of knowledge. The Peter Kenyons and David Deins of this world don't have a monopoly on good ideas. We also need to encourage more ethnic minorities and young people into the game. Britain is a multi-cultural society, but football crowds are still predominantly working and middle class white males. That has to change. It needs to be led by the FA from schools upwards."

Supporters' trusts have already done football the power of good, although the debate is split on whether it would be a good thing for all clubs. Premier

League chairmen Dave Richards doesn't think it would work at the top level.

"I think having fans on the board is good," he says. "But I think there's a level where the fans can own the club. If you want to progress, you need investment. You need to have the money. It's difficult for the average guy in the street to write a cheque out for £100,000. When you're on a board, you have to do that."

However, having experienced the way supporters' trusts work first hand, AFC Wimbledon chairmen Kris Stewart is in no doubt that if football wants to progress, every club should have a trust.

"Supporters' trusts are the way forward," he says. "Every club should have supporters involved. You'd struggle to impose that model on the Premiership clubs, but it works for the rest of football. Mind you, Barcelona has shown that it doesn't have to be confined to small clubs. Supporters being involved in an organised way can only be good for football. Look at the money supporters have brought into football and the clubs they've saved. The support from government for Supporters Direct is a big plus."

However, if something is not done very soon, a pair of brogues smoking on the pavement is all that will be left of Planet Football. With the top few clubs around Europe harvesting all the cash and everyone else fighting for scraps, with players earning an average man's annual salary in two days and with some clubs charging 50p a minute to enter the ground and watch, the game will surely implode.

First up redistribution, which did so much good for the game as a whole until it was bypassed by the creation of The Premiership, needs to come back in some form.

"A football match requires two clubs," says Kris Stewart. "Man U can't play if Birmingham aren't there. It takes two teams to make a game. Football has been in a mess since gate sharing ended. Governance stuff needs looking at too. Turnover, capital and salaries need bringing back into kilter. The money clubs spend has to relate to turnover. We won't be where we should until there's a more even distribution of TV money and talk about gate sharing for league games."

Player salaries need looking at drastically. It's insane that okay Premiership players like Shola Ameobi should live like Hollywood stars. His appearance on *Footballer's Cribs* in 2005 revealed Shola, the scorer of two Premiership goals in the 2004/05 season, to live in what one internet poster called a "palace with two seven foot projector screen cinema rooms and two rather large motors."

Drastic measures are obviously needed and are now under serious consideration. Wigan chairman Dave Whelan called for Premiership clubs to back a salary cap in September 2005. In the Football League, the jungle drums are beating even louder, with caps coming high on the discussion list of the AGM in June 2006.

"For the long-term good of the game it is something we have to look at and consider," said Norwich chief executive Neil Doncaster, a year after his club's relegation from The Premiership. "You show me the clubs that break even in the Championship – there are not many. It has worked very well in some other sports, it has enabled those sports to have better competition within their leagues."

Unsurprisingly, the man who fought so hard to free players from the shackles of the maximum wage is dead against the return of salary capping. Instead, says Jimmy Hill, clubs need to take the responsibility themselves and pay players what they can afford.

"I've never changed my view," he says. "Footballers should be free to earn what clubs can afford to pay them. What is happening at the moment is clubs are paying players more than they can afford. It's because of pressure from spectators

Nobody can impose common sense on the game

to win. If the clubs don't, the supporters don't turn up. Nobody can impose common sense on the game. The FA can't interfere on this."

The fear of fans not turning up in the future is very real. With astronomical ticket prices brought in to keep up with player wage demands, few young people – the future of the game – can afford to go any more.

"We need a successful top level of football with cheap prices," says FC United's Jules Spencer. "Look at Germany, in their top division prices are a third of what they are here. Football needs to be accessible for kids, families and working class people."

To encourage and enforce change, football needs strong governing bodies. As the FA has shown time and again, it has the fear factor of a night out with Joss Stone. Its ham-fisted attempt and failure to secure the services of Luis Felipe Scolari as England manager caused former England boss Graham Taylor to lambast the "absolutely pathetic nature of their amateurish search" for a new boss. Headlines such as "bumbling FA go back to Brit rejects" ensued, whilst *The Sun* labelled the affair a "totally complete and predictable shambles."

This is clearly going to have to change if the FA is going to have a chance of bringing the powerful elite at the top of the game to heel. One way to

Football needs to take action to save itself

stiffen up the stiffs, according to Jimmy Hill, would be to get some ex-players involved.

"I would like to see more ex-professionals involved in the FA," he says. "There's 90 people on that committee and not one of them would be guaranteed to hit the back of the net from the penalty spot. I'm not knocking the FA. They do a good job but it would do them good to have some members who'd played the game at the highest level. I partly blame the PFA for this. It's a campaign they should be producing."

Thankfully not all governing bodies are as lily-livered as the FA. The summer of 2006 saw UEFA, standing alongside the European Union, prepare to go into battle with Europe's top clubs and G14 over the future of the game. Acting on the findings of the Independent European Sport Review, a body made up of EU sports ministers including Richard Caborn, UEFA plan to target salary caps, distribution of cash, numbers of foreign players and dodgy agents to save the game from its biggest danger: predictability, caused by a growing wealth gap between clubs.

"It is not too dramatic to say that football needs to take action to save itself from going down the road of the closed circus that G14 would introduce if their view prevailed," said UEFA chief executive Lars-Christer Olsson in May 2006. "The independent review should help in striking the right balance between football being a sport and a business, and save European football's future."

However, G14 hit back, pointing out that the clubs who are successful now are the same ones who have always been on top of the pile.

"Go back 30 years and look who was dominating the leagues," says G14 general manager Thomas Kurth. "It's the same clubs, but nobody thought it was bad then. It's normal for a small club to have difficulties in winning the league. There are strong rules to guarantee unpredictability and maintain balance. Chelsea could buy the 100 best players in the world, but they'd still only be able to put 11 on the pitch. You can only use 11 players at one time. And you have to look at how many matches each team plays. Some clubs don't play in Europe, so they have more breaks between games. That gives a balance. Big clubs have more pressure. They have to have more players to be at the same level as those not competing in Europe."

UEFA v G14 is the latest in a long line of fierce battles to determine the future of football. We've seen professionalism triumph over amateurism, the players defeat the maximum wage and England's top clubs cakewalk into The Premiership. What next – business or pleasure? Good or evil? Shit or bust? Time will tell, but in the meantime, here's something to ponder:

"We need to reclaim the idea that grounds are for all of us and football should be reclaimed as a sport," says David Conn. "Within that, we need a strong FA, money spread more widely and evenly, moderation of ticket prices and grass roots should be looked after. But you can distill all that down to one point: football clubs should be football clubs."

Simple enough really innit?

Now, over to you.

Acknowledgements

I would like to thank my mum, dad and all my friends for all their support, especially Scott Royal for his valuable insight, all at MK Communications, Dewi Lewis Media and last, but by all means first really, My Fiona without whom, I am frankly, a bit rubbish.

Paul French, September 2006

I would like also to thank all the following who were generous enough to give me time and allow me to interview them.

Bella Abrams
John Birley
John Blackwell
Alan Bloore
Dr Adam Brown
Mark Bushell
Phil Carling
Paul Child
David Conn
James Cooper
Dr Graham Curry
Bryony Dixon
Gethin Evans
Stephen Froud
Jamie Guthrie
John Harding
Mike Harris
Shaun Harvey
Jimmy Hill
Stephen Holroyd
Andy Hosie

Lamar Hunt
Peter Hunter
Dave Jenkins
Angharad Jones
Thomas Kurth
David Litterer
Brian Lomax
Sam Maher
John Moules
Phil Neal
Ken Ramsden
Dave Richards
Nick Robinson
Jules Spencer
Jeff Stelling
Kris Stewart
Dr Rogan Taylor
Richard Tims
Phil Thornton
Tony Williams
Mark Wylie

I would also like to acknowledge the following sources of information which proved invaluable in the writing of the book.

Hard Tackles & Dirty Baths: George Best
History of Football: The Beautiful Game
DVD
Living to Play: John Harding
Sheffield FC 1957 centenary history
[special booklet]
Not so bleak up north: the early development of football in Sheffield: Dr Graham Curry
When Saturday Comes: issue 208
Pilgrims Patter

www.11v11.co.uk
www.alliwantisronaldo.free.fr
www.answers.google.com
www.bbc.co.uk/northyorkshire
www.biz.thestar.com.my
www.btinternet.com
www.businessweek.com
www.cigarettecards.co.uk
www.clarets-mad.co.uk
www.confguide.com
www.en.wikipedia.org
www.essex.ac.uk
www.footballeconomy.com
www.footballforumuk.com
www.football.guardian.co.uk
www.football-league.premiumtv.co.uk
www.football-research.org
www.freespace.virgin.net
www.krysstal.com
www.g14.com
www.labourbehindthelabel.org
www.le.ac.uk
www.makingthemodernworld.org
www.mg.co.za
www.middle-east-online.com

www.millwall-history.co.uk
www.news.bbc.co.uk
www.newsco.com
www.newsletter.co.uk
www.playthegame.org
www.poppiesfans.com
www.premierleague.com
www.sakhalintimes.ru
www.sirc.org
www.soccerhall.org
www.soccer.mistral.co.uk
www.sover.net
www.the-english-football-archive.com
www.thefa.com
www.radio.cz
www.Rivals.net
www.Saints-alive.co.uk
www.songfacts.com
www.surfingseadog.co.uk
www.timesonline.co.uk
www.urban75.org
www.webjcli.ncl.ac.uk
www.wikipedia.com
www.wotsat.com
www.wsc.co.uk

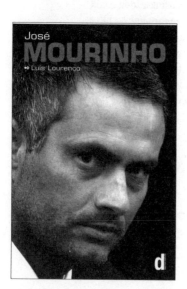